Praise for *Be UPFRONT*

'Equal parts rebellion and roadmap—Lauren Currie shows us how confidence really works.'

—Zoe Blaskey,
Author and Host of Motherkind

'Both a manifesto and a guide, *Be UPFRONT* will change the way you think about confidence and show you exactly what you need to do to uncover yours. A world of confident women will be a changed world for everyone.'

—Stephanie Harrison,
Bestselling Author of *New Happy*

'This book isn't just about confidence. It's about women across every race and culture—owning the truth of it and carrying it as a light for the world.'

—Dr Meenal Viz,
Author of *Power of Protest*

'*Be UPFRONT* is a manifesto for collective power. Lauren Currie helps the reader develop the type of personal confidence that becomes a social movement. She shows us how courage expands through connection and collaboration instead of completion. I am excited for this guidebook to be in the hands of women who are ready to take their position upfront!'

—Tamu Thomas,
Author of *Women Who Work Too Much*

'Most books on confidence tell women to adapt to broken systems. *Be UPFRONT* dares us to do the opposite, to trust the women we already are and use our voices to change the rules entirely.'

—Stacey Grant-Canham,
Founder of Black and Beech

'Galvanising, compassionate and pragmatic. This is a rare book that doesn't shy away from the societal difficulties faced by women, but takes them on. Empowering and exciting. I will be recommending to all of the women in my life'
—**Dr Sula Windgassen,**
Health Psychologist and Psychotherapist

'Finally, a book that treats confidence as what it really is— not a personality trait, but a skill. Lauren Currie gives us the tools to build it lesson by lesson.'
—**Nishma Patel Robb,**
Chief Sparkle Officer, Glittersphere

'Hyping women is my love language. And so, *Be UPFRONT* spoke to my soul. Practical, passionate and precisely pertinent, Lauren turns the idea of "confidence" from a nebulous intangible into a daily practice. A must-read (wo)manual for women everywhere.'
—**Erin Gallagher,**
Author of *Hype Women*

'Every leader needs this book. Lauren Currie redefines confidence as a skill we can all build and in doing so, she gives us the tools to transform not just ourselves, but our teams and organisations too.'
—**Kylie Reid,**
Founder of EGG

'The confidence manual every woman should read.'
—**Gill Whitty-Collins,**
Author of *Why Men Win at Work*

Lauren Currie OBE

'Everything you need to learn and
unlearn about confidence.
Truly inspiring.'

Viv Groskop

'This book will change
how you think about
confidence forever.'

Dr Soph

BE

UPFRONT

24
Rules
for Life
Changing
Confidence

CAPSTONE
A Wiley Brand

Registered Offices
John Wiley & Sons, Inc., 111 River Street, Hoboken, NJ 07030, USA
John Wiley & Sons Ltd, New Era House, 8 Oldlands Way, Bognor Regis, West Sussex, PO22 9NQ, UK

For details of our global editorial offices, customer services, and more information about Wiley products visit us at www.wiley.com.

The manufacturer's authorized representative according to the EU General Product Safety Regulation is Wiley-VCH GmbH, Boschstr. 12, 69469 Weinheim, Germany, e-mail:Product_Safety@wiley .com.

Wiley also publishes its books in a variety of electronic formats and by print-on-demand. Some content that appears in standard print versions of this book may not be available in other formats.

Library of Congress Cataloging-in-Publication Data is Available:

ISBN 9781907312694 (Paperback)
ISBN 9781907312717 (ePDF)
ISBN 9781907312700 (ePUB)

Cover Design: Lauren Currie

Set in 11/14pt and Sabon LT Std by Straive, Chennai, India.
Printed and bound by CPI Group (UK) Ltd, Croydon, CR0 4YY

C9781907312694_020226

*This book is dedicated to the past version of me,
thank you for being UPFRONT before you
had the words. And to you, thank you for choosing
to learn how to be UPFRONT. This choice
will change you, and it will change the world.*

Contents

Contents **xi**

Foreword

Confidence.

Everybody wants it. Surprisingly few people believe that they have it. And many women think they never will. Which is where Lauren Currie comes in.

Be UPFRONT is your step-by-step manual to unlocking everything you've ever wanted, by removing everything that's been holding you back.

The genius of this book is that Lauren takes entrenched time-honoured rules and reframes them in ways that will make you completely rethink what you've always believed.

That little voice in your head? No problem. Lauren has an answer for every single thing it might be saying to you, that's getting in the way of you living the life you really want to live.

You have so many treats waiting for you in here. You'll learn the UPFRONT version of 'Try before you buy'—'Try before you believe'. You'll find out how to get rid of your Imposter Syndrome once and for all. You'll schedule your self-doubt to overcome it. You'll discover the power of 'woohoo' (and how that changes your brain for the better—really!). You'll be inspired by stories of other women living their lives by these principles (full disclosure, I'm one of them).

You'll find you can indeed choose confidence; you can practise it, you can protect it and, importantly, you can pass it on.

And you'll find, by the time you reach the end of this book, that you've arrived where you've always wanted to be. UPFRONT.

Cindy Gallop
New York
September 2025

Introduction

B e UPFRONT.

Adjective
bold, honest, and frank.

Noun
*a business and a movement dedicated to upskilling
10 million women in confidence, visibility, and power.*

Verb
*to step forward before you feel ready; to build
ladders for yourself and for others*

This is a book about confidence, but as you'll learn in the pages ahead, not the kind of confidence that comes in neat bullet points, staged photos or vague advice. This book is about confidence as a practice. A rebellion. A way of showing up in a world that profits from your self-doubt.

When I say 'confidence', I'm talking about confidence that grows like a muscle, strengthened in daily reps, sometimes sore, sometimes shaky, always worth the work. The kind of confidence that will feel uncomfortable, inconvenient and messy. The kind that changes you and, by extension, changes the world around you.

I'm going to tell you exactly how to build it.

To Be UPFRONT is to give your confidence the attention it deserves. It's a way of moving through the world, boldly, unapologetic and rooted in truth, even when it's difficult. UPFRONT is also a real place. A beating heart. A movement made up of thousands of women all over the world, in digital rooms and Zoom squares, practising confidence together. At the centre is the *Bond*—UPFRONT's six-week online experience where women gather to dismantle the old rules of confidence, unlearn the scripts we've been handed and replace them with ones rooted in power, self-trust and community.

The word Bond is no accident. It's the collective noun for a group of women. It's how we describe the connection, accountability, laughter, tears and breakthroughs that happen when women commit to unlearning together. Women who might have been strangers on Day 1 become mirrors, allies and cheerleaders. They call themselves Bonders. What started as one course is now a learning ecosystem of Bonds. Bonds for leadership, freelancing, money, public speaking, personal branding and more, all grounded in the same belief: confidence grows faster when we grow it together.

Whether you're a Bonder or have never heard of UPFRONT until now, these pages will meet you where you are. Each chapter follows a rhythm:

1. **Old Rule**—an outdated belief or expectation you've likely been living by, often without even knowing it.
2. **New Rule**—an UPFRONT alternative, drawn from lived experience, scientific research, community stories and the slow, courageous work of unlearning.
3. **UPFRONT Moment**—a reflection and an invitation to practise the New Rules in your own life.

This rhythm of Old Rule, New Rule is a practice of reframing. It will teach you how to see differently, to choose consciously and to build confidence—not as a fixed trait, but as a skill you are practising. Every interaction, every conversation and every decision is an opportunity to Be UPFRONT in your daily life.

This book isn't meant to be read once and put back on a shelf. Not on my watch!

Be UPFRONT is designed as a practice—something you return to, experiment with, over decades! Confidence grows through action, reflection, and connection, and it's always easier to build it together.

If you'd like to explore the ideas in this book alongside other readers, to reflect, practise, and share what you're learning, you're invited to become a Book Bonder.

Book Bonders are readers who want to take these ideas beyond the page and into their everyday lives, in whatever way works for them.

You can join at any point by scanning the QR code below.

There's no right pace, no fixed path, and no pressure, just an open invitation to practise confidence together.

Being UPFRONT doesn't happen overnight. It unfolds through hundreds of small choices, acts of noticing and moments of practising confidence. That's why each chapter ends with an UPFRONT Moment—a reflection or invitation to help you put what you've learned into practice. These are not tasks to tick off. They're moments of pause. Tiny turning points. A chance to connect with yourself, your story and your confidence.

There's no right or wrong way to meet these moments. Take your time and trust what comes. The first step is to show up, the second is to stay in the moment long enough to do the work. Confidence is built, not born, and building takes work. These UPFRONT Moments are your training ground. Your reps. There's no skipping and no shortcuts. You'll be asked to question old stories, to listen harder and to believe bigger things.

Journalling is the tool I've chosen for you in these moments because this is a conversation only YOU can have with yourself. You are the authority on what your confidence looks, feels and sounds like. You are the guide. You are the inspiration. No one else can define your confidence and no one else can reclaim it for you. This is the nature of confidence. Your confidence and your UPFRONT life is totally unique to you.

Our rhythm is more than structure. It's a learning pathway. A gentle map for unlearning. A way to dismantle the invisible rules that have kept you small, and replace them with ones that make you visible, vocal and free. You'll become UPFRONT.

Confidence is not a one-size-fits-all skill. Your identity—including your race, class, sexuality, culture, or disability, among other aspects—shapes how the world responds to your confidence and how you respond to the world. This diversity isn't a challenge to our movement, it's the movement's strength. The more we understand each other's truths, the more powerful our collective confidence becomes. Some chapters may feel like they were written with your life in mind; others may not. That's OK. Take what resonates. Leave what doesn't. Honour the truths you don't carry.

We live in a world where 90% of people hold biases against women.[1] That means when you speak up in a meeting and your idea is ignored until a man repeats it, you're not imagining it. When you lead and are called 'cold' or 'bossy', you're bumping into the same bias that says men are more deserving of jobs, power and pay. Confidence doesn't exist in a vacuum, it exists inside these systems. That's why at UPFRONT we say: we're here to change confidence, not women. The problem we're here to solve is not that women and girls lack confidence, but that we live in a world that does not reward, celebrate or encourage confidence in women.

I have written this book for you and your daughters, your granddaughters and every woman who comes after us. Together, we are breaking generational cycles. Together, we are setting the old rules on fire, and we're making new rules along the way. Nobody is off the hook. This work needs all of us.

Before we dive in, I want to tell you my story. Because this book isn't just built on research, science, practice and community; it's built on lived experience. My confidence didn't arrive fully formed. I'm living it. I'm stumbling through it. I'm rebuilding it. Again and again. The truth is, this book wouldn't exist if I wasn't walking this path myself, practising confidence daily, falling on my face sometimes, dusting myself off and doing it again, better.

I'm not writing from the mountaintop. I'm right here in it with you, learning, unlearning, showing up and being UPFRONT even when I'm scared. This book is a match. Your voice is the spark. Together, we're going to burn the old rules down and Be UPFRONT.

Take my hand.

Let's begin.

Note

1. United Nations Development Programme (UNDP) (2020). Almost 90% of men/women globally are biased against women. 5 March. https://www.undp.org/press-releases/almost-90-men/women-globally-are-biased-against-women.

Part I

Unlearn

My Confidence Story

Old Rule: Your confidence is a problem

New Rule: Your confidence is a catalyst

This is my confidence story. One version of what it looks like to unlearn everything you were told about confidence. I had to unlearn the belief that confidence is too much, selfish or sometimes dangerous. I learned that confidence is a tool for positive change, both personal and systemic.

My confidence has soared and shattered and shape-shifted since I began building UPFRONT in 2016 into what it is today. When I was wee, I was totally unafraid to take up space. I was proud of how clever I was. I talked, sang and performed from the moment I woke up to the moment I went to bed. I used to line up all my teddies in a row and give them instructions. My mum likes to tell the story that I used to point at her and make demands before I could talk. I also had a whole other imaginary life that I would spend hours telling my granny about. When I was three or four, I had a husband called Jim, and I had three kids who were always leaving the cupboard doors open. I used to record my own radio show.

I used to interview imaginary guests. I was confident. I was a confident wee girl.

I want you to think about the young, confident girl in your life right now, maybe your daughter, your niece, maybe your sister, maybe cousins, children of friends. A young girl who's in your life right now, who is full of confidence. It might even be your younger self. I want you to imagine her face, imagine her bright eyes, imagine how confidently she says no when you ask her to do something she doesn't want to do. I want you to connect with how utterly herself she is and I want you to say her name out loud.

When I became a teenager, I learned to hide my confidence and my face. I remember my face used to burn so red and hot I thought I was going to burst into flames and die. I refused to go to school on the day of show and tell, and I used to hand-write answers and rehearse what I would say if a teacher put me on the spot and asked, 'What did you do at the weekend, or what music do you like to listen to?' Back then, the safest thing I thought I could do was to stay quiet. Being noticed felt dangerous.

I learned to hide my cleverness. I stopped putting my hand up and I learned quickly that what I looked like was far more important than what I said or what I did. I learned that what everybody else thought about me was more important than what I thought about me.

But despite all these new rules I absorbed from the women around me and the patriarchal world we live in, I did excel academically. I tackled every single project with the mission to be the very best. And it was around this time that I started to learn and understand the hatred that other girls had for me.

I could taste their disgust with me, they would scowl at me every time I walked down the corridor. They wrote messages to me and about me on the toilet walls and they threatened me with violence most lunch times. Why? Because they said I thought I was better than them.

Every single young girl is born with all the confidence, creativity, energy, determination and resilience that she needs, and then someone or something takes it away.

The problem we are here to solve isn't that women lack confidence. It's that confident women are not rewarded in this world, and this starts at a very, very early age. I wonder if something like this ever happened to you? Chances are high your answer is yes. Because we know that by the age of eight, girls are already less confident than boys. We also know by the time they reach adolescence, their confidence drops by 30%.[1] Every day I wonder—if we don't interrupt this pattern, who will?

Let's fast forward through my product design engineering degree, the maths, the physics, to the day I met an amazing woman who changed my life. We did amazing things together. We made the *Kilmarnock Standard*, and anyone reading from Scotland knows how big a deal the *Kilmarnock Standard* is (weekly print circulation of 1,533). We were both the first in our families to go to university. We were both ambitious, driven, hard-working, and we were on a mission to do work that would make Scotland better, make the world better. She became my business partner and together there was nothing we couldn't do. Together, we were unstoppable. Then she became my friend. This was my first taste of entrepreneurship. It was 2008, six businesses ago! I was 23.

We built a team. I hired and managed people who were older than me. We built a home for the business above a tea room in Glasgow. My mum came up with the business name. My dad built all the furniture. We won a Young Scot award, and I was leading. I was building. I was confident, and I loved being on stage. I loved being on the radio. I loved performing. I was telling stories and people were listening. I was no longer hiding my cleverness and I was in a place where this confident version of me was being rewarded. She was useful to the world. She was celebrated and she was necessary.

But sometimes no amount of smarts or grace can protect your confidence, because we live in a world where women are pitted against each other and our businesses and our relationships fall apart.

I want you to think about the woman in your life who is no longer in your life because the system made you think that there wasn't enough room for both of you. Maybe it's your friend from high school, maybe it's your first boss. Maybe it's a colleague. Imagine her face. Remember how good it used to feel when you were vibing and it was the best. I want you to say her name out loud.

You can meet one person, one woman, in your life who can change the course of your confidence forever.

The problem is not that women lack confidence. The problem is we are rewarded for knocking each other down. What would a world where that doesn't happen look like? Where women are celebrated and we are encouraged to lift each other up, where we are genuinely cheerleading and supporting each other?

It looks like being UPFRONT.

The Birth of a Movement

UPFRONT began on 13th November 2015.

I was the only woman on the conference programme. Back in 2015 I knew that was not OK, but I didn't really have the language, the knowledge or the insight to articulate why it wasn't OK. Society wasn't talking about gender, we weren't talking about sexism or inequality or oppression the way we are now. But I knew I was tired of going to conferences and seeing the same, below-average presentations, by the same middle-class white dudes. I believed the fallacy of meritocracy I'd been taught. I believed that good work spoke for itself. I believed that hard work always paid off. But if so, where were all the women? I couldn't understand it, so I put a Post-It note in the women's toilets, on the mirror. It said: 'Do you want to be on stage? Tell me about it'.

The Post-It note that started a movement
Source: Zara Alexandra Kwok

When I came off stage I had a queue of people waiting to talk to me about public speaking. That was the day I realised this problem was damn complicated. I learned that people were incredibly afraid of being on a stage but also desperate to overcome that fear. The designer in me fought for solutions. What would bridge the gap? I broke it down and thought about how I could provide the experience of the stage without the anxiety of having to perform. The answer was a big red sofa. I invited people with stage fright to sit on a sofa alongside me as I presented on stages around the world.

They could sit and experience the stage without the scary bit; they were tiptoeing along their confidence journey. They would sit UPFRONT—figuratively and metaphorically.

I first tried it out at a conference called Silicon Beached. We had over thirty people who wanted to sit on stage with me. The couch obviously couldn't take thirty people so we had to find some deck chairs to add to the stage and just shuffle them in. They absolutely loved it. For some of them, it totally transformed how they were thinking about being on stage and encouraged them to potentially give talks themselves one day. They were hooked!

They asked me for a workshop, a book, a podcast. Anything that could help them continue on their journey towards being a confident public speaker. I had none of those things. I was busy running my other businesses and working a full-time job. But I wanted to help them. So I went looking. I searched for resources I could point them to—tools, courses, books that spoke to women about confidence in a way that felt true. What I found was overwhelming in quantity but narrow in value: products and messaging designed by men, for men, built on the idea that confidence is an individual personality trait rather than a systemic issue. There was nothing that reflected women's lived experiences. Nothing that understood that low confidence in women is not a personal flaw, but the outcome of cultural conditioning and bias.

I decided to build it myself.

I had a brilliant employer who let me use their studio on weekends to run UPFRONT workshops. I hand-made UPFRONT name badges, carried my kettle and my books from home and turned it into a workshop space. I sold tickets for £30 and spent my Saturdays teaching women confidence. It wasn't unusual for the attendees to cry. They told me on their feedback forms this one afternoon had changed their life. I knew I was building something extraordinary.

What happened next was the start of something amazing. Something that weaved together all the things I was good at. A synergy between me and my vision—something I'd not felt since my very first business in Glasgow. I wanted to build a world where confident women were rewarded and celebrated. My idea worked and women queued up for more. A movement had begun. UPFRONT was born. They felt braver. They did new things. Started projects, quit jobs and travelled abroad solo. They started wearing bright colours and ordering first in restaurants. They found the confidence they'd been taught to hide. UPFRONT was my favourite side project. A fantasy even—imagine if I could do this work every day? NEVER! It would never work. I could never feel this good every day. This kind of impact, purpose and ease could never be a 'proper' business. Could it? I didn't believe in myself enough. Yet.

The room I used could only fit twenty people in it, and I was only one person. I needed every woman in the world to have this experience. I wanted to build a world where low confidence was never the reason a woman did not do the thing she wanted to do. Scale was an issue. There was only one thing for it. I had to make this happen online. It took me years instead of months—thanks to my full-time job, other businesses, a global pandemic, pregnancy, a baby loss, giving birth, PTSD from birth trauma and raising a small human—but I did it.

I built an online version of the workshop. I wanted to teach women how to be on stage, how to unlearn all of the backwards ways we've been taught to think about our own confidence and how to understand that low confidence is a direct consequence of the patriarchy. In August 2020, the very first Bond was born (it wasn't called a Bond then). I had 223 sign-ups for our first Bond. But then I did another Bond, and another Bond. . .

At first, when you bought a Bond ticket, I put a Post-It note with your name on my wall. I can't do that anymore, because there are too many of you. I grew a tiny team and started to launch Bonds for organisations. We hosted a fantastic Bond for Nike teams spread across the United States and Asia. In summer 2024, we welcomed over 2,000 women from 24 time zones to the Bond. The Bond has developed into a six-week online programme where you unlearn everything you've been taught about confidence and you learn how to transform your own confidence and the confidence of the women around you. We now work with clients from all over the world, in the private, public and third sector. And of course, if you've not done a Bond, there's a Bond place with your name on it. Come join us.

Women leave a Bond changed. You earn more. You step up to lead. You parent better, you show up at work better. And the stories—I mean, this is one reason I'm writing this book, because there are thousands of UPFRONT stories we can all learn from. Women like Donna Patterson, who single-handedly took Morrisons, the fifth largest supermarket chain in the United Kingdom, to court for discriminating against her because she was pregnant. She won the case with a settlement of £60,000. To folks like Trisha who are talking out in the open about why bosses need to stop telling women to be more confident. To folks like Laura, who was head-hunted and negotiated a relocation package to move her three children to the other side of the world. She also added three zeros to the end of her salary because of what she had learned in the Bond. The average salary increase for Bonders is 49% and Bonders are 80% more likely to apply for a leadership position, with 92% of them feeling more secure and confident in their current roles. This is powerful, not only for me as a side hustle that became a business, but powerful as a movement. What would the world look like if the statistics we see coming out of UPFRONT were applied to all women everywhere?

But this is where my confidence story turns a little dark. I knew the more successful UPFRONT became, the more men were going to get annoyed. I thought men would come for me, the patriarchy would retaliate. But the people who have come for me, and the people who are still coming for me now, are women.

I have been called a fascist, a dictator, a homophobe, a racist and a capitalist. I have asked every single one of these women who are throwing stones at me to have a conversation, and not one of them has taken me up on that offer, but yet they continue to throw stones, spread rumours, regurgitate myths and mistruths.

There have been days where I have felt like giving up. And maybe this is the patriarchy fighting back, the internalised misogyny it breeds into all of us. But I will not give up. I will never give up because I can see the change that UPFRONT is capable of making in the world. And I know the legacy of this book and the conversation me and you are about to have together has ripple effects that will span the globe and generations.

We cannot genuinely build a confidence revolution without dismantling the internalised misogyny that lives inside all of us.

I want to ask you something personal, what would you go and do if you genuinely and unequivocally had the support of every single woman in your life? Take a moment to really think about it. Write your answer in the margin.

It's up to me. It's up to you. It's up to everyone reading this book right now to build a world where you can go and do *that* thing, the thing you're scared of, the thing you dream about, the thing you think you're not ready for. Whether that's asking for the promotion, starting the business, speaking up in the meeting, walking away from the toxic job or finally calling yourself an artist, a leader or a founder.

Nobody else is going to come and make this happen for you. There is no superhero moment. No golden ticket. No permission slip. And yet, you are not alone. We do this work together. Confidence is not a solo project. It's built in community, shoulder to shoulder.

This work is urgent. And the data backs this urgency: women are promoted at slower rates than men at every stage of their careers, especially women of colour.[2] The World Economic Forum estimates it will take 131 years to close the global gender gap if we continue at the current pace.[3] We simply cannot wait for systems to catch up. We have to act now.

And when we do, we create ripples. Studies tell us that when one woman speaks up in a team, it increases the likelihood that others will speak up too, especially those who have been quiet before.[4] Confidence is contagious. Confidence is collective. This is how we change the world, not in one big leap, but in small UPFRONT choices, multiplied across thousands of people, day after day.

Learning to live differently, building new habits and unlearning old beliefs is not a quick fix. It's not a weekend workshop or a 60-second reel. It's a long-term process. A lifelong journey. And the good news is you've already started.

I have a tattoo on my left arm. It's a spiral representing the Fibonacci sequence. It's there to remind me that I have time, even though I do plan to live until I'm 100 years old, and I plan to be as cool as Cindy Gallop when I'm 60. I also know that I could die tomorrow. This is the tension that we're living in. You cannot fight time. You cannot fight life. Life is going to steal your confidence over and over and over again, but every single time you will get it back, and every time you do it will get easier. You will wake up each day and you will keep going. Because your relationship with confidence isn't a destination. It's a commitment. Your relationship with confidence is lifelong.

My story is just one version. This book is about your story and how we rewrite it, together. My plan is to activate your confidence and the confidence of 10 million women. UPFRONT's plan is to build a world where confident women are rewarded, celebrated and never punished for being confident. What's your plan?

This book is how you find out.

Notes

1. According to a major study by YPulse, Kay, K. and Shipman, C. (2018). The Confidence Code for Girls Study.
2. McKinsey & Company and LeanIn.org, *Women in the Workplace 2024*.
3. World Economic Forum, *Global Gender Gap Report 2023*.
4. Dasgupta, N., Sciricle, M.M., and Hunsinger, M. (2015). Female peers in small work groups enhance women's motivation, verbal participation, and career aspirations in engineering. *Proceedings of the National Academy of Sciences* 112 (16): 4988–4993. https://doi.org/10.1073/pnas.1422822112.

1

You Were Always Teachable

Old Rule: Confidence is something you are born with

New Rule: Confidence is a skill you practise

Maybe she's born with it. I was five years old. Maybelline had just launched their iconic *'Maybe she's born with it. Maybe it's Maybelline'* campaign. Now I'm no advertising exec but the reason this campaign became such a significant part of pop culture isn't because the word *maybe* is very close to *Maybelline*. It's that women are taught that the key attributes and skills that fuel confidence, progress and power are innate.

You are taught that confidence is a natural gift bestowed upon the lucky few and there's no hope for the rest of us (unless you buy their product of course).

So you tell yourself, every damn day, you were not born with it. You concede to moving through the world without actively learning confidence. This is exceptionally good news for the status quo because for as long as you think confidence is unteachable and unlearnable you stay exactly where you are. Knowing that you are capable of so much more, and not knowing where or how to begin. This book is where you begin.

Without confidence, you are far less likely to challenge authority, to speak up against injustice, be wealthy, be in a position of authority and be taken seriously. Psychologist Albert Bandura called it 'self-efficacy', and the research is clear: people who believe they can do something are far more likely to set bold goals, keep going when it gets hard and grab the opportunities that lead to power, wealth and influence. Without confidence, you leave money, power and opportunities on the table. Researchers call it the 'confidence pay penalty', and it's costing women like you thousands over your lifetime.

How would your daily life change if confidence was not a fixed trait but something you could learn? How would our world change if every single woman in the world learned confidence?

We're going to find out. Together. Me and you. Because confidence is a skill you can learn and this truth changes everything.

With practice, you can and will develop the confidence you need to do anything you can possibly imagine. It's a muscle. It's a muscle that you build, stretch, tear and grow. What's more, the world is your gymnasium. The reps are saying yes to the opportunity. The weights are the moments you choose to step outside your comfort zone.

'Maybe she learned it' doesn't have the same ring to it. But it's the truth. And actually I kind of like it: 'Maybe she learned it, maybe it's confidence'.

A real-world example—and not one bathed in celebrity—is the simple act of driving. I wasn't born knowing how to drive, children can't drive at all. At first, it felt impossible, so many things to think about at once. Do you remember? My hands were tense on the wheel, my foot hovered nervously over the clutch, my eyes darted between mirrors, signs and the road ahead. Driving demanded coordination, judgement, presence and trust in myself—skills I didn't know I had yet.

Little by little, I learned. I practised staying calm in chaos. I learned to anticipate problems, to make quick decisions, to trust my instincts under pressure. I learned how to take up space on the road and in my life. Driving isn't just physical; it's mental and emotional. You have to manage fear, assert yourself and believe you belong, especially when you're merging into fast-moving traffic. That's confidence.

And that's the point. Confidence, like driving, is a skill made up of many smaller ones—awareness, self-trust, risk-taking and repetition. You weren't born knowing how to drive, but you learned. You practised. You got better. And now you go places.

Even if you haven't learned to drive (yet or ever), the point still stands, right? Think of anything that once scared you, that felt out of reach until you tried—riding your first bike, booking a solo trip or creating a formula in excel. Confidence is never just one thing. It's a collection of learnable skills: self-trust, presence, risk, resilience. You weren't born with it. You built it.

Now we have some real-world examples. Confidence isn't a personality trait reserved for the lucky few. It's a learned behaviour. Something that can be built, grown and shared in many ways, and science says so too.

The Science

A meta-analysis of over 100 studies in STEM (science, technology, engineering and mathematics) fields found that confidence is shaped by mastering experiences, encouragement, observation and emotional regulation.[1] In other words, you gain confidence by doing hard things, seeing others do them and hearing 'you can do this' from people who believe in us. Can you hear me shouting 'you can do this' in my best Billy Connolly voice? I really do believe you can do it, with all my heart.

Across 26 studies, researchers found a strong link between self-efficacy and behaviour, proving that confidence grows when it's nurtured early. When children are given the space to try, fail, try again and be supported through it, their belief in themselves grows.[2]

And it doesn't stop there. In second-language acquisition, students who believed in their abilities performed better. Confidence doesn't just follow success; it fuels it. Believing in yourself makes everything better and easier.

In perhaps one of the most sweeping studies, a meta-analysis of over 16 million students confirmed that targeted interventions aimed at boosting self-belief significantly improved academic outcomes.

So if you've ever questioned whether confidence can be learned, the answer is a resounding: yes.

Now you know you can learn it, what will you do with that power?

UPFRONT Moment

As I shared in the Introduction, these UPFRONT Moments are invitations. Invitations to pause. To listen in. To have a conversation with the person who knows your confidence better than anyone else: and that's YOU.

There is no right or wrong way to journal here. Use pen and paper. Use your Notes app. Doodle in the margins of this book. The format doesn't matter, your honesty does.

If you feel resistance when you read the question, that's a signal. It means this question *needs* your attention. Nobody is going to read what you write. You don't need to explain it, share it or make it sound clever. This is not school. You won't be graded. Spelling doesn't matter. Neatness doesn't matter. Coherence doesn't matter. Mess is welcome here.

If you're new to journalling, your inner critic might clear her throat and step up to the mic. That's OK. Let her speak, then hand her a cup of tea and tell her to take several seats. She has *no idea* what's coming.

Unlearning is hard. It's sweaty, heart-opening, confidence-building work. And that's what makes it so powerful. Let's begin. I'm rooting for you.

1. **What were you taught about confidence as you were growing up? What are the inherited stories you've absorbed about who gets to be confident, what confidence looks like and what it means if you *have* it (or don't)?**

    Things you might want to consider as you think about this question:

    - What did the adults around you model?
    - Were you praised more for being quiet or for speaking up?
    - Was confidence seen as admirable or as arrogance?
    - Were boys and girls encouraged differently?
    - What did school, culture, media or religion teach you?
    - What were you told about bragging, boldness or ambition?
    - Did anyone ever call you 'too much' or 'not enough'?
    - Whose confidence were you taught to fear, envy, admire or shrink from?

    Write it all down—the big moments, the throwaway comments, the family mantras, the classroom rules.

These are the roots of your confidence story. This is where you start. With seeing them clearly and honestly so you can choose what to carry forward and what to leave behind.

2. **What does your *confidence* look like, not the version you were taught to admire or aspire to, but the version that feels like yours?**
   In this chapter, we talked about the myth that confidence is a fixed personality trait—you either have it or you don't. And you've started to unravel that myth. But there's another layer to explore: even when you *do* pursue confidence, you often chase a version that doesn't belong to you. The kind that's always loud, always extroverted, always 'on'. The kind that speaks without pausing. Wears suits and heels every day. Stands at the front of the room. Says yes to everything without thought. This is what culture taught you confidence looks like. But your confidence is unique to you. Go deeper—what does your confidence feel like in your body, in your voice; when does it show up in your daily life?
   We're moving to a place where confidence isn't something you *have* or *don't have*. It's something you *do*. Where it shows up in your body, your voice and the choices you make every day.
   So try asking yourself:

   • What does my body feel like when I feel confident?
     Maybe your shoulders are back, your eyes are up, your stomach feels calm, or maybe it's full of butterflies, but you're still doing the thing anyway.

- What does my voice sound like when I believe in what I'm saying?

  Is it loud? Is it soft? Clear? Do you speak faster or slower? Do you ask questions, or share ideas even when you're nervous?

- What are the moments when you feel most like *you*?

  Specifically in the moments when you try something new? When you help someone? When you're learning with others?

Confidence looks different for everyone. It's not always about being the loudest or the first. So what does *your* confidence look like?

Write it all down. Get specific. Make it yours. This is how you begin to build confidence that's UPFRONT. Confidence that fits you like your skin, not a cheap costume.

Notes

1. Sheu, H.-B., Lent, R.W., Miller, M.J., Penn, L.T., Cusick, M.E., and Truong, N.N. (2018). Sources of self-efficacy and outcome expectations in science, technology, engineering, and mathematics domains: A meta-analysis. *Journal of Vocational Behavior*. https://doi.org/10.1016/j.jvb.2018.10.003.
2. Holden, G. (1990). Self-efficacy of children and adolescents: A meta-analysis. *Psychological Reports* 66 (3): 1044–1046. https://doi.org/10.2466/pr0.1990.66.3.1044.

2

You Are a Confidence Cultivator

Old Rule: Confidence grows by winning

New Rule: Confidence grows by lifting others

Picture this, I'm on stage standing in front of 300 people. I'm about to give a keynote. There's a red sofa on stage with me. I've popped a cushion on there saying 'UPFRONT' (hand-made by mum—thanks mum!).

I've invited every woman in the room with stage fright to come and join me on stage. To sit on the soft, safe, red sofa and feel what it's like to be on a stage. So many women want to take part, we're scrambling to find deck chairs to fit them all on stage with me.

The sofa was called the UPFRONT couch. Over the span of three years, the UPFRONT couch appeared on stages in every continent and supported hundreds of women to get over their stage fright. This is the origin story of how UPFRONT came to be.

I believe there is enough room for all of us to be on stage. I believe a spotlight's shine is infinite. I believe there is enough. Enough space. Enough time. Enough love. Enough money. Enough homes. Enough confidence. For all of us. But it took me a long time to get here. And on days when I'm pissed off or hungry or tired, I can slip back into the dark place of scarcity. I don't belong there. You don't belong there.

You've no idea of the absolutely deliciously incredible possibilities that will come for you when you choose to reject scarcity. Rejecting the lie of scarcity is a radical act. Especially when it comes to confidence. Especially if you are a woman. Right now, we are making a collective choice, me and you, to believe there is enough confidence for every single one of us.

I've learned this truth the hard way. I've spent too much of my precious time snarling because she has the book deal and I don't. Grumbling because she got invited to the fashion awards and I didn't. Whining because she got a mortgage effortlessly and I didn't.

And these stories are part of the reason we don't make art or money or progress or joy. We don't write songs. Or tell stories. We don't speak up against injustice. Or ask the question. Because we believe someone else has already done it, so what's the point? Do you know how many books about confidence have been written? Well I do and it's a big number. Over 10,000. And here I am writing another one and here you are reading it. Do you see? It wouldn't matter if there were a million books about confidence, none of them was written by me.

Scarcity is one of the darkest tricks the patriarchy is teaching you. It's at the very root of the internalised misogyny that lives inside all of us. What a tragedy we've been taught to believe confidence is a finite resource. We're living in a system where hoarding, storing and grabbing confidence is rewarded. Where we constantly feel like we need more and we need to grab the confidence someone else has and steal it away like a hungry wind.

Maybe you don't praise, compliment or give credit to others because it might diminish your own. You sit tight on knowledge, skills or advice, thinking that sharing it might make others 'too good' or better than you. You avoid showing vulnerability. Instead of sharing your struggles, growth or setbacks, you present an image of perfection, which breeds insecurity in others.

The system is working exactly how it was designed to. Not only are we walking through the world thinking confidence is something you are born with, we then crack the code and keep it to ourselves.

Not on my watch! When your confidence grows, you are not taking confidence away from someone else. When you use your light to light someone else's torch, your light does not shine any less. The confidence you do have? No matter how small, I want you to share it with others. Shout it from the rooftops.

How would your daily life change if you intentionally shared your confidence with other women and girls? How would our world change if every single woman shared confidence in her workplace and her home?

When confidence is shared, like fire, it's multiplied, and when you keep it to yourself, it diminishes. I dare you to find an act more joyful than giving confidence to another woman, of watching her eyes change when she starts to believe the words you are telling her. When she starts to realise that you are right. That she is good enough for the job. That she does deserve to book the holiday. That her story is important. When she starts to see herself as the giant you always knew she was. There's nothing like it.

Build Ladders, Not Walls

The most powerful, radical act you can do in your work, your friendship groups and your community is build ladders, not walls. Ladders lift people up. Walls shut people out. Women already face enough barriers in the workplace, not to mention the rest of the world. The last thing we need is to be building more of them.

Building ladders isn't some feel-good statement, it's a power move. When you support other women, you're not just helping them, you're strengthening your own position, creating allies and shaping a culture that works for you, not against you. In a workplace this looks like advocating for the women around you and making sure their contributions are seen and valued. In your friendship group this can be encouraging a friend who's starting a new business or supporting a friend to leave an unhealthy relationship.

You've taken action to rise up by reading this book. You're here, working on your confidence. As you do, I want you to build ladders around you to continually lift other women up. You'll continue to keep each other motivated and keep each other strong. Take a moment now to think about what those ladders look like in your life. Where can you put them? How can you grow them? Where can you find ladders to help you reach even higher heights?

Bringing Others with You

When Smriti joined the Bond, she was on maternity leave and found herself considering her professional future:

> *In the period leading up to my maternity leave, I experienced professional challenges. When I shared*

THE MOST POWERFUL, RADICAL ACT YOU CAN DO IS BUILD LADDERS, NOT WALLS.

the news of my pregnancy, professional opportunities vanished. One of the best things about joining the Bond was meeting so many women from different walks of life who opened my mind to the possibility of thriving in the face of uncertainty.

This has prompted a period of self-reflection where I'm asking myself what impact I wish to make in the world upon going back to work. The Bond also made me realise that I had stopped owning the great work I had done and was doing. I was not taking up the space I deserved. Another big realisation to come out of this process is that I want to use my voice and my experiences to empower other mothers and women of colour to achieve leadership roles.

Smriti has already taken steps in this direction by updating her LinkedIn headline, which previously only reflected her work in making the governance of World Heritage more inclusive.

I added two things; first that I'm looking to empower mothers and women of colour to achieve leadership roles and, second that I'm currently on maternity leave. Both were very big steps for me. Now I'm working to build up my voice and gradually talk more about these themes, in addition to sharing my professional expertise in the cultural heritage management sector.

Smriti hasn't stopped at LinkedIn updates.

One of the priceless pieces of advice I picked up on my Bond journey was to start implementing before I'm ready, and I am. I'm working on a project to interview mothers in leadership roles in the cultural heritage sector in Germany, to shine a light on their experiences. I am asking each of them to share the top skills they've acquired for their leadership roles through being a mother. We're discussing what unspoken biases they faced when returning to a leadership position or applying for leadership roles post-maternity leave. I'll be posting these interviews on LinkedIn. I'm excited and curious to see what comes out of the process.

I not only want to make these women's experiences more visible, but also to reach out to other women who may be going through similar situations. I would like to share advice about what to do while they're on maternity leave to ensure they remain in touch with their professional lives and support network. My aim is to bring together the women who have already walked this path and those who are seeking some guidance.

Smriti is building her own ladders to help other women and in doing so is building her own confidence. It's a virtuous cycle. It's UPFRONT in action.

Turn on Your Light

I once heard Oprah Winfrey talk about what it was like when she saw Barack Obama at a conference. '*So, did Barack Obama light up the room?*' the interviewer asked. Oprah replied, '*Yes, the room got lit up, but not in the way you think, because he got all of us to switch our own lights on*'.

It's a really simple idea on the surface but it stuck with me because there is an immense difference between being a leader who's prioritising turning your own light on versus being a leader who is working with intention and thoughtfulness to get other people to turn on their own lights.

Mary Follett, a pioneering American social worker, management consultant and organisational theorist, talks about power and how it isn't a scarce resource. It's something you make together with other people. Something we make together. You and me. You and your colleagues. You and your friends. You and your family. If we work together and collaborate, we are in community with each other. We share. We lead. We support others on this journey and in doing so we grow together.

Let's hold onto a powerful truth: confidence isn't just something we build, it's also something we can give to others. And when we share it, it grows. This isn't just a feel-good idea, it's backed by solid research.

The Science

Studies tell us that women who have a strong inner circle of other women are two-and-a-half times more likely to land high-ranking leadership positions.[1] This effect is not just about receiving support, offering encouragement and sharing strategies with other women, it also boosts the giver's confidence, creating a sense of competence and belonging. The researchers emphasise that mutual empowerment among women, particularly through networks of trust and shared experience, creates a feedback loop of professional and personal growth. This aligns with the 'Helper Therapy Principle', which shows that providing support enhances the self-esteem of the supporter as much as the recipient. Together, these findings affirm that when women uplift each other, everyone benefits.

CONFIDENCE
ISN'T JUST
SOMETHING WE
BUILD, IT'S ALSO
SOMETHING
WE CAN GIVE.
AND WHEN
WE SHARE
IT, IT GROWS.

Share your confidence. Celebrate your confidence. Let someone borrow it. Because confidence isn't a scarce resource. The more you give, the more you get. When we model confidence, when we name it in others, when we pass it on, we don't just grow individual confidence. We build collective power. And that's not just beautiful. It's science.

The truth is there has always been enough confidence for everyone, if you share it with intention.

Now you know this, what will you do with that power?

UPFRONT Moment

Think of UPFRONT Moments as your confidence reps—moments of practice, reflection and honesty that only you can do, and do over again. They are designed to be part repetition and part challenge. This isn't about finding the 'right' answer. It's about building your awareness, one rep at a time. Consistent practice is your best friend. Confidence isn't something someone else can give you. It's something you grow through doing this work, with yourself, for yourself.

You are the expert on your experience. No one else knows what it feels like to speak with your voice or carry your stories. That means no one else can define confidence for you.

So this is your invitation to slow down, check in and keep showing up for the most important conversation of all: the one with yourself.

Where is scarcity showing up in your life?

Take a moment to notice the places where you feel like there's not enough. Not enough time. Not enough money. Not enough opportunities. Not enough space for your voice, your ideas, your joy.

Now go deeper, where does scarcity show up in your work? Maybe you are afraid to ask for a raise, or worried

SHARE YOUR CONFIDENCE. CELEBRATE YOUR CONFIDENCE. LET SOMEONE BORROW IT.

there's only room for one person at the top? Do you find yourself competing instead of collaborating? Do you hold back on sharing your ideas because you're scared they'll be dismissed or stolen?

Go further, where does it show up in your friendships? Do you believe there's only so much love or attention to go around? Do you feel jealous when good things happen to others, even if you're happy for them too? Do you shrink yourself so you don't take up 'too much' space?

Get really personal, where does it show up in your dreams? Have you convinced yourself that success is for other people, not people like you? Do you lower your hopes so you won't be disappointed? Do you keep yourself small because you're scared there's only so much success, or someone else got there first?

Now ask yourself this beauty: what would it feel like to believe there is enough for all of us? Enough time. Enough confidence. Enough support. Enough space. Enough joy. Enough opportunity.

Write about what would change:

- In how you speak to yourself
- In how you show up at work
- In how you treat your friends and other women
- In how you imagine your future

You don't have to feel abundance to start practising it. In fact, feelings are almost always a product of action or inaction, not the other way around. But just begin by noticing where scarcity lives and where you're ready to let it go.

How does it feel to imagine power not as something we *take*, but something we *make together*?

So many of us were taught that power is limited. That for one person to rise, someone else has to fall. That it's a race. A hierarchy. A crown passed from one hand to the next. But what if that's not true? What if power is something we *build* and *share* together? What if your confidence doesn't just serve *you*, but it serves everyone around you?

Take a moment to reflect on this question: what happens when you share your confidence? Ask yourself:

- Do people around you speak up more?
- Do you give others permission to be bold, messy, curious or brave?
- Do you model something that helps someone else feel less alone?
- Do you feel stronger when you're helping others rise, not just trying to rise alone?

Now finish this sentence, in as many ways as you can:

'When I share my confidence, I . . .'

Try:

- 'When I share my confidence, I give others permission to speak'.
- 'When I share my confidence, I lead with joy'.
- 'When I share my confidence, I remember how far I've come'.
- 'When I share my confidence, I help build a different kind of world'.

And remember you don't need to have a 'platform' of 'followers' to share your confidence. You just need to show up as yourself, with your voice, your boundaries, your support and your ideas.

Note

1. Yang, Y., Chawla, N.V., and Uzzi, B. (2019). A network's gender composition and communication pattern predict women's leadership success. *Proceedings of the National Academy of Sciences* 116 (6): 2033–2038. https://doi.org/10.1073/pnas.1721438116.

3

You Are Practising Confidence

Old Rule: Confidence is about big moments

New Rule: Confidence is about small moments

Let me tell you a story about a girl.

She grew up on a steady diet of Disney films, magazine quizzes and 'you can be anything' slogans, as long as that 'anything' was a perfectly dressed, high-achieving, effortlessly likeable woman. You know the type: married, maternal, rich-but-not-rude, sexy-but-classy, funny-but-never-too-loud. She makes six figures, keeps white cotton bedding clean, drinks smoothies before sunrise and always, *always*, sends thank-you notes.

Sound familiar?

Somewhere along the way, we were sold the idea that *real confidence* comes from checking off the milestones. Nail the job. Nail the relationship. Nail the aesthetic. (Don't forget to actually have pretty nails, too. French manicure preferred.) We were conditioned to believe confidence is the trophy you get for achieving the unachievable.

What an utterly ridiculous idea. To have us believe that confidence resides in these big moments of achievement, moments of promotion, buying fancy cars and clothes. What's so damn clever about this particular lie is that it makes confidence feel too big for us to reach. It's unattainable. Too far away. Too mysterious. So we concede to a life without it. Moving through the world at half mast. 'It's for those other people. The confident ones', we say.

Or the other story for the few of us is that we persist. We keep fighting and pushing until we get the big job and the big car. Then, Boom! Confidence whiplash. We realise those big moments don't deliver the lasting confidence we've been waiting all our lives for. Think of your friend who's spent years working towards a promotion, finally lands it and then feels even more anxious in her new role. Or your friend who loses weight, thinking it will bring her joy, but still struggles with self-esteem. In addition to these big moments largely being unattainable, if they are attained, the goal posts move. The promotion, the big car, the house, the beauty standard is followed by an infinitely bigger, better, even more unattainable version.

It's an emotional rollercoaster, a perpetually cyclical machine that gets us nowhere. And it's one I've spent too many hours on. It goes a little something like this:

- **The Build-Up:** I focused all my energy on achieving a particular revenue number for my business, convinced if I got there everything would feel better. I poured everything I had, every ounce of focus and every waking thought into chasing one specific revenue goal. I was convinced that if I could just hit that number, everything would finally slot into place. I'd feel safe. Settled. Worthy. It became the answer to every anxious thought I had: '*Just get there. Just get there*'.

- **The Achievement:** I bloody did it and it was scary and amazing. I got such a rush, for a short time. It was electrifying, a wave of adrenaline, pride, disbelief. I cried.

I laughed. I felt like I could breathe for the first time in months. For a little while, I rode the high like it would never end. I thought: '*This is it. I've made it*'.

- **The Letdown:** To celebrate, I booked a solo trip, my treat to myself for surviving the climb. I imagined feeling radiant, powerful, basking in the joy I'd earned. Instead, sitting alone in a strange hotel room, the silence pressed in. The rush evaporated. In its place: guilt, confusion, loneliness. I kept thinking, '*Well I don't really deserve this. It wasn't even that hard so why am I celebrating? It probably will never last and this is just a high before the fall!*' I felt like I was letting myself down, like I had ordered something off a menu, waited months for it to arrive and now that it was here, it didn't taste like I thought it would.

- **The Doubt:** I felt like I was back where I started or even worse, like there was something wrong with me for not feeling the way I thought I would. I felt *broken*. '*Why isn't this enough? What's wrong with me? Was all of it for nothing? What am I even doing?*' Instead of basking in pride, I was spiralling. I felt like I was right back where I started—or maybe even further behind, because now I knew the finish line I'd been chasing was never going to save me.

Confidence whiplash happens because these big moments, the achievements, promotions and compliments, are all about other people. The audience. The observer. They might boost our confidence for a feather of time. But it doesn't last. Confidence has been sold to you as a *destination*, a finish line you cross when you achieve enough. When that finish line keeps moving it's exhausting. The idea that confidence comes from 'having it all' or 'being enough' is a myth. Even when and if you check off societal milestones, you will probably still feel inadequate.

Let me show you a different way.

The Power of Small Moments

Confidence isn't tied to what you *have* but how you *feel*. The answer is swapping big moments for small moments. Teeny tiny moments that happen multiple times over your days. How you talk to yourself when you make a mistake and what you tell yourself when you look in the mirror. How you react when you're given an opportunity. And do you know what the absolute best part is? The big moments will still come, but when they do they will be about YOU, not other people. I'm grinning so wide my face hurts because I cannot wait for you to get stuck into these small moments and feel the shift. Here are some of my favourites:

1. Asking myself, 'What's the best thing that could happen?'
2. Wearing bright, bold, jewellery that makes me feel like a walking celebration.
3. Being a believing mirror for the women in my life. The term *believing mirror* was coined by Julia Cameron, the author of *The Artist's Way*, a beloved guide to unblocking creativity. She describes a believing mirror as someone who reflects back your most hopeful, most possible self, especially when you're struggling to see it yourself. It's an incredible thing: being seen, not just for who you are now, but for who you could become.
4. Saying 'yes' to a project that scares and excites me at the same time.
5. Letting myself take up space in a conversation, speaking slowly, with no rush to shrink or finish.
6. Gifting myself a solo date just because I can.
7. Sending a text to a friend telling her the specific thing I admire about her.

8. Celebrating a small, unseen victory with as much joy as a big one.
9. Making a brave request instead of assuming the answer will be no.

From Moments to Meaning

Focusing on the small moments is important because it's these moments that help you stay connected to your truth and your values. When you're connected to who you are and what you believe in, you are connected to your own power. When you can find those small moments in every day, you are consistently building your confidence, one moment at a time.

I shared some of my small moments, but the beauty of this practice is that there is no real limit to what your small moment can look like. You need to find your own version of these, so you can recognise them, day in, day out.

What Confidence Looks Like in Real Life

Katell found a writing practice through the Bond:

> *Throughout the Bond we were encouraged to journal (something I found challenging) and to support one another (which came easily and felt genuinely rewarding). At the end of the program, we were asked to write a poem or at least, to show up in some way. To my surprise, I ended up*

writing a substantial acrostic poem. Not only did I finish it, but the content made sense to me. I was actually proud. Still, I had no intention of sharing it, definitely not with the community. But then I remembered everything we'd learned about confidence and visibility. So I did the unthinkable: I posted the poem in UPFRONT Global for everyone to see or hopefully miss. It was the wee hours of the morning, and I figured most people wouldn't even notice it. Wrong.

Another Bonder who had also written a poem and was asked to perform it invited me to join her. My sarcasm, the trusty shield I've always used, kicked in, and I joked about how I didn't even want to write anything, let alone perform it. But inside, I was spiralling with anxiety. And then something clicked. I realised that if I didn't take that step in the safest place I could possibly take it, I'd be holding myself back again. It wasn't about perfection. It was about showing up. So I performed the poem. Full of nervousness. Full of self-judgment. But I did it. And now here I am, writing again. And actually enjoying it. Me, the one who didn't even want to write a poem a couple of weeks ago.

Remember these are small moments; Katell's bigger moment of performing her poem started with the small act of journalling. You might not go on the same journey Katell did, but practising small moments like this are essential for your confidence, and might just take you somewhere amazing. Learn what you can from each small practice and keep going. Keep trying new things or going back to old hobbies, until you find the thing or things (you can have more than one) that make you feel confident.

Then work out how to introduce these moments to your life more regularly. Cold-water dips once a week? Great. Spending 10 minutes drawing in the morning? Fantastic. Taking 30 minutes after collecting the kids from school to play silly games with them around the house? Amazing. Do what makes you feel good.

But often the problem we see time and again isn't necessarily the finding of these moments. A little reflection on your happiest moments might get you there. The problem comes when we try to take time for ourselves, time just for ourselves and our small moments. Because often for women, we can only take time for ourselves by saying no to spending time serving others. Whether that be supporting our partner and our children or simply doing household chores. Let me introduce you to *Positive Selfishness* via my UPFRONT Moment podcast guest Francesca Specter, author of *Alonement*. Here's what she had to say:

> *Sometimes when we advocate for ourselves and it's not hurting anyone else, it's a really positive space. And if we're not meeting our needs, if we're not at least giving that to ourselves as women, as humans, then that's going to come out somewhere, we're going to resent our children or our partners. We're going to hold it against them because we all have these things within us, whether you call it a soul or a natural human passion and curiosity. But if we feel too guilty to do it, then we're not really leading a meaningful life. For many women, the very idea of carving out time to be selfish, to invest time in me, is an alien idea because it's not something that they've been brought up witnessing and it's also not something our society rewards or celebrates.*

Selfing

You can embrace positive selfishness however works for you. It might mean making time to cook yourself a delicious meal. It could be taking a whole day out for yourself. Or it may be 15 minutes of uninterrupted peace to enjoy your morning coffee. At UPFRONT we call the act of positive selfishness **Selfing**. Think of it as self-care meets positive selfishness. And we define Selfing as anything which incorporates looking after yourself and prioritising yourself. So not only taking uninterrupted time out, or taking the day for yourself. But also going to therapy, having a regular exercise routine, taking a course or even just actively eating a healthier diet. When you are Selfing you are working on you, for you. I want you to embrace this concept as you navigate through this book, as this is what you are doing right now. You are engaging with yourself for yourself, the UPFRONT way, you are *Selfing*.

Going from small moments of confidence to Selfing is different for everyone. We see such variation in Selfing from our Bonders that I would be committing an injustice to those Bonders if I didn't share some of their stories here. Meet Stacey:

> *I'm looking at my Bond graduation certificate. I'm going to print it, frame it, and display it. This is my new story. When I received my testamur for my Doctorate in the mail, I barely glanced at it. I felt nothing. No pride, no happiness, nothing in response to this tangible reminder of my enormous achievement. Celebrating my wins was something quashed from me early on. When I'd graduated with my Bachelor's degree, my father took my testamur 'for safe keeping'. I didn't live with my parents then. They didn't finance me to get to that point.*

In fact, during those years of study, my father intentionally made my life more difficult than it needed to be. I lived away from my parents, in a different state. Yet, he refused to sign a simple government form acknowledging that he wasn't supporting me financially. Because I was under a certain age, and because his income was above a certain threshold, the government assumed he was supporting me. I had no power to claim otherwise, without his signature on that form. Without it, I couldn't receive any financial support. 'I don't want people to think I can't support my daughter', is what he'd said. While not supporting his daughter.

And so, for all those years, I lived in poverty, supporting myself through multiple casual jobs, living in unsuitable share houses, grateful that I was vibrant and pretty, because it meant a lot of dinner dates, and that meant eating more than just apples and porridge. All the same, he took my testamur. It was made of vellum. The replacement, which I paid for years later, was printed on paper.

When an article based on my master's research (my first ever academic publication) was accepted into a high-ranking journal, the new man who controlled me yelled and yelled at me about his own achievements until I shrunk into a sad mass of nothingness.

Of course, these are not the only reasons for my lack of celebration. By nature, I prefer the process over the outcome. That's enough reason, isn't it? Until I made a conscious effort not to, I'd only experienced nothingness when people congratulated me. Mostly, I hid my achievements. Learning to celebrate my wins has come only recently. And sharing some of my smaller wins along with

UPFRONT has encouraged me to further embrace the joy, to celebrate, to acknowledge the outcomes of my effort. I nurture this practice every single day.

Stacey's story is a powerful reminder that confidence doesn't always look like shouting from rooftops or taking up physical space. It begins as the quiet small decision to take your own success seriously, perhaps for the first time. To reframe your story not through the lens of those who diminished you, but through your own eyes. For Stacey, printing and framing her Bond graduation certificate is more than a gesture, it's reclamation, it's Selfing. It's saying this matters. I matter. After a lifetime of conditioning and being treated poorly taught her to mute her joy, shrink her worth and accept control disguised as care, Selfing is radical. That's what learning confidence can look like—a deeply personal shift from silence to celebration. Not big and flashy but small and sacred.

Sometimes, that rewrite shows up in academia. Other times, it shows up at the front door, with shoes on, kids waving goodbye. Magda is a Bond graduate whose experience of Selfing is exactly that. Here's her story:

I went out in the evening for drinks and food with fellow mums, leaving my gorgeous children in the care of their dad. This might seem like a small thing, but for me, it was massive. Since becoming a mum five years ago, I've always been the one doing bedtime. I haven't been out in the evenings, not even once. I had mixed feelings about it. A part of me felt guilty but another part knew that if I don't give my husband the space to work out his own strategies and connect with our children in his way, then I'm holding us all back. And if I never carve out time for myself, I'll burn out. I had such a nourishing, wholesome evening. We shared stories, talked about all sorts of interesting things, and I felt like me again, not just a mum but a whole person.

And you know what? My kids were fine. They saw me leave, they were happy because they were with their dad, who loves them deeply, and the world didn't end. It wasn't a disaster. It was a milestone!

Magda's story lives in the same truth. One night out. One bedtime routine passed over to her partner. One small, brave step into Selfing. Not a huge act but an utterly transformative one.

Both stories show us that confidence is not a single leap but a series of small moments. A daily discipline. Practising confidence doesn't always mean public speaking or asking for a raise, it's also saying *yes* to yourself and *no* to guilt. It's framing the certificate. It's walking out the front door. It's making a bolder small choice today than you did yesterday.

These small acts accumulate. They reshape your identity. They shift how you see yourself and how others respond to us. Over time, they lead to big changes. A new story. A stronger self. A life built on chosen confidence not inherited silence. This is the work. This is the practice. Confidence is not who you are. It's what you do. Every single day and Selfing is how you do it.

UPFRONT Moment

Confidence isn't something you gain once and keep forever. It's a practice.

Take a moment to think about what that means. Picture your confidence not as a prize. Not a moment. Not a final exam you either pass or fail. Picture your confidence as a practice. Something you return to. Something you build through repetition, self-trust and care.

Ask yourself:

- What small daily action could feel like an act of *devotion* to yourself?
- Is it starting the day with silence? Wearing lipstick that makes you feel electric? Taking 10 minutes for a solo walk before your world needs you again? Saying no to an invitation without explaining and guilt? Saying yes to rest without explaining and guilt?
- What would change if you treated your confidence like something alive, something that needs tending, feeding and rest?

Write it all down. Let your answers be as practical or as poetic as you need them to be. This is about *your* practice, *your* pace, *your* power.

When you were growing up, what 'Big Moments' were you taught would bring you confidence? Pause here and try to name them. Write them down one by one. Was it:

- A wedding?
- A degree?
- A job title?
- A salary level?
- A weight on the scale?
- A house, a baby, a ring?

And now ask:

- How many of those 'big' moments still influence your choices?
- Are you still chasing any of them, even if they're no longer your dream?
- What would it feel like to gently put one of them down?

You were sold a story that confidence comes in one big, shiny moment. But you're here now, unlearning that story. Rewriting the rules. Start by noticing which rules are still living in your body and which ones you're ready to leave behind. It's time.

4

You Are a Match for Your Discomfort

Old Rule: Confidence is comfortable

New Rule: Confidence is uncomfortable

Every day I choose an uncomfortable path. I chose to be an entrepreneur in my twenties, which, needless to say, meant choosing stress, sleepless nights and permanent uncertainty. I choose to live in Sweden with next to no support network. I choose parenting away from my family and constant unfamiliarity. I choose leadership which is often isolating and lonely. I choose no playbook and constant growth. I choose all of this on purpose, intentionally. It's incredibly uncomfortable sometimes. But one of the beautiful by-products of these choices is confidence. Confidence and discomfort are the best of friends. Discomfort is a sign you're stepping into uncharted territory and trying something new, pushing boundaries or showing up in ways that stretch you. Discomfort is the price of entry. My discomfort is a badge of honour I wear proudly.

Trying is required, especially trying new things. Trying on a new version of yourself, like a gorgeous heavy vintage coat that's slightly too big for you. If you're really trying then it's inherently uncomfortable. But, do you know what else trying is? Trying is sexy. It's caring, it's living, it's achieving—and that's regardless of the result. If you are trying you are succeeding. For so long, I believed the women I admired weren't trying. I watched them build companies, raise families, speak on stages, write books, rest, and do it all with seemingly no effort. They made it look so easy. Natural. Certain. Sure. The opposite was true. They were all trying. Hard.

Ironically, I am now a woman who other women think of in this way. A friend kindly let me into the version of me she holds in her head; I'm a woman who gets out of bed every morning feeling *very sure*. I'm flattered (I think) but the truth is I'm not sure. It's been over a decade in the making to be OK with this. My sureness isn't 100%, and I don't think it ever will be, or should be. But the last 15 years of shipping, showing up and building businesses have helped me get to where I am. I'm committed to building UPFRONT. There have been red threads that I've always been sure of: you learn by doing, action builds confidence and design is the best process I have to make change happen. But there have been mountains of things I have been unsure about. The mountain grows the more I learn and the more I progress, and this is a good thing.

Being certain is dangerous. Our political parties are full of incompetent men who are sure *and* wrong. It's up to you to take action despite not being sure; ironically it's the only time action should be taken. 'Sure' should be your warning system for missing something. To move forward while holding onto the curiosity that reminds you of how much you don't know is the aim. The benchmark of progress is discomfort; the product of progress is confidence.

Some questions to ask yourself:

- How uncomfortable are you right now?
- Where are you waiting to be sure?

- Have you thought about the cost of waiting?
- What would feeling more sure mean to you?
- Are you using someone else's level of sureness as a barometer for your own? This last one is a dangerous game to play as nobody is honest about their level of sureness. Nobody's TikToking about being unsure.

There are three levels of being sure in the UPFRONT Sureness Scale:

1. Completely unsure (you know absolutely nothing)
2. You know enough (the sweet spot)
3. Completely sure (you know everything)

Here's the magic that's actually just good sense. You'll never know everything for sure so level three is a dangerous illusion. If you're here then maybe listening to people who don't sound like you is good advice, and maybe this book isn't right for you after all. You should be questioning what you think you know. If you're sitting at level one, completely unsure, then it is risky to move forward with your ideas—but this is also very rare. If you feel you're in this spot then you should similarly question what you think you know, or don't. This leaves almost everyone, and I'm betting this includes you, in the sweet spot. Yes, some amount of knowing something is enough, a speck of knowledge is enough to get going. Because you become more sure and more confident by taking action. This is the gold in this rule of thumb. It's not sureness that's important. It's action. And all of this is to tell you squarely that you know enough to be sure enough, to make a move, to take the first step. It's uncomfortable, and it should be.

Let's talk about practice, it's the 'get good' in the immaculate advice of '*get going, then get good*' from artist, designer and founder Jack Butcher. The 'get going' is the speck of knowledge, the speck of sureness you already have. The get going is practice and no, practice doesn't make perfect, that's just another handy word that starts with a p. Practice doesn't make perfect, that's a fallacy, practice makes confidence. And if there is anything you take away from this book, let it be this. You have to practise confidence to be confident. That is to say, you have to practise being uncomfortable.

Let's take a tangible example: comedians. Their job is to make you feel comfortable, laugh and hang on every word of their story. But here's the thing: every line, every pause, every stumble over a word, every drop of a prop, even when it looks like an accident, is planned. It's been rehearsed, sometimes for years. Yet when you watch them, it feels spontaneous, it even feels like they're winging it sometimes. It looks effortless and natural. It's all practised.

Like the women I looked up to when I was younger, what looks effortless is often the result of extraordinary effort. The more polished it seems, the more work has gone into making it look that way. Confidence isn't magic. It's practice, repetition and showing up again and again. The real question is: how much practice are you willing to put in?

Learning confidence is not easy or comfortable—if it was I wouldn't be writing this book. Building confidence is not effortless or certain, it just looks that way sometimes. It is messy, scary and difficult. But if you can master the skill of being OK with discomfort you can do anything. *Anything.*

Comedians have mastered the skill of being OK with discomfort and turned it into entertainment and successful careers. But what happens if you master the skill of discomfort and apply it to social and political change? You step up. You have to. You change the world. Here's Dr Meenal Viz's story of doing exactly that.

Stepping Up

Dr Meenal Viz stepped up and out of comfort during the COVID-19 pandemic in 2020. Meenal is an NHS doctor who went viral for her one-woman protest outside Downing Street; she was calling for more to be done to protect front-line health workers. She was six months pregnant and was being confronted by the severity of the situation every day. '*I found myself in a very difficult position*', she told me when she joined the *UPFRONT Moment* podcast.[1]

> *I felt like I wanted to speak up, but I didn't have the language. How do you say, 'This is not right and something needs to be done'? In my head I had people from Instagram and on TED Talks with these inspirational messages and I thought I can't speak like that. But my gut feeling was that if I didn't speak up, I would probably regret it for the rest of my life.*

Meenal knew that pregnant healthcare workers in particular weren't being protected and more specifically that those from ethnic minority groups weren't being heard. This was despite all the evidence showing that they were disproportionately affected by the virus. She was threatened by the NHS for speaking up, and knew that doing so meant she could lose her job and her medical licence. Meenal was also under pressure from her family to stay quiet.

The trigger that pushed her to her one-woman protest outside Downing Street was the death of pregnant nurse Mary Agyapong. Mary Agyeiwaa Agyapong, 28, died after giving birth at Luton and Dunstable Hospital, where she also worked.

*Her husband lived across the road from us and she
left behind her newborn baby and her two year old.
I saw the grief that hit this family . . . I don't know
if it was my pregnancy hormones or my gut feeling,
but I said, 'I have to do something about this'. So
that's when I went and protested outside Downing
Street.*

The newspapers picked up Meenal's story, and a photo
of her standing alone, heavily pregnant and wearing a mask
outside Downing Street went viral overnight. She was holding a sign that simply said: *'Protect healthcare workers'*. Meenal was inundated with messages of support, including from
a number of retired doctors who encouraged her to take the
government to court over the lack of PPE (personal protective equipment) being provided to healthcare workers. Meenal took a huge step outside of her comfort zone and into
discomfort yet again to start legal proceedings.

*'At the time, because there was such a sense of urgency,
I had to ask people for help and I wasn't afraid of doing that'.*
This was a huge change for Meenal, who admitted she has
historically been very bad at asking for help. *'I think it's part
of the culture of being a doctor. You want to feel like you can
do everything by yourself'*, she explained. *'But I realised that
despite what the world tells you, or how it tries to make you
feel as though nobody wants to help and nobody wants to
listen, people will listen, they will help'.*

Meenal received thousands of pounds in donations to
help with the legal challenge. The whole process took over
eight months before the government finally agreed to change
the guidelines and make it a legal requirement for the NHS to
provide protective gear for workers.

Dr Meenal Viz's story powerfully illustrates what can
happen when we learn to be OK with discomfort and unsure-
ness. But look closely at Meenal's story. Where did Meenal sit

on the Sureness Scale? If Meenal didn't practise being uncomfortable, maybe she would have looked at the legal battle with the NHS as a non-starter, as something she knew nothing about—Meenal is a medical doctor after all, not a lawyer. But she knew how the government was behaving towards PPE for their workers was not OK; she knew enough to act. She was in the sweet spot of the Sureness Scale, and that's all she needed. The next step was action. Then a dramatic and important change occurred. Meenal is a shining beacon of an example of what we teach at UPFRONT, and pertinent to the teaching in this chapter. Practising being in discomfort leads to confidence, which leads to action, which leads to change.

Meenal's story is huge, complex and fast-paced. This makes Gilly MacArthur's story of paying the cost of entry to confidence a beautiful contrast. Gilly meets discomfort daily, and in cold water.[2] Here's her story.

Meeting Discomfort in Cold Water

Gilly MacArthur didn't grow up dreaming of icy lakes. In fact, she jokes that she was once the person bundled in down jackets all year round. But when she moved to England's Lake District in her forties and found herself craving connection to nature, she decided to give cold water swimming a try.

The first time she entered the frigid waters of Windermere, wrapped in a wetsuit, it was hard, brutally hard. But when she got home that day, she noticed something surprising: a deep, buzzing pride. A sense that she'd done something brave, something different. She returned the next day, ditching the wetsuit, and she hasn't stopped since.

Nine winters later, Gilly is a cold-water swim coach, helping hundreds of people, especially women, lean into discomfort for their mental and physical well-being. She describes cold swimming as a daily 'reset', a way to reconnect to the raw sensations of nature and to her own body.

Gilly knows first-hand that confidence isn't built by being comfortable, it's built from showing up again and again, even when it's difficult and uncomfortable. It's exactly about being OK with discomfort. Even now, she often stands at the water's edge and needs to have a pep talk with herself to get in. '*It doesn't get easier*', she says. '*But you learn about strength in community and with that confidence!*'

For Gilly, discomfort has become a portal to personal power. Cold water isn't just something she endures, it's something she welcomes—a reminder that she can do difficult things, and that every time she chooses discomfort, she grows.

Her confidence didn't stop at the lake's edge either. When a serious rock climbing fall left Gilly with a broken back, she faced another choice: retreat into fear and inaction, or rebuild her relationship with risk and discomfort. Through months of recovery, she intentionally shifted her focus towards what was still possible, refusing to let her accident define her. When she eventually returned to climb in the very same place where she fell, it wasn't because the fear had disappeared, it was because she had learned how to carry it differently. It was because she spent many years practising being in discomfort on her own terms.

Today, Gilly is a coach and a mentor, helping hundreds of people meet their own fears at the water's edge. She doesn't promise it gets easier. She promises you will get stronger. Confidence, she teaches, isn't a feeling you wait for, it's a muscle you build by stepping into discomfort again and again.

Gilly's story reminds us that confidence doesn't come from comfort, and growth isn't supposed to feel easy. Readiness is a complicated myth. It's action, not waiting for a high level of sureness, that changes you. Powerful transformations often start when we stop waiting to feel completely sure and start trusting that we are already a match for our discomfort. You are in the sweet spot and it's time to do the thing.

Bonders Doing the Thing

Gilly is one of many women showing us what it looks like to act before you feel ready. To trust that discomfort is the cost to confidence and growth. The Bond is full of thousands of women who've done the same, women like Emily.

Here's what Emily had to say about her Bond journey and how sitting with discomfort led to her confidence and growth.

> *The Bond is what helped me to get started on my patient ambassador journey. When I did the Bond, I had recently applied for and been accepted as a volunteer patient ambassador at MedicsForRareDisease. I was so keen to support this charity as I'm very passionate about the cause, a focus for medics on rare disease with the aim of shortening the diagnostic odyssey for rare disease patients. Despite my enthusiasm, I was also nervous about making myself vulnerable and sharing my own experience as a rare disease patient.*
>
> *I felt conflicted about wanting to share what I'd been through, and also not wanting to relive it or seem attention-seeking. As a result, I procrastinated over simple tasks like creating social media posts to promote and support the charity. The Bond's approach to confidence and 'doing the thing' spurred me on to get that first LinkedIn post written, and I did! It didn't feel comfortable, but I did it anyway and the Bonders gave me some lovely feedback. This was the first step on my journey to feeling better about what I was doing and I haven't looked back since. The opportunity to talk on a podcast came up shortly after and I did that too. I was asked back on the podcast for a second time, and I accepted.*

*I now have three of these under my belt and really
enjoy doing them; something I never thought I'd
do or say!*

When we think of 'doing the thing', we often picture
bold leaps, like pressing publish, stepping on stage, saying
yes to something new. But sometimes, doing the thing means
choosing not to. Saying no. Speaking up. Drawing a line. Setting a boundary. These actions can feel just as, if not even
more, uncomfortable. And yet, they are just as vital to our
growth, our confidence and our ability to change.

Boundaries

Sometimes, doing the thing means saying no. Sometimes, it
means protecting your time, your energy and your values,
even when that feels deeply uncomfortable. This kind of
discomfort is quiet, but it's powerful. It asks us to face our
people-pleasing, our perfectionism and our fear of being perceived as difficult or unhelpful.

Abbie's Bond journey is a brilliant example of what this
looks like in real life, leaning into the discomfort of boundaries and resisting the reflex to say 'yes' too quickly:

*This week, I've been dedicating more time and
energy to specific things rather than constantly
feeling like I'm jumping backwards and forwards
across a whole heap of different tasks. I've been
setting myself time to complete or progress on a
particular element. I've been using my calendar to
'book in time' for key things and I've made sure
that I don't have Slack and emails sitting open on
my screen.*

The biggest win, and the thing that's made a big difference, is that I've been pushing back more. I've been clearer about my priorities and time-frames. It's a hard habit to break. And it's been uncomfortable. I've always been such a 'yes!' person, the second anyone asks me to do anything. But I know that all that means is that I feel like I have open tabs and then more open tabs, other people's tabs, and nothing ever gets closed!

I've ended the week feeling so much better about my priorities and my ever-growing to-do list. But I do feel a little anxious knowing that it's Monday again tomorrow and I need to focus on not falling back into the 'yes, right away!' safety zone, I need to keep practising being in discomfort. Need to keep being UPFRONT. No one ever got anywhere by being comfortable, right?

Abbie's right of course—learning confidence isn't easy or comfortable. Building confidence isn't effortless or certain. But it is worth it. It's amazing how much your life will change when you realise just how much it's worth it. I need you to hear me. Trying despite the discomfort, despite the uncertainty, despite the barriers, despite the messiness is where the richest rewards are.

Because you, too, just like Gilly, Meenal, Abbie and Emily, are a match for your discomfort.

UPFRONT Moment

We're often told to 'wait until we're ready', to 'trust our gut' or 'know when the time is right'. But let's be honest: how often does that mythical feeling of total readiness actually show up?

Waiting to feel 100% sure before we leap can keep us stuck for months, years, sometimes forever. Not on my watch!

Confidence grows not from waiting, but from acting. From doing the thing while your hands shake. From taking the next step even when you're still figuring it out. That doesn't mean being reckless. It means recognising when you're sitting comfortably in the sweet spot and choosing to move forward anyway.

Take a moment to reflect on this:

- Where in your life are you waiting to feel 'sure' before you leap?
- What is that waiting costing you? (In energy, joy, time, opportunity?)
- What would happen if you acted now, even while feeling unsure?
- Who or what are you waiting for and why?

Write it all down. Let it be messy. No censoring. Get honest with yourself about what's keeping you in the waiting room. Then ask yourself: is it time to walk out the door?

Confidence often begins with trying. Trying on a bigger version of yourself before you fully believe she's yours.

Think about when you were a child and built a den. You didn't wait for someone to tell you what to do, you experimented. You acted 'as if'. Confidence is the same. It starts with trying. It starts with imagining yourself as the person who says the bold thing, leads the project, presses send or sets a boundary. At first, it might feel awkward, like a coat that's a size too big. But with practice, it begins to fit.

This is your invitation to try.

- Picture yourself trying on a 'bigger' version of you. What is she doing?
- What does it feel like in your body? Where does it feel thrilling? Where does it feel awkward?
- What would it take to grow into this version slowly, gently and bravely?
- What old beliefs do you need to let go of in order to own this version of yourself?

There is no 'right' fit. There's only your next, more expansive shape. Keep trying. I'm rooting for you.

Notes

1. How to successfully challenge the status quo, *UPFRONT Moment with Lauren Currie* [Podcast], 2023.
2. Choosing confidence and cold water, *UPFRONT Moment with Lauren Currie* [Podcast], 2023.

5

You Were Never the Imposter

Old Rule: You have imposter syndrome

New Rule: You don't have imposter syndrome

Self-doubt gets a bad rap. Entire industries exist to try and banish it. It brings shame, fear and the urge to hide. You go to great lengths to make it disappear. To pretend it's not there. You ignore it. You see it as a big flashing neon sign that you are doing it wrong, or worse, you give up entirely. Self-doubt can become too heavy to carry. But self-doubt isn't the enemy. Self-doubt is a natural part of progress and growth. You can't learn confidence without it.

I refuse to live in a world where self-doubt is seen as a flaw. Instead, I see it for what it really is—a sign that you're building confidence. Self-doubt always gets a seat at my table, it does not get banished in my world. I've learned to dance with it, knowing that its presence means I'm heading in the right direction. When she arrives, we to-and-fro like old friends. The key to dancing with your self-doubt is not letting her stop you from doing the work, she's just coming along for the ride. She's your partner in crime. Every time she whispers a negative thought like '*You don't belong here*' or '*You're going to get it all wrong*', it's a push to the left. Your only job is to correct to the right. You reply kindly with, '*Yes, I might get it wrong and that's OK*'. Your reply says that you're here to try, to progress regardless. The world will try to tell you that you don't belong, you'll get it wrong or you're not the right person for the task. Every time I swing left or right and dance with my self-doubt, I'm proving to myself that self-doubt doesn't hold the power. I do. She and I are building my confidence as we dance, we are one. Trying to block her out or fight her only slows your growth. Acknowledge her, smile when she arrives even. Then do your dance.

Later in this chapter, I'll show you how I've learned to schedule my self-doubt so it doesn't run the show. Self-doubt is not something to crush, it's something to carry with care. I desperately wish some of the people in power had more self-doubt. The politicians taking away women's rights or the far-right groups protesting against progress—where is their self-doubt? They've ignored it, and now they're dangerously narrow-minded. But I see self-doubt hanging out in schools, universities, offices and living rooms full of young girls and women with bright ideas who've been taught to doubt themselves to an unhealthy extreme. I'm here to redress this balance. Imagine if we could redirect all that self-doubt to the men in power, those who hold the reins and make poor decisions time and again. Wouldn't that shift the world into being a better place? Of course it would.

The biggest mistake I see women in the Bond make is mistaking their self-doubt for a lack of competence. Most of the time you are doubting yourself because you're learning or you're in a totally new situation. When you really lean into this idea, self-doubt lessens its grip and becomes a signal of growth.

Research backs this up: a 2010 study found that people with moderate self-doubt tend to develop higher self-awareness, stay more motivated to learn and show stronger long-term performance, especially when they feel safe and supported.[1]

You Deserve to Be in the Room

Let's talk about imposter syndrome. It's become a pop psychology buzzword, especially in spaces focused on women's development. Everywhere you turn, there's a workshop promising to 'help you overcome imposter syndrome'. It's trendy. Familiar. Yet, the way we use this term deserves deeper scrutiny.

This framing, as if women are somehow flawed, is where the lie begins. For years, this concept has been used to describe nagging feelings of not deserving our success, that we're somehow faking it or don't belong. It's often framed as a psychological issue that needs to be fixed within the individual. It labels women's doubts and insecurities as something inherently wrong with them, a syndrome no less, instead of questioning why so many women, especially women of colour, feel this way in the first place.

I need you to believe me when I say **you do not have imposter syndrome**.

You have self-doubt. You have fear. You have hesitation. These are all normal reactions to doing hard things, to stepping into the unknown, to navigating systems that were never designed for you, especially if you're a woman, a person of colour, neurodivergent or living at the intersections of these identities. But calling these feelings a *syndrome*, as if you're broken, sick or flawed, is not just unhelpful. It's harmful.

Here's how the confusion started: the term *imposter phenomenon* was coined in the 1970s by two psychologists studying high-achieving women. It was never intended to become a blanket label for every woman who has ever second-guessed herself. And yet, over time, it morphed into imposter syndrome, a diagnosis, a tidy explanation and, often, an invitation to fix *yourself* instead of the world around you.

But how can this be an individual issue if 82% of women report experiencing it? That number doesn't suggest a personal flaw. It reveals a pattern, one that's especially sharp for women of colour. Here's what systemic erasure can look like in real life, as told by Talisa Lavarry in her book, *Confessions from Your Token Black Colleague*. She was leading a high-profile event with a major keynote speaker, none other than former president Barack Obama. On paper, she was the perfect person for the job. But behind the scenes, she faced relentless bullying and questioning of her abilities, all of which stemmed from systemic racism and bias. Lavarry's colleagues, the majority of whom were white, repeatedly undermined her despite glowing praise from the client. She began to question her own competence, doubting whether she was qualified, even as she excelled at the task. Eventually, she was demoted and erased from the project altogether. The professional damage was terrible, but the emotional toll was far greater. She became consumed with anxiety, self-doubt and even suicidal thoughts.

This wasn't imposter syndrome. It was a direct result of facing systemic racism in the workplace. Lavarry was the only Black woman on the team, and her experiences were shaped by her race, not a lack of confidence. This is the reality many women face: being told they don't belong, being excluded or undermined and then being labelled as an 'imposter' when they start to doubt themselves. We can't pathologise a natural and expected reaction of the vast majority of people. We can't tell women they're broken for feeling uneasy in spaces that make them uneasy because they were never built for them in the first place. We have to stop pretending imposter syndrome is an individual flaw. Because when you're expected to over-perform, be liked at all costs and constantly self-edit your tone, of course you feel like an imposter. That's not a syndrome. That's a response to inequality.

What we call imposter syndrome is often just being human, learning, growing, trying. And yes, being scared sometimes. But that fear is often a signal, not a stop sign. It tells you you're stretching. It means you care. What's far more dangerous than self-doubt is the shame we attach to it. Shame makes you small. And imposter syndrome, as it's often presented, becomes just another tool to keep women small, another reason to doubt our brilliance, our place and our power.

So no, you don't have imposter syndrome. You have evidence of progress. You have a signal that you're changing. That's not something to fix. That's something to honour.

At UPFRONT, we believe the feeling of being an imposter is real, but a syndrome it is not. Here is a list of imposter syndrome symptoms that are actually signs you are a considered human being who wants to do good work:

- Considering whether your work is good enough or not.
- Thinking about how others will perceive your work.
- Reflecting on what you said and how it made others feel.
- Being aware that there's always more to learn.
- Questioning your decisions to make sure they're well thought out.
- Feeling out of place when you're in a new environment.
- Noticing others' strengths and using them as inspiration.
- Wanting external feedback to confirm you're on the right track.
- Being cautious before diving into new challenges.
- Caring deeply about doing quality work.
- Wanting to double-check your work to avoid mistakes.

- Feeling motivated by high standards and self-improvement.
- Taking time to process feedback, even when it's positive.

These are not flaws. They are signs of care, growth and emotional intelligence. As we navigate the patterns of imposter syndrome it is vitally important to remember to flip the script from seeing imposter syndrome as a personal flaw back to a systemic and environmental effect.

The Patterns of Imposter Syndrome

These patterns show up so often that they've been studied and categorised. Dr Valerie Young created five personas to help us recognise these feelings and see them for what they are: signs of a system, not of failure. These are not flaws or fixed identities, they're patterns of behaviour shaped by the world we live in.

The Perfectionist: Nothing less than perfect feels like success.

The Superwoman: You overwork to prove your worth.

The Natural Genius: If something is hard to learn, you think you're not smart enough.

The Soloist: You refuse to ask for help, thinking you should do it all alone.

The Expert: You feel like you never know enough and fear being exposed.

If any of these sound familiar, pause before blaming yourself. Let's remember that these identities were based upon making the problem about you by a system built to keep you where you are. Remember to take them as a symptom of an external problem, and ask yourself, where are these beliefs coming from? Who benefits when I doubt myself to the point of inaction?

You are not broken, but your environment might be. Your place of work, the public spaces you frequent, your online spaces, the media you consume, what about your living room? There's a name for what you're experiencing. It's called cognitive dissonance—the discomfort that arises when your lived experience clashes with society's or social expectations. Women are constantly working to meet moving targets that aren't real. We are measured by standards that shift whenever we get too close. And we feel that disconnect.

It gets very personal for me too. I remember feeling what I now know as cognitive dissonance when I was juggling the demands of running multiple businesses while raising a family. There were moments when I was working late to hit a target or preparing for a big pitch, only to face judgement for not spending enough quality time with my son. I couldn't win, if I dedicated time to work, I was told I wasn't being a present parent, but if I focused on family, I felt the pressure to do more in my business. That constant tension between what I was doing and what others expected from me was exhausting. Was I supposed to choose between being a good mother or a good founder? It felt like a lose-lose.

The right answer was a resounding 'neither'. We should reject the premise. I did. I let go of those external judgements and worked on defining success on my own terms, focusing on what truly mattered to me rather than trying to meet a standard that didn't fit my reality. This was part of my confidence journey, and now I want to teach you how to do the same. The reason these patterns feel so familiar is because they're applied to us all by a system that wasn't designed for us:

- Do you feel like a failure because no matter how well you do, you aren't rewarded the same way as others?
- Are you trying to do it all because you feel that's what's expected of you?

- Do you feel like you need more knowledge, even though you already add value?
- Do you feel someone else gets the credit for your work?

If you answered yes to any of the above then it's time to start believing in your excellence.

Believing in Your Excellence

I want you to stop equating confidence with competence. Overconfident, arrogant white male leaders often get the benefit of the doubt, regardless of their actual skills. Studies show that overconfidence often pays off for leaders, particularly white men, who are more likely to be rewarded for arrogance and self-promotion, even when their actual skills don't measure up.[2] Yet women are frequently held to a higher standard, where our confidence is often scrutinised or dismissed. Women of colour, in particular, are seen as either too confident, threatening or not confident enough. This hyper-focus on how women present their confidence ignores the deeper issue. Which is that confidence is being judged against an outdated and biased model of leadership, one that rewards traits more often seen in men than women, and especially white men. I love this quote from Jennifer Jackson—she nails the context of where we sit in this system and how incongruent personal imposter syndrome is:

> *Whatever you think you can't do, just know that there is someone who is confidently doing it wrong right now. They have no plans at doing it better either and people are paying them to do it. Please believe in your own excellence as much as they believe in their mediocrity.*

From Redundancy to Reconnection: Katell's Story

Shortly after her redundancy, Katell discovered UPFRONT. For Katell, joining the Bond proved to be a life-changing experience:

> *For as long as I can remember, I've felt off-kilter, like I needed to apologise for simply existing. Despite being loud, chatty, and seemingly very social, I often felt misunderstood and out of place. I never truly felt seen or heard, always carrying a fear of rejection deep within me. People would sometimes tell me I was clever, kind or talented, but those compliments always felt more like noise than validation. As a child, kind words would often overwhelm me to the point of tears.*
>
> *As an adult, I learned to deflect that discomfort with irony and self-deprecation. Professionally, I struggled with imposter syndrome. Appraisals were excruciating. I would often try to reschedule them. When they were positive, I couldn't hide my surprise, and managers would often comment on my facial reaction. No matter the job, I always felt like the odd one out. Still, I stayed in roles for years, better the devil you know, I'd tell myself. There's a strange comfort in the predictability of discomfort. Becoming a teacher was no different. I loved working with children, but I hated the structure and politics.*
>
> *It wasn't just the fear of management anymore. There were also parents to worry about. I had to contend with not just appraisals but inspections, writing curriculums, planning lessons from scratch*

*and being periodically observed with my perfor-
mance, judged by colleagues who had no experience speaking nor teaching a second language to
primary school children. There was always a trail
of paperwork threatening to expose me as a fraud.
I taught for seventeen years. Honestly, I might still
be there if redundancy hadn't come as the unex-
pected gift it turned out to be.*

At this point a friend recommended that she attend one
of our webinars. Katell explained that this was when she recognised confidence was something she needed to work on.

*The timing felt significant, too. I had just lost my
job and was staring down a vast unknown. What
did I even want anymore? What didn't I want?
Could I, at this age, really reinvent my life? So
I logged into my first Huddle & Bond expecting
to be talked at from the safety of my computer and
maybe sold something at the end. Boy, was I wrong.
This one felt different. It was different.*

*From the very beginning, the content and
structure of the session were engaging and genuinely supportive. The facilitator created a welcoming space, and then, to my surprise, I found myself
placed in a small virtual room with a group of ran-
domly selected women. We were there to discuss
the question put to us. It was intimidating at first.
These women had what I considered impressive
careers and important job titles. I felt like an out-
sider, unsure of what I could possibly bring to the
conversation. But instead of judgement, I was met
with kindness, support, and real understanding.*

When they learned about my redundancy and where I was in life, they didn't brush it off or change the subject. They empathised. A few of them mentioned something called a Bond saying I should absolutely join the next one. They believed it could help me figure out my next steps and reconnect with what I truly wanted for myself. I just so happened to be diagnosed with ADHD shortly before. It explained so much, my past struggles, my present challenges, but I still had to learn how to navigate life with that new awareness and develop myself. What struck me about UPFRONT was how openly it acknowledges that we're all different. It embraces neurodivergence rather than expecting everyone to fit into a neat box. So for me, joining felt like a no-brainer. I joined and completed the Bond. And I loved it. My biggest takeaway: visibility means showing yourself and your work to the world before you're ready. It's about learning to embrace your failures as much as your wins and discovering that you're OK exactly as you are.

Katell's story shows us how high levels of self-doubt can make us feel less connected to who we truly are if we don't acknowledge it and explore it. Her story shows us what's possible when we stop seeing self-doubt as a stop sign and start treating it as a compass. Like Katell, I've had to unpick the difference between what I was told I was bad at and what I actually needed support with.

Self-doubt thrives in the gap between who we are and who we've been told we should be. This is what I discovered when I examined the areas of my own business where I believed I lacked competence.

Where Do You *Think* You're Bad?

The areas where I think I lack competence fall into two categories: firstly, the things I told myself I was bad at, based on what society and the world had taught me to believe about myself; and secondly, the things that I'm genuinely bad at.

Let's start with the first version. For years, I told myself I was 'bad at money'. I didn't want to think about it or talk about it. The very thought of a spreadsheet made me feel sick. I was full of money doubts. In my first business, I had to manage payroll every month and it was such a source of stress, I'd cry every time I had to do it. It constantly chipped away at my confidence and made me question my ability as an entrepreneur. The truth is I'm actually incredible at making money, selling and building businesses that generate revenue and profit. What I needed to realise was that money isn't something I needed to shy away from. I needed to surround myself with people who are great at the details, like spreadsheets. My zone of genius is at the whiteboard, dreaming big and moving fast, not buried in spreadsheets.

One of the biggest challenges for me right now is navigating the shift from being a founder of a small team to being a CEO of an organisation. A founder sparks the idea and brings the creative vision; a CEO turns that vision into a scalable, sustainable business. Where founders thrive on innovation, CEOs need a rounded skillset in strategy, leadership, operations and financial acumen, to lead people, make decisions under pressure and keep the entire machine running smoothly. One starts the fire, the other keeps it burning.

I'm a fire-starter. At the time of writing, I've been full-time in my business for four years and it's time to scale, to expand my product, my role and the business as a whole. This requires a different kind of energy and skillset. It requires the CEO skillset, which I've been sneakily convincing myself I'm not good at. But that's a lie. The truth is, I've just never done it before. It's outside of my comfort zone because my expertise lies in creation, vision and turning ideas into reality. I'm leaning into that discomfort now and reminding myself that growth requires stretching into new territory. I'm building new confidence muscles.

Then there's the actual stuff I'm terrible at. Organising. When I tell you I run my day to day from a desktop with no folders, no file names and no system in place, I'm not kidding—it's the wild west. I'm absolutely terrible at detailed project management. I'm the person who'll come up with an idea in the morning and have a prototype built by the evening. Process? I used to think I didn't have time for it. But I've learned that sometimes that lack of organisation slows things down, and that's not a good thing. So my team is building systems around me, not to change who I am, but to support how I work.

The lesson is this: not every moment of self-doubt is a warning that you're failing. Not every uncomfortable feeling means you're on the wrong path. Most of the time, self-doubt is simply a flashing neon sign that says: **you are building confidence.**

Growth feels awkward. It feels uncertain. It rarely feels polished or easy. But that's not a sign to stop, it's a sign you're stepping into new territory. If everything felt smooth and certain all the time, you wouldn't be growing. You'd be repeating. But you are here to build something bigger, not to stay where you are.

When you feel self-doubt rising, it's not a reason to retreat. It's an invitation to stretch. When you feel that uncomfortable itch of uncertainty, it's not proof that you're in the wrong place. It's evidence that you are stretching your confidence muscles.

Schedule Self-Doubt

How would the world change if we all accepted that self-doubt is a very natural sign of learning, confidence and growth? We'd see more women in leadership, more new ideas in the world and workplaces, governments and communities shaped by women who used to talk themselves out of even showing up. Yes please!

My self-doubt gets louder the more I care. If it disappeared I'd be worried. But I have learned to do the thing, with my self-doubt, every day, for over 15 years. You can learn to manage your self-doubt, welcome it and own it too. My favourite way to do this is to schedule it.

Set aside a fixed time in your day to be with your self-doubt. You are going to look it RIGHT in the eyes. You are going to sit with it and learn from it. Dedicate 10–15 minutes at the start or end of your day or the last Friday of the month—whatever works for you! Set a timer. This is a time where you can allow yourself to think through what's bothering you, what fears you have, and reflect on them. This is your *self-doubt session*. The goal is never to eliminate the feelings but to acknowledge them in a structured way. It works every single time because it gives you control over the time you give self-doubt. It takes her negative power away but leaves her lessons.

Comedian Tom Allen once described himself as '*confidently insecure*'. I love this. He is acknowledging that he has insecurities, like we all do, but he's not letting them get in the way of what he does. This is why scheduled self-doubt works. You're not trying to deny that you have insecurities. You're not expecting to get rid of them. You're sitting with them. Welcoming them in. Acknowledging them, but not giving them the power to derail what you are doing.

Now you know, the goal isn't to wait for self-doubt to disappear. It rarely does. The goal is to schedule it and do the thing anyway. You were never the imposter, you were always the signal of positive change. The world taught you to call it imposter syndrome. But what you really have is ambition. Doubt is your signal and confidence is your reply.

UPFRONT Moment

This chapter is inviting you to unlearn one of the loudest, most stubborn lies we've been told: that our self-doubt is a flaw, or worse, a diagnosis. These UPFRONT Moments are here to help you pause, reflect and rewire. This moment is an invitation, gentle but clear, to think differently about what self-doubt means and what it's really trying to show you.

Because unlearning 'I am an imposter' takes time. These prompts are not about fixing you, they are about carving out the time and space to realise the lessons and value in discomfort.

Go slowly. Be kind to yourself. Let's ask:

When was the last time you mistook self-doubt for a lack of competence? And how might you reframe that moment as evidence of growth instead?

What story does your self-doubt try to tell you?

Write it down in as much detail as you can. What does that voice in your head say when you're about to take a risk or step into something new? Does it sound like someone you know? A parent, a teacher, a boss? Does it warn you, belittle you or try to keep you small?

What new story could you start telling yourself instead?

Imagine you're rewriting the script. What would you say if you were your own biggest cheerleader? How would you speak to yourself if you fully believed you were capable, prepared and deserving? What would I say back to your self doubt? Borrow my voice.

Now start writing it. Let it be messy. Let it be bold. Give yourself the words you wish someone had said to you years ago.

Notes

1. Woodman, T., Akehurst, S., Hardy, L., and Beattie, S. (2010). Self-confidence and performance: A little self-doubt helps, *Psychology of Sport and Exercise* 11 (6): 467–470. https://doi.org/10.1016/j.psychsport.2010.05.009.
2. Chamorro-Premuzic, T. (2013). Why do so many incompetent men become leaders? *Harvard Business Review*. https://hbr.org/2013/08/why-do-so-many-incompetent-men.

6

You Were Never Sorry

Old Rule: You are sorry all the time

New Rule: You are sorry when it counts

I'M NOT SORRY. There I said it. Do you ever say 'sorry' when you've done absolutely nothing wrong? Do you apologise when someone bumps into you? Do you say 'sorry' before you say 'no'? Sometimes we even apologise when we take up space with our voices, our bodies, our boundaries. This isn't politeness, it's conditioning and it's the result of generations of being told to shrink, stay small and not rock the boat. It's internalised patriarchal ideas in action.

You don't need to apologise for existing and you don't need to justify your no. So let's stop handing out apologies you don't mean. Let's replace 'sorry' with confidence. Because you were never meant to walk through life like an apology. You are meant to lead, to take up space, to own your power unapologetically. Sorry is a really beautiful and important word so let's only use it when we mean it.

I have a long list of times I've caught myself apologising when I wasn't at fault. Let's see how many you can tick off and then reflect on the lessons in this list. Here's a non-exhaustive list of moments I have said sorry unnecessarily:

1. **When someone bumped into me:** A very large man bumped into me while I was waiting for my train home. Despite being the one who was jolted, I instinctively said, '*sorry!*' I immediately caught myself, realising I had apologised for something that wasn't my fault at all.

2. **For standing in a queue:** I apologised in the queue to board a plane, even though I wasn't in anyone's way. It's like I feel the need to excuse myself for taking up space.

3. **For asking for directions:** I asked for directions whilst in Barcelona, apologising before even asking. '*Sorry to bother you, but can you tell me how to get to...?*' As though needing help or guidance was somehow a burden to the person I was asking.

4. **For crying:** During a very stressful period in my life, I started crying on the street. Saying '*sorry*' to nobody in particular, as if I needed to apologise for showing emotion.

5. **For laughing:** In a conversation at university, I laughed loudly, and instantly I said, '*sorry, my laugh is so loud*'. I worried that my laughter might annoy people.

6. **For being overdressed:** I once arrived at my neighbour's dinner party wearing a fancier outfit than everyone else. Feeling out of place, I immediately apologised for being 'overdressed'. I tried to downplay my appearance to make others feel more comfortable.

7. **For being underdressed:** On the flip side, I've also apologised for being 'underdressed' in situations. At an event, I didn't realise it was a more formal occasion and apologised for wearing trainers, even though no one else had noticed or commented.

8. **For eating:** I've found myself apologising for eating in public, especially when having a snack or meal in a shared space like an office or on a plane. '*Sorry, I'm eating*', is something I've said more times than I care to admit.

9. **For being hungry:** On several occasions, I've apologised for needing food, as though my hunger inconvenienced others. '*Sorry, I just need to grab a quick snack*', I'll say, as if eating were something I should do quietly and out of sight.

10. **For being tired:** There have been times when I've apologised for expressing how tired I am, particularly at work or social events. '*Sorry, I'm just really exhausted today*', I'd say, as though my fatigue were something I should hide or feel bad about.

Why We Apologise

Language is one of the most powerful tools we all have access to. The words we use matter. How and when we say sorry matters. When we say sorry at times we are not at fault or don't actually feel regretful, we are taking a subordinate role. We are saying, here's my agency and here's my power, take them, they're yours. This might infuriate you and it might be unfair but it's true.

We live in a world where 90% of all people have a negativity bias towards women.[1] This means from a very young age we learn to communicate in a way that will keep us safe. We learn to use apologetic language and speak in a way that prioritises us being liked.

I want to live in a world where women understand how to communicate to make people listen. Where women know to tell stories that create change. Where women know how to pitch ideas that become reality. I do this by encouraging you to notice how you use language to make yourself and your ideas small.

This is not *tone policing* nor is it asking you to speak like anyone other than yourself. This is teaching you how to speak as your confident self, instead of the version of you who has been taught to hide by oppressive systems.

Yes, workplaces and policies need to change and those things are changed by human beings, like me and you. But we will never be in a position to change policy, influence laws or cultural changes if we continue to apologise for existing.

What are we going to do about it? You are going to unlearn everything you've been taught about apologising. Let's look at the root of the problem. Maybe you're trying to smooth interactions and get rid of tension? You might be terrified of being called bossy, rude or a show off. You bet I've spent half of my adult life obsessing over how to avoid being called a show off, instead of obsessing over my joy and my growth. What a tragedy. (And yes, my next book will be called SHOW OFF.)

Who are you in the context of unnecessary sorrys? Maybe you're a perfectionist. Where are my recovering perfectionists at? Join the club! Maybe you say sorry for the tiniest of mistakes, the smallest of errors because you constantly fixate on those things, instead of all the things you do well. Maybe you carry an exceptional amount of guilt. Guilt for having needs and desires. Guilt for being tired. Guilt for being busy. Guilt for wanting a holiday. Guilt for wishing for more money. So you say sorry. . . All the time.

It might just be a habit. Maybe all the women around you say sorry, your mother, your friends, your mentors. So now, you do too. Sometimes you say it and you don't even feel sorry, it just slips out of your mouth like a verbal tic.

Ultimately, we say sorry to make sure the people around us don't feel threatened or intimidated by us. Sorry is a beautiful and important word. It's vital you learn to use it properly. When you say sorry unnecessarily, you are shouting 'I don't believe in myself, I don't rate what I have to say, I am deeply uncertain and unsure'. How other people feel about your confidence is actually none of your business, it's nothing to do with you, and it's all about them. Leave the judgement with them.

Should You Even Be Sorry?

You often hear that women say sorry more than men. But here's what's really interesting about women saying sorry. We only say it more often because we have a lower threshold for an *offence* that warrants an apology. One study asked a group of men and women to write down any offences they committed or experienced, and how often an apology was offered. Women not only said sorry more often, they also said they committed more offences.[2]

But did they really? No. The men in the group just didn't see certain behaviours as offences. They offered no apology because they didn't feel the need to. Look back at the list I gave you at the start of this chapter. Can you imagine the men in your personal life and professional life apologising in any of those situations? Then why are you?

Sorry is not a word to use lightly. It's a word to use intentionally, when it matters. But for many of us, 'sorry' has become a habit. It's a habit we need to break. It's also worthwhile pointing out the damage that excessive apologies do to your actual apologies. How meaningful can your sorry at the right time be, if you say sorry at the beginning or end of every other sentence?

As sociologist, author and TEDx speaker Professor Maja Jovanovic said in her excellent TEDx talk on this topic: *'If you are beginning and ending your sentences with "sorry" ... don't be surprised if there's nothing left of your confidence at the end of the day'.*[3]

From Sorry to Strength

Kat knows this better than anyone. She spent 3.5 years in a relationship that undermined her confidence completely and it took her several years to build it back up once she left and rediscovered who she was.

> *One of the things I realised looking back is that I apologised for everything in that relationship. I moved in with my boyfriend quite quickly, in another country too. It was his house, and after a few months I felt like I didn't have any space of my own. I remember asking if he could make more room in the closet for me. I started my request with, 'I'm sorry, I know it's a pain for you to move your things, but I could do with some more space for my stuff...' I got another shelf in the closet, but it wasn't enough.*

That was far from the only thing Kat found herself apologising for. Her boyfriend got hung up on her past relationships, so she apologised for those too, even though she hadn't known him at the time. To avoid arguments, she stopped talking about whole periods of her life because she'd shared them with another partner and knew mentioning it would only lead to arguments.

'*When I left that relationship, I realised how much of myself I'd lost. Not all of that came from saying sorry, but I spent a lot of time apologising for things I definitely shouldn't have*', she shared. Learning not to say sorry all the time has been really important for her as she's built a new life. '*I value myself a lot more now that I don't say "sorry" for things I can't control or simply don't need to apologise for. I also feel much more confident asking for what I need, not just in romantic relationships, but in life in general*'.

Maybe some of Kat's story resonates with you. Maybe all of it does. Do you apologise when you shouldn't and make yourself smaller in the process?

Here's another example from Toni in the Bond; she says:

> *This week I'm proud of myself for doing a job interview ahead of the end of my maternity leave. I'm terrified of interviews and have never got a job from one, ever. I'm a mess before it begins. This time, I handled it with confidence and felt calm and able to talk competently about what I do (not even a shaky voice!). I've started noticing a transformation in my confidence as I apologise less. I am allowing the discomfort of sounding more assertive and I find it freeing which I absolutely did not expect. I love working on this and feeling a steady flow of confidence coming in which is so uplifting.*

Yvette in the Bond says: '*I have noticed that I am now saying "Thank you for waiting for me/us" if I or my children are late, and I'm thanking people for pointing out very unserious mistakes I may have made instead of apologising for them*'.

These shifts might seem small, but they're everything. Each time you swap sorry for strength, you are teaching your brain and the people around you that you deserve to be here. That your needs matter. That you don't exist to make yourself smaller for the comfort of others. This is how UPFRONT confidence is built. So how do we shift this habit? How do we unlearn what we've been taught? We start with our words.

Breaking the 'Sorry' Habit

I'd like to share a simple, but really effective exercise you can use to break the habit of saying sorry when you don't need to. Over the next week, pay close attention to your language. Whenever you feel yourself going to say 'sorry', flip the statement and instead thank the other person.

Instead of saying '*sorry for ranting*', say '*thank you for listening*'.

Instead of '*sorry, I'm feeling emotional*', say '*thank you for trying to understand something difficult*'.

Instead of '*sorry I'm late*', try '*thank you for waiting*'.

Instead of '*sorry to bug you*', try '*do you have ten minutes for a question?*'

Start today. Notice what you say and how you use the word sorry.

You were never sorry. You were just taught to be. That ends now.

Say what you mean.

You are not sorry.

UPFRONT Moment

Think of this as a moment to turn down the noise of expectation and tune into the clarity of your own voice. This is your rep, not for being right, or perfect or polite, but for being *honest*. With yourself. For yourself.

We are taught, especially as women, to apologise so often and so early, we forget we're allowed to exist without permission. You can and do exist without permission.

This is your invitation to lay that heavy weight down.

Start here:

Think about the last time you said sorry, and you didn't mean it. Maybe it slipped out automatically. Maybe it gained you safety or time or belonging.

- What were you really trying to express?
- What would you have said if you felt safe and comfortable?

Now explore:

- How often do your apologies take away your confidence?
- When do you apologise for being human? Being tired, hungry or confused?
- How often do you apologise for your ambition? Your opinions? Your ideas?
- Where are you saying sorry just to make others more comfortable?

Take a moment to rewrite some of your most common apologies.

Try:

- 'Sorry if I'm being annoying' → 'I care deeply, and I'm speaking up'.
- 'Sorry for asking' → 'Thanks for taking the time, this matters to me'.
- 'Sorry I'm late' → 'Thanks for waiting'.

Now close your eyes and picture the you who no longer says sorry unnecessarily.

- What does her posture say?
- What does her presence feel like in a room?
- How does she feel day to day when she makes a mistake?

Finish this sentence, again and again, until it feels like truth:

'I am not sorry for. . .'

Try:

- 'I am not sorry for needing rest'.
- 'I am not sorry for dreaming big'.
- 'I am not sorry for taking up space'.
- 'I am not sorry for using my voice'.
- 'I am not sorry'.

Let this be the beginning of your un-apology. A reclamation.

Notes

1. UNDP Gender Social Norms Index (GSNI), 2020.
2. Schumann, K. and Ross, M. (2010). Why women apologize more than men. *Psychological Science* 21 (11): 1649–1655. https://doi .org/10.1177/0956797610384150.
3. Jovanovic, M. (2019). 'How apologies kill our confidence'. TED Talk, TEDxTrinityBellwoodsWomen. Video, 17 min., 56 sec. https://www.youtube.com/watch?v=G8sYv_6uyss.

7

You Were Never Meant to Be Fearless

Old Rule: Confidence means fearlessness

New Rule: Confidence means running with your fear

When was the last time you had horses in your tummy? You call them butterflies. I call them horses. Credit to my little boy who coined the term aged six. I use the horses in my tummy as part of my confidence compass. The horses are bringing me important messages: you really care about this, you've never done this before, you're scared.

I was scared when I ditched my pseudonym, Redjotter, and decided to use my real name online in February 2020. I was scared when I did my first stand-up comedy gig in March 2017. I was scared when I led an 8,000-person protest through the streets of London. I'm scared right now writing this book for you. But I am doing it anyway. And that's what confidence is. Trying. Taking action despite the fear. Running alongside the horses.

The moments that supercharge my career, and bring me immense pride and joy, all begin with fear. They begin with doubt. What if I can't do it? What if they laugh at me? What if I look stupid? I don't think this fear ever really goes away. Every step outside your comfort zone comes with its own recipe of fear.

I have taught thousands of women how to learn confidence. I have built a business that builds confidence infrastructure in organisations all over the world. And I have days when my confidence feels inadequate and vulnerable. These are often the moments when I'm levelling up. I am going to a place where I don't have confidence. I'm writing a book, buying a puppy or teaching my son fractions.

Confidence is like a passport. It gets you far, but every time you go somewhere new, you need to collect fresh stamps. New places, new people, new challenges, they all ask you to prove yourself again. But the beautiful, incredible thing is we're never starting from scratch. Every time I do the thing despite feeling scared I'm building new muscle. Collating evidence. I'm a person who can do hard things. I am a person who takes action despite feeling scared.

So how do you learn to run alongside your horses?

You stumble, then you fall, then you wobble, then you run. There are no shortcuts. The only way to build confidence is by taking action before you feel ready. Have you ever seen an actual horse being born and learning to run? They run within an hour of birth. This is because they are not so different from their ancestors in the wild who had to run within the first hours of being born or they would be eaten by a predator. We live in relative comfort now and we aren't going to be eaten if we don't write the book, start the project or apply for the promotion. But the same lesson applies. Action has to come first or you will never run; and the best places to run are the places where you have the least confidence. This is where your stumbles and falls happen the quickest, and in return where your confidence growth happens the most.

Zara's Brave Ask

As a new mum, Zara had a lot to get to grips with. Being a mum is hard work. Babies are beautiful, but that doesn't mean it's easy. Still in the early stages of her maternity leave, she was feeling a little isolated when she joined the Bond. She wanted to get to know some other mums in her local area and build a support network.

Choosing to run with the horses doesn't always mean doing something that's big and scary like standing on stage in front of hundreds of people. Sometimes it is what can seem like a small action, like inviting your neighbours to go for a walk with you. But that doesn't make it any less significant, or any less scary.

'*I asked a group of moms I barely know if they wanted to come for a long walk, despite fearing that the answer would be no*', were Zara's words. To her surprise, and delight, one said yes immediately and another decided to join them at the last minute. She felt the fear of being rejected, but she took a leap of faith. By asking the question, she took the first steps towards building a community of mums with babies at a similar age to hers.

How easy would it have been for Zara to keep quiet, to not invite these other women to join her for a walk? To surrender to the fear that they'd say no? To save herself the pain of assumed rejection by not asking at all? But she didn't do what was easy. She chose to run with her horses.

There Are Always Horses on the Horizon

The truth is that no matter how many times you do this, you will never feel ready for the next time. You might get more comfortable with public speaking, or voicing your opinions in meetings, but there will always be something else that requires you to stretch your confidence muscles.

It is tempting to wait until you feel ready, but ready is sneaky. It always stays a few steps ahead of you. If you keep waiting for ready to lead you by the hand into the spotlight, you'll be stuck in the waiting room forever, and that is no fun at all.

Too often I see women like you waiting to be given permission. Waiting to be tapped on the shoulder and told, '*It's your turn now*'. Waiting until they feel 100% ready. Women hold just 23% of C-suite positions.[1] That's not because we aren't capable of leading businesses. One of the reasons is the decisions we don't make along the way. The opportunities we step aside for, watching them thunder past.

Every time we delay a decision or talk ourselves out of something, we let an opportunity to run with the horses pass us by.

Where Will the Horses Lead You?

At 23, I started my first business. No safety net, no investors, no fancy connections, just action. People told me I was too young, too inexperienced.

At 33, I moved to Sweden during a pandemic. A whole new country, no network, no roadmap. Again, people said, '*Why would you do that?*' But I knew I wanted to build a bigger life.

At 38, I wrote and self-published a children's book called *Taylor Meets The Trick* to teach children and the grown-ups around them about the patriarchy. No publisher waiting for my manuscript. No one giving me permission. Just a deep belief that this story needed to exist in the world. So I made it happen. I chose action, even when it felt terrifying and I had no idea what I was doing.

If I'd waited, I'd still be in a little town in Scotland, where the high street is paved with dog shit, playing small, waiting for someone to pick me. Instead, I picked myself. I ran with my horses.

I want to give you a challenge now. Be honest about what you're scared of. If you're not sure, answering this question is a good starting point: What are you not doing because you're scared? Now tell a friend, tell a group of people you trust, admit it to yourself without judgement. Write it in the margins.

Instead of thinking, *What's the worst that could happen?* Ask yourself, *What's the best thing that could happen? What would you do if you weren't afraid? How would your life be different?*

Donna Did It Scared

Donna Patterson is an UPFRONT Bond graduate who was dubbed 'the Erin Brockovitch of Bradford' in 2022 after taking her employer Morrisons to court for maternity discrimination and winning.[2] What makes Donna's story even more remarkable is that she represented herself in court because she couldn't afford legal representation. Before taking that step, she tried to resolve the issue informally through the company's process, but when that didn't work she had a decision to make: raise a claim with an employment tribunal or walk away and put it down as a bad experience. Donna told me:

> *I read somewhere that children learn what's important to their parents by seeing how their parents behave. I constantly try to teach my boys to do the right thing and make good decisions, and understand the outcomes of those decisions. That really played a part in me pursuing my claim because how could I possibly tell my children to do what is right, to stand up for what is right, if they don't see me doing that myself?*

Her other motivation was to raise awareness of maternity discrimination. That meant she wasn't prepared to go for a settlement agreement, because they often come with non-disclosure agreements attached. When all the legal quotes she received were astronomical, she decided her only option was to represent herself.

This was when Donna joined the Bond. Her fears weren't unfounded. Of the 77% of women who experience maternity and sexual discrimination, only 1% of them raise a claim.[3] That statistic alone shows you how brutal the system is. It's a system that's designed to make you give up. But she didn't quit.

The weekend before the tribunal started, Donna rewatched some of the Bond course content, a video about charisma versus stage fright.

> *I knew there would be so much information in there that would help me for the week ahead. I listened to what was said. There was lots in there about your body, how you position yourself, where you put the weight on your feet. And there was an element about the dynamics of a room and how to control that. I knew I was going to need to control the room because as a legally unrepresented person, I was the least qualified in that room, and that's a really frightening position to be in.*

The way Donna coped was to use a lot of the techniques she'd learnt in the Bond about breathing, taking the time she needed, remembering to pause and to always have water available. '*I kept reminding myself why I was doing it, reminding myself that while I was the least legally qualified, I was the one person in the room who knew the story better than anyone else. Nobody else knew it end to end the way that I did, because I was the only person who had experienced all of it*'.

At the end of a gruelling week, on a Friday afternoon, the judge delivered his verdict that Donna had won.

I felt so emotional because I had won and all my effort had been worth it. But more than that it was the validation that someone impartial said 'yes, what happened was wrong and it also broke the law', which up until that point I didn't know. I knew what had happened was morally wrong, but I wasn't sure it met the criteria to have broken employment law and the Equality Act.

I burst into tears when I got the news of Donna's win. It hit me right in my heart. Donna cross-examined eight witnesses on her own, and it took her five days to do it. Five days of sheer confidence.

I've written this book to serve women like Donna. Donna isn't grandstanding, she isn't putting people down to get ahead, Donna isn't dominating or imposing. Donna's confidence isn't about being loud, or what others say or do. Donna's confidence is about Donna, it's the voice in her head that says, 'You can do this'. It's her voice that says, 'I know who I am, I know what I can do'.

Being UPFRONT teaches you this. You are learning how to do things you used to think were impossible. You are learning who you are and you are realising your potential. You're taking action. You're doing things that scare you. You become a woman who uses her power. Against huge multi-million pound institutions. And you win.

Donna's win is a huge win for all of us. Donna's win is a huge win for every single one of you who have picked up this book because your confidence has been crushed by toxicity, discrimination, systemic injustice—Donna's win is a huge win for the hundreds of maternity leave Bonders who join us because they're utterly terrified to go back to work. Donna's win is a huge win for every single one of you who's ever been dismissed, ignored and punished for having a baby.

She was scared, but she did it anyway. She showed us what's possible when you choose confidence over comfort.

Fear shows up in many forms. For Donna, it was the fear of taking on a legal system alone. For others, it might be the fear of speaking up in a hospital ward or questioning authority in the most vulnerable of moments.

That was the case for Agnes Agyepong. Her story, like Donna's, begins with fear and transforms into something extraordinary.

Agnes and the Power of One Step

'The fear didn't go away. I learned to run with it. And every time I did, new doors opened'.

—Agnes Agyepong

Agnes Agyepong never set out to be a founder or a social entrepreneur. Her journey into activism and leadership began with trauma: experiencing neglect during her labour, navigating postnatal and prenatal depression and facing the stark realities of Black maternal mortality rates in the UK. Agnes could have easily retreated into silence. She could have accepted the broken system as it was. Instead, she chose to run with her horses. She chose to feel the fear and act anyway.

She began with one small act of confidence: refusing to leave the hospital without speaking to a matron about the care she had received. From that conversation, Agnes realised the power of using her voice, not just for herself but for other women too. One action led to another. She became a Maternity Voices Partnership Chair. She founded the GloMama Awards, an annual celebration of mothers on social media. She co-founded the Fatherhood Awards. She created the Global Black Maternal Health Institute.

And she did it all without a grand business plan, without investors, without waiting to feel ready. She launched GloMama with zero pounds, no website and no tech platform, just her phone, her Instagram DMs and her fierce belief that mums deserved to be seen, celebrated and valued. In her words, '*I was pooping my pants with fear. But I did it anyway*'. Today, Agnes's work has touched thousands. She's been featured in national media. She's created powerful spaces of joy and justice, all by taking one shaky, courageous step at a time.

Agnes's story reminds us that you don't need to feel fearless to take action and you don't need a flawless plan to begin. Confidence isn't the absence of fear, it's moving forward with the fear beside you. Agnes ran with the horses. She still does. And because of that, she is changing lives, including her own.

Now it's your turn.

Run with your horses and let them guide you somewhere new.

UPFRONT Moment

Fear doesn't mean stop. It means this matters. It means your body is paying attention and there's something here worth stretching for.

You were taught to treat fear like a red light. But what if fear is a green light? This is your confidence rep. Not the absence of fear, but the act of moving with it. The horses in your tummy aren't trying to scare you. They're trying to show you the way.

Start here:

Close your eyes and call to mind a recent moment when you felt that flutter in your tummy, the rustle of nerves, the kick of adrenaline.

- What were your horses trying to say?
- Did you listen, or did you try to quiet them down?
- What did that moment need from you?

Fear is not your enemy. It's your compass.
Write your own best-case scenario.

- If you showed up despite the nerves, what becomes possible?
- If you spoke up, pressed send, stepped in, what might happen next?

Now gather your evidence:

List three moments from your life when you were afraid, and you *did it anyway*.

- What did those choices teach you about yourself?
- What did they make possible?

Finish these sentences:

- 'Fear shows me. . .'
- 'When I run with the horses, I. . .'
- 'I don't wait to feel fearless. I choose to feel. . .'
- 'Confidence feels like. . .'

Now picture the version of you who rides the wave of fear instead of waiting for it to disappear. The horses are waiting to run with her. Oh, the places you'll go!

Notes

1. McKinsey, *Women in the Workplace 2024: The 10th-anniversary Report*. https://www.mckinsey.com/featured-insights/diversity-and-inclusion/women-in-the-workplace.
2. Meet the Erin Brockovitch of UPFRONT, *UPFRONT Moment with Lauren Currie* [Podcast], 2022.
3. Equality and Human Rights Commission, *Pregnancy and Maternity Discrimination in the Workplace,* 2016. https://www.equalityhumanrights.com/sites/default/files/pregnancy_and_maternity_recommendations.pdf.

8

You Can't Graduate Confidence

Old Rule: Confidence is a destination

New Rule: There is no finish line

What if confidence isn't a milestone, but a daily practice? There's no finish line. No shortcuts. Waiting to arrive somewhere only makes us forget to show up for the work. I cannot have that. It's a waste of your precious time and energy.

I start every class I teach in the Bond by reminding our Bonders not to put me on a pedestal, because I am on my own confidence journey and always will be. Every single new milestone requires confidence. I do the reps every day. We know that confidence is like strength training, you have to keep showing up, doing the small consistent actions that build over time. My reps look like: sharing my work online, saying yes to opportunities that feel scary, choosing the difficult path of entrepreneurship. The list is very long. I've done the homework, read the science and lived the truth. From Bandura's self-efficacy theory to Dweck's growth mindset and the neuroscience of habit formation, the evidence is clear: confidence isn't a trait you're born with, it's something you build through practice, repetition and showing up again and again. If I woke up one day and announced, *'I'm ready! I'm confident!'* I'd be lying.

In summer 2023, I ran the Stockholm Marathon but in 2020 I didn't even own running shoes. Nor does anyone in my family run. I had no confidence and was a total beginner. I knew that if I kept showing up, my confidence would come. Yes, I made mistakes, yes it was horrible at times, but now I am a confident runner, and I will tell my grandchildren I ran a marathon (fuelled by Dolly Parton and potato salad).

But confidence wasn't a finish line I crossed at the end of the marathon. It didn't magically appear on that day, fully formed. It grew slowly, in the early morning runs, when the aching muscles healed, when I grew through the feeling of nausea and not knowing, and during the moments of doubt when I wanted to quit. It was the small moments of action that produced a change in my confidence. Even now it's not permanent, just like the muscle that grew in my legs, and the conditioning my lungs had adapted to. Everything that was a new challenge, whether it was running a different distance, training in new conditions or just putting my running trainers on, was a challenge to my confidence.

No One Is Confident All the Time

One of the confidence myths we talk about in the Bond is that confident people are confident all the time. Wrong. Confidence ebbs and flows. Often we are very confident in one area of our lives, but lacking in others. This is true for everyone. For me, I can stand on a stage in front of hundreds of people and get a standing ovation. But when I do anything new that's physical, like climbing or playing football, I can feel completely out of my depth and try to escape the situation. Confidence isn't all-or-nothing. It's situational, it's fluid and it's allowed to be messy.

It's far too easy to fixate on all the ways you're not confident. But take a moment now to think about an area of your life where you are confident. Maybe it's your ability to do the best for your children as a mother. Perhaps you feel confident speaking up in a team meeting at work. Or you're confident in setting boundaries with your partner. You might be confident at going to the gym on your own, navigating to a new place or cooking delicious, nutritious food. If you're not confident in every area of your life, that is more than OK. That is normal.

Embracing the situational nature of confidence is liberating. You don't have to approach every situation with unshakeable self-assuredness. Instead you can learn to navigate those situations with self-belief and compassion.

Belief that you will do your best, with the resources you have right now. Belief that you can and will learn. Compassion that you will be kind to yourself, because you can't know everything. We are all on a journey. We learn our lessons in different ways and at different times. Embracing that journey is liberating too. It gives you permission to practise, learn and take action, knowing that you won't get it right all the time. No one does.

Sometimes we lose confidence in ourselves. This is also part of you learning to Be UPFRONT. A bit like taking a wrong turn when you're driving. Through this book, and through UPFRONT, I want to give you tools to face the inevitable obstacles in your path and to rebuild your confidence if and when it does take a knock.

Keep Going

Confidence isn't something you graduate from; it's something you practise, lose and rebuild in different ways throughout your life. Running has taught me that confidence is a moving target—some days you feel unstoppable, other days you feel like you're back at square one, questioning everything. The key is to keep going, knowing that confidence isn't about reaching a destination, but about showing up again and again.

So, whether it's running, speaking, leading or learning something new, know that confidence isn't a final achievement. I think of it as my lifelong companion and I'm genuinely buzzing with excitement when I think about the things we'll do together in the future.

The danger of the finish line story is that it tells us once we reach the finish line the work is done. This becomes an excuse. An opt-out. A permission slip to step down. I'm here to ask you to opt-in forever. When you expect confidence to be permanent, natural setbacks like a rubbish job interview or a bad date will make you feel like your confidence is gone forever. It's never gone, it just ebbs and flows.

So let's make a deal; no more waiting, no more opting out. Confidence isn't waiting for you at the finish line, it's built in every messy, imperfect step you take right here, right now.

Joyeeta Das, co-founder and CEO of Samudra Oceans, explained why focusing on confidence as a destination is so damaging when we spoke on the *UPFRONT Moment* podcast.[1]

> *I personally find that when you're very fixated on the type of outcome you want, it really eats away at your confidence. It gives you a lot of tenacity and direction, but there's a lot of fear because you wake up every day paralyzed about what if ABC*

doesn't happen? I've found that it's much easier to influence ABC as an outcome if you stop thinking about that as the only goal and make the journey the means as well. If you're really enjoying the journey, then the outcome is an emergent thing that happens or doesn't, but at least you had a good time along the way! That really helps bring in confidence.

Letting go of perfection is often what unlocks our ability to keep going. That's where UPFRONT confidence lives, not in how flawlessly we perform, but in how fully we participate.

Letting Go of Perfection

How many times have you stopped yourself from doing something because you feel if you can't do it 'well' or 'perfectly' you don't see the point in starting? This is a trap we can fall into when we focus on the destination instead of the journey. What I want you to remember is that there's so much joy in the journey and you can learn to enjoy it. Here's a great example from Rachel who was part of the Bond.

I finally picked up my paint brushes. I've had a massive mind block as I haven't painted in ages and had this deep feeling of 'if I can't create something perfect, then there's no point', which obviously removes the joy of it as well. I think it's also tied to my self-worth.

But I found a picture to copy and had fun experimenting with colour mixing and zoned out listening to my book. It definitely wasn't perfect but I enjoyed it and desperately needed that first step to head back towards creativity and being more playful with it. Hopefully it's also a step towards me letting go of 'perfect all the time' when I go back to work.

And here's one from my own life: I've started learning guitar. Right now, I can play three chords and one song, Bob Marley's *Three Little Birds.* It's slow, clunky and my fingers hurt, but I'm still doing it. Every time I pick it up, I get a tiny bit better—and that's the joy.

Confidence isn't a diploma you hang on the wall. It's not something you earn once and keep forever. It's a living thing, shaped by the choices you make every day. You build it in the mess. In the moments you show up even when it's awkward, unglamorous or slow. You build it in the reps.

So no, you can't graduate confidence. But you can commit to it. You can honour the journey. And you can choose to keep showing up, again and again.

UPFRONT Moment

We've been taught to think of confidence like a medal, something you earn and keep forever. But we're learning it's more like a muscle, something you build through effort, rest and repetition.

Start here:

Think about an area of your life where you've grown in confidence over time.

- What did your early steps look like?
- What setbacks or doubts did you have to move through?
- How did your confidence grow, not in one moment, but in many?

Now reflect on this:

- What are you *waiting to feel ready for* right now?
- What story are you telling yourself about when you'll be 'confident enough'?
- What action are you avoiding because you think you need to feel more sure, more perfect, more prepared?

Confidence doesn't come before the action. It comes *because of it*.

Try finishing these:

- 'Confidence doesn't mean I have no doubt, it means. . .'
- 'I am confident when I. . .'
- 'When I show up consistently, I. . .'
- 'My confidence is growing in the moments when. . .'

Now take a moment to imagine your future self, not the 'perfect' version, but the one who has kept showing up. Is she proud? Strong? Determined? What has she learned by staying the course?

You're already in motion. And that counts.

Note

1. Why confidence is like flying a plane, *UPFRONT Moment with Lauren Currie* [Podcast], 2024.

9

You Are Building Confidence in a World That Doesn't Want You To

Old Rule: Confidence upsets people

New Rule: May our confidence upset them

This might be hard to hear, but the sweet spot you're searching for doesn't exist. You want to be confident but don't want to annoy anyone. You want to speak up but don't want Angela at work to think you're too big for your boots. You want to stand up for yourself at dinner but still want your mother-in-law to like you. You want to share your ideas at work but want the leadership team to think you're nice. You want to earn more money but don't want your mum to think you're ungrateful. You want to pursue your dream of being an artist but don't want your wife to think you're daydreaming. Do you see the problem here?

Your confidence will upset people, period. You cannot be confident without ruffling feathers.

Seth Godin calls it causing a ruckus. Brené Brown calls it daring greatly. Roxane Gay calls it being a difficult woman. I call it being UPFRONT.

The world is not kind to confident women.
The world does not like confident women.
The world is often cruel to confident women.

Study after study shows that women are penalised for the exact traits that make men successful—traits like assertiveness, ambition, decisiveness. In one landmark experiment at Harvard Business School, researchers presented students with a case study of a successful entrepreneur. Half read about 'Heidi', the other half read about 'Howard'. The only difference was the name. While both were rated equally competent, Heidi was seen as less likeable, less trustworthy and *not someone you'd want to work with*.[1] This is not a one-off. A Carnegie Mellon study found that women who negotiate are viewed as demanding or difficult, while men who negotiate are viewed as strong leaders.[2] In politics and the workplace, confident women are called 'bossy', 'abrasive' or 'too much', while men are praised for taking charge.[3] We learn early that too much confidence, too much power, too much visibility makes us a target. And often, we shrink ourselves to avoid the backlash.

That is exactly why choosing to read this book is an act of rebellion. That's why supporting confident women is radical. That's why choosing confidence, even when it upsets people, changes the world. I know it's scary. It's scary to imagine not being liked and scary to think about upsetting people.

But the alternative is a world where we stay quiet, stay small and the status quo remains unchallenged. A world where we play along instead of leading. That's not a world I want to live in. I choose confidence, knowing full well that hundreds of people don't like it.

Do you know what keeps me choosing it? For every one person my confidence upsets, there are ten, twenty, maybe even fifty others who feel activated by it. They see it as an invitation, as permission, encouragement, as a reminder of what's possible. Confidence is contagious.

Tall Poppy Syndrome

Let's talk about Tall Poppy Syndrome, the cultural phenomenon where high-achieving women get cut down by their peers. It's society's way of saying *don't be too confident.*

Nearly 90% of women in the workplace have experienced this.[4] Tall Poppy Syndrome leads to increased stress, diminished mental health and reduces your productivity. When success becomes a double-edged sword, we all lose.

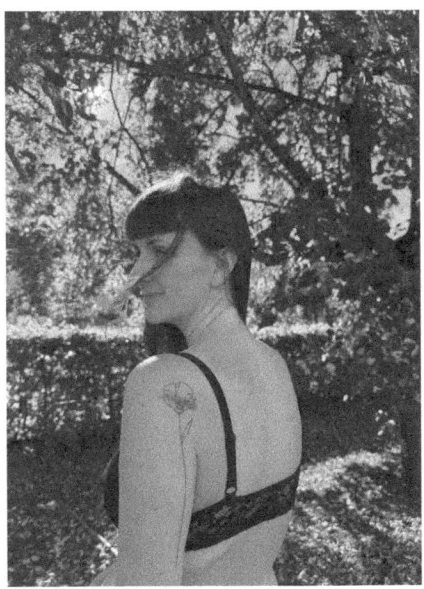

My Tall Poppy tattoo

Research links this behaviour to traits like social dominance orientation and authoritarianism. In simpler terms, some people feel threatened by others' confidence and act out to restore a sense of equality or dominance.

I've experienced Tall Poppy Syndrome in such a severe way that I got a tattoo of a tall poppy on my arm to remind myself to accept that I am a tall poppy. And that is my power and my gift.

For so long, I held myself back because I didn't want to stand out. I didn't want to make others uncomfortable. I feared what people, especially other women, would say. But as my business grows, I'm learning that being a tall poppy has consequences and that's OK.

I know it stings when other women put you down or judge you. It's tough to put yourself out there and risk rejection. But I've learned what we fear most is often the thing we need to lean into most.

When hate from other women happens, I try to pause, take a breath and remind myself that this isn't about me. It's about them. Their own shame, fear and bias that they haven't yet processed. Responding with empathy and curiosity, and without internalising their behaviour, has helped me grow. I've also learned that some people simply don't know how to celebrate another woman's success.

You cannot solve this problem for other women, you can only solve it for yourself. Your only job is to keep showing up. Keep trying. Keep being UPFRONT. Because when you do that, you give others permission to do the same. And the world needs that. So, embrace your tall poppy, and let others see you do it. If they can't handle it, that's their work, not yours. Always hold space for others to be confident, but never dim your confidence to make someone else comfortable.

This isn't a personal problem, it's a structural strategy. If confident women are seen as threatening, it becomes easier to keep them out of leadership, decision-making and influence.

After the Bond I got promoted, I started speaking more confidently in meetings. Within weeks, I was pulled aside and told I was coming across as 'intimidating' and that I should soften my tone, feedback none of my male peers received. I almost shrank back. But instead, I chose to keep showing up fully. I'm not going to mute myself to soothe other people's discomfort.

(Casey, Bond graduate)

Understanding Your Fear

Zoe Blaskey, founder of the *Motherkind* podcast, talked to me about how easy it can be to give in to your inner critics that are screaming at you not to stand up tall.[5] Not to put your head above the parapet. Zoe shared that her confidence got squashed as a child and that she was quite badly bullied at secondary school. It didn't happen in a vacuum. It happened in a world that taught her, and so many of us, that being visible means being vulnerable, and being confident means becoming a target.

The outcome is that whenever she gets offered opportunities to speak up on TV or elsewhere in the media, she says:

The young part of me freaks out. That young part of me is like, why would you put your head above the parapet? Why on Earth would you expose yourself? Because the young part of us always wants safety and the equation got a bit mixed up because of those experiences. It thinks the way to get that safety is to be small, and that's what I did throughout school.

I've done quite a lot of work with professionals on this, and it's got to the point where I can just observe it. It's not about telling the younger part of myself to 'do one'. It's about saying we're on this mission now. I get that a part of you feels really afraid. That makes sense given what happened. . . But the adult part of us is going to take over now and you are safe and you are loved. I like watching that dynamic within myself and telling her that she can come along.

This kind of reaction won't always be conscious. As Zoe said, she's done a lot of work to get to where she is now. If you are making yourself small, or saying no to opportunities that come your way, take a moment to reflect. Ask yourself why? Gently dig into where that response has come from. Is there a part of you that is trying to keep you safe? And how can you communicate with that part of you so that she feels safe even when you're stepping outside your comfort zone?

You are building confidence in a world that benefits when you stay small. Your confidence might ruffle feathers, unsettle rooms or earn side-eyes from people who'd rather you stayed quiet. Let them be unsettled. Let them whisper. Your confidence is not the problem, it's the antidote. So keep rising, keep speaking, keep showing up. Not because it's easy, but because it's how we change everything.

UPFRONT Moment

Let's not sugar-coat it. Confidence comes at a cost especially when you're a woman and especially when you don't fit the mould. You've probably already paid some of that cost: the eye-rolls, the gossiping, the snarky comments.

And yet. . . here you are. Reading this book and doing the work. You're still showing up and that really matters. I'm proud of you.

This moment is your rep. Together, we're building the kind of confidence that upsets, inspires and liberates all the right people.

Start here:
Think of a time when your confidence *upset someone.*

- Who was uncomfortable?
- What did they say or do?
- How did it make you feel?
- How did you respond? (Did you shrink? Did you soften? Or did you hold your ground?)

Now go deeper:

- What part of you still wants to be liked, accepted, approved of at all costs?
- What stories were you told about being 'too much', 'too loud' or 'too ambitious'?
- Whose voice is criticising you when you are writing these answers?

Then ask yourself:

- What would it feel like to ignore that voice? To instead listen to Lauren's dulcet Glaswegian tones ;)
- Who misses out on your leadership, your creativity, your ideas if you prioritise being liked?

Try these:

- 'When others feel uncomfortable with my confidence, I remind myself. . .'
- 'I'm not here to be liked. I'm here to. . .'
- 'Being a tall poppy means. . .'

Now, meet the part of you that's scared, the inner child, the bullied schoolgirl, the younger self who just wanted to be safe. She's still with you. And she needs reassurance, not rejection. Talk to her like you'd talk to a little bird with a broken wing, or use the voice you'd use to read a bedtime story to a young child you love with all your heart. Speak out loud to her.

You might want to say:

- 'I know you're afraid, and that's OK'.
- 'But now, we're on a different mission'.
- 'You can come with me. I'll keep us safe'.
- 'You don't have to lead, but you don't get to be in charge anymore'.

I'm not about pretending it's easy. It's not. I want you to do it anyway. Let this be your mantra: 'I am building confidence in a world that doesn't want me to, and I'm doing it anyway'. Feel the sting. Feel the fire. The world needs you standing tall and being UPFRONT.

Notes

1. Symons, L. and Ibarra, H. (2014). *What the scarcity of women in business case studies really looks like.* https://hbr.org/2014/04/what-the-scarcity-of-women-in-business-case-studies-really-looks-like.
2. Rouvalis, C. (2016). *Gender divide.* https://www.cmu.edu/cmtoday/artsculture_business/gender-pay-gap-research/index.html.
3. Tiedens, L.Z. (2001). Anger and advancement: The role of anger and gender in negotiating status. *Journal of Personality and Social Psychology* 81 (1): 86–94. https://doi.org/10.1037/0022-3514.81.1.86.
4. Women of Influence. *The Tallest Poppy.* (2023).
5. Matrescence and confidence with Zoe Blaskey, Motherkind, *UPFRONT Moment with Lauren Currie* [Podcast], 2022.

Part II

Relearn

10

You Are Cringing Forward

Old Rule: Avoid cringe

New Rule: Cringe forward

C ringing. My oldest friend from school calls it 'the knee twist'. You know that feeling when you're lying in bed, trying to fall asleep and then, bam, you remember something embarrassing you did or said. Your body twists, like it's trying to fold in on itself, or escape the feeling, the cringe, the knee twist, classic.

But why are we so afraid of cringing? Awkwardness isn't fatal, nobody dies from it, it doesn't even actually hurt. You'll be just fine. Yet, we make huge, life-altering decisions, how we spend our time, who we hang out with, how much we earn, just to avoid that one feeling.

> *I laughed when Lauren said that no-one ever died of awkwardness, because I remain convinced it'll be my cause of death! Yet we're all still here. . .*
>
> (Rachel, Bond graduate)

I get it. I've had my fair share of knee twist moments and I still do, all the time. But in those moments I'm also smiling. A little secret smile between me and me. Because I know something that most people don't: cringing means I'm growing. Cringe isn't the enemy of confidence. It's the evidence of it.

I'm calling bullshit on the idea that cringing is something to avoid. Cringe is the price of learning confidence. No one gets to skip it. It's the signal that you're stretching, reaching and living. So instead of running from it, let's learn to love it. Cringe forward.

When was the last time you cringed? Congratulations! I am cheering for you wildly. That's a strong signal you're pushing boundaries and stepping outside your comfort zone. If you've never cringed or can't remember the last time, chances are you aren't taking enough risks, you aren't stretching yourself and you certainly aren't living an UPFRONT life.

I distinctly remember my last cringe, it wasn't a biggy but I felt it in the moment. I was on a call with one of the world's biggest fashion brands, talking about a Bond to support their teams. They mentioned a 'watch party' for the staff who couldn't be at the runway show in Paris and who would instead gather together to watch the show on a big screen. I immediately blurted out, *'Can I come?'* I can barely write this to you because I want to hide under the table. Their faces. But guess what? Nothing bad happened and I think they were a little surprised, maybe even a little admiring of my audacity? They politely explained that it was for staff only. There it was, bang, the cringe. Nothing catastrophic happened. And what if they'd have said sure to coming along? I lost nothing either way, but gained a maybe in the process. Cringe forward.

When you embrace cringe, you take away its power. When you are at peace with your own cringe, no one can ever call you cringey. No one can use it against you when you own it.

Even cultural icons agree: cringe is inevitable. And more than that, it's instructive. As Taylor Swift, a Grammy-winning singer-songwriter, wisely puts it, '*No matter how hard you try to avoid cringing, you'll look back and cringe at some point in your life. That's just part of the journey*'. She's right. We all have those moments when we look back and think, *What was I even thinking?* And that's OK.

Emma Watson, the actor and activist best known for playing Hermione in the *Harry Potter* films and for her work on gender equality, echoes this sentiment beautifully: '*I use the word "cringe" a lot. I've always had a tendency to cringe when I look back at things I've said or done*'. She reminds us that even the most thoughtful, accomplished women are not immune to that knee-twist feeling. And yet, they keep showing up.

If you're like me, you might feel that deep sense of exposure when creating something personal. Whether it's a piece of writing, a podcast or even a social media post, there's something very vulnerable about putting your thoughts, your heart, your ideas and your voice out there for the world to see. It can feel like standing naked in front of an audience, where the world can see every flaw, every mistake, every imperfection. This is EXACTLY where you want to be.

Austin Kleon, a writer and artist known for his books on creativity, says, '*If your work makes you feel exposed, vulnerable, or even a little bit ashamed, you're on the right track*'. He's onto something. Personal work is the most vulnerable, but it's also the most transformative. When you expose yourself, whether it's your thoughts, emotions or creative work, you invite others to see you for who you truly are and that's where real connection happens.

When I first started writing this book, I was terrified. The first few chapters? Cringe central. I stumbled over words. I threw tantrums. I announced to my family I'd never be able to do it. But the more I kept showing up, the more I allowed myself to feel that discomfort and push through it, the more I realised that of course I could do it. It's in those cringy, exposed, raw moments that we uncover new layers of our confidence.

> *Confidence has always been a massive challenge for me, I'm guilty of being one of those people that is put off by 'over' confident people, cringes at the idea of promoting myself and can find a million excuses to stay small and isolated. It's time to change things up.*
>
> (Jenny, Bond graduate)

I implore you to find the confidence to cringe. Yes, you are going to be embarrassed by some things you say or do, but that is a good, gorgeous, generous thing. That's why I believe cringing is a sign you're doing something brave. And let me tell you, I've cringed my way through some of my proudest moments.

In October 2022, I did something that still gives me the knee twist. March of the Mummies took place in London and across ten other UK cities, organised by Pregnant Then Screwed, a grassroots charity that campaigns for the rights of mothers and caregivers, and fights against the systemic disadvantages faced by pregnant women and working parents. This Halloween-themed protest aimed to highlight the challenges faced by parents, especially mothers, regarding high childcare costs, inadequate parental leave and limited flexible working options. Over 8,000 people showed up. And guess who was at the front with a megaphone, a huge top hat and a painted face? Yes, you guessed it. Me.

March of the Mummies, 2022. Photo by Donna Ford.

When the founder asked me to lead the protest, I said YES so fast you'd think I was being offered a backstage pass to see Taylor Swift. It wasn't a thought-through yes, it was a cartwheel-out-of-my-mouth yes. But then, cut to me, actually standing there, megaphone in hand, a thousand expectant faces looking my way, reality hit hard. It was terrifying. I'm forever grateful to Sophie Walker, founding leader of the Women's Equality Party and a lifelong campaigner for gender justice, for seeing something in me that I couldn't quite see yet and for giving me the gentle shove I didn't know I needed. Her belief steadied me, rooted me, made me lift my chin.

I'm so proud of myself for showing up with my whole heart, even as I cringed inside. We got coverage on every UK news channel and landed on the front cover of *The Guardian*. There's a photo of me leading that march, painted face, huge hat, voice cracking with purpose, framed on my living room wall. Someday, I'll tell my grandchildren about that day. It's one of my proudest, brightest, loudest moments.

The UPFRONT philosophy is this: Cringe is the bridge to confidence. Think of it this way, each time you cringe, it's a step towards who you're becoming. Every awkward moment, every mistake, every vulnerable piece of work you put out into the world is a sign that you're growing, stretching and building something bigger than yourself. You can't skip the cringe if you want to build your confidence muscle.

That's why at UPFRONT, we say cringe forward. It's not about avoiding the cringe or pretending it doesn't exist. It's about leaning into it. Cringe isn't a bad thing, it's a rite of passage. It's the badge of honour for those who are brave enough to put themselves out there and grow. So the next time you feel that uncomfortable flush of embarrassment, remind yourself that this is where the magic happens. Embrace it, learn from it and cringe forward, because that's how you build confidence, one cringey step at a time.

Making your dreams come true is the most embarrassing work in the world. It's sweaty and ugly. Mortifying. You'll say the wrong thing and cry in toilets. Share something that makes you cringe later. You'll be misunderstood, judged and underestimated. But still you'll keep going.

You're building confidence, one cringey, brilliant step at a time. I'm proud of that, and I'm proud of you.

UPFRONT Moment

Cringe is proof you're trying. Writing those words down is how you'll remember that. This chapter might've made your shoulders tense. Maybe your cheeks flushed remembering that thing you said, that post you shared, that email you wish you could unsend. Good. That means we're in the right place.

Cringe isn't something to avoid, it's something to pay attention to. This moment right here is where we stop just thinking about it and start doing the work. So please, don't just nod along. Pick up your pen. Open your notes app. Get it out of your head and onto the page. Let this be the moment you stop waiting to feel ready and start moving through the awkward.

Messy is fine. Cringey is expected. But silence won't get you anywhere. Write it down. Cringe forward. You're doing great.

Start here:

- What's the last thing you did that made you cringe?
- Saying yes too quickly?
- Asking for something you wanted?
- Sharing your art?

Take a breath. Write it down. Don't flinch. This isn't about fixing or erasing. It's about honouring the fact that you *showed up*. That matters.

Now go deeper:

- What did that moment make possible, even if it made you squirm?
- What might you have missed out on if you hadn't cringed your way through it?

- What are you not doing right now because you're afraid of cringing again?

Then try this:

- Write a thank-you note to your cringe. I'm serious!

Try:

- 'Thank you, cringe, for showing me. . .'
- 'Thank you, cringe, for teaching me. . . .'
- 'Thank you, mortifying memory, for reminding me I was brave enough to try'.

Now finish these:

- 'When I cringe, I know I've. . .'
- 'The cost of avoiding cringe is. . .'
- 'If I wait until I'm not embarrassed, I'll miss out on. . .'
- 'The version of me who cringes forward is. . .'

The most extraordinary people you admire are cringing too but they're still showing up. So the next time you feel your stomach twist, your face flush or your brain scream why did I say that, pause and remember that's the sound of your confidence muscle stretching.

You're doing it. And I'm right here, whispering with my whole chest: Cringe forward, baby. I believe in you!

11

You Were Never Meant to Shout to Be Heard

Old Rule: Confidence is loud

New Rule: Confidence comes in all volumes

We live in a world that rewards extroversion. It's a big problem and I say this as your most extroverted Scottish friend. When the loudest voice always wins, we start aspiring to be the loudest. The result is a society drowning in noise, with a lack of competence and an intense absence of true leadership. Watch any presidential debate and you'll see it play out in real time. Meanwhile, the quiet and calm among us are constantly dismissed, overlooked and told to be louder.

For women, this is just another trap in the game of damned if you do, damned if you don't. 'Be louder', they say, until we're told we're too loud, too much or taking up too much space.

My extroversion is one of my greatest superpowers, yet it has been a source of shame for most of my life. I've been told my laugh is too loud, I talk too much, I play music too loudly and I interrupt too often. At the same time, every month, I welcome thousands of women into the Bond, who have been shamed for the exact opposite. They're told to speak up, be louder and have more opinions.

The truth is, it doesn't matter if you're loud or quiet, you will still be criticised. Research backs this up: studies show that women who speak up are often seen as less like-able, while women who stay quiet are seen as less competent.[1] It's a rigged game. One study found that when women spoke more than men in collaborative settings, they were judged as less 'team-oriented', even when they were simply contributing equally.[2] This double bind means that no matter where you sit on the volume dial, you've likely felt the sting of being too much or not enough. So the goal isn't to please them, it's to free yourself. Free yourself from chasing the perfect pitch and instead commit to owning your voice, whatever its volume.

Quiet Doesn't Mean Low Confidence

Let's imagine for a moment that confidence is like a volume dial. Society tells us that to be successful, we have to crank those speakers up to full blast. So you try. Maybe it feels like you're pretending. Or maybe you push, only to discover your dial doesn't go past 50%.

Confidence isn't about blasting the speakers to the max. It's about knowing where your unique setting is on the world's volume dial. Some of us thrive at full volume, others feel most confident when we're at a quieter, calmer level. Both are equally powerful.

I've learned a lot about confidence by parenting, rais-ing and loving an introverted child, while being a very extro-verted mother myself. My son has taught me that confidence isn't always loud. And his confidence definitely doesn't need to look like my confidence to be real.

Here's what I now know:

1. **Introverts talk a lot, and can be very loud, when they feel safe.** It's not about how much they speak, but who they're with.

2. **Shyness is not a personality trait.** It's a feeling. A state. It's not fixed.

3. **We live in a world that constantly rewards extroversion.** It shows up in who gets attention in classrooms, meetings, politics and leadership. This is one reason I wrote this book for you—to shift that narrative.

4. **Trying to give your child what *you* would want in a moment of discomfort often makes things worse.** Especially when you're projecting extroverted expectations onto an introverted nervous system.

5. **Our home is often quieter and slower than I would instinctively choose, and now I see that as a gift.** It's made space for gentler joy, deeper thinking and richer rest.

6. **Happiness doesn't always sound like loud laughter or look like overt celebration.** Just because someone's joy doesn't match your own expression of it, doesn't mean it's not joy.

7. **Extroverts and introverts are equally capable of being confident.** There is zero correlation between being outgoing and being self-assured or between being reserved and lacking confidence.

8. **Introversion is often mistaken for rudeness.** But what if we all slowed down long enough to look again? We'd see care, depth, reflection. All vital forms of leadership and connection.

These lessons have softened and stretched me. They've helped me become a better parent, a better leader and a better listener. Most importantly, they've helped me understand that confidence comes in all volumes, and none of them are wrong.

SHYNESS IS NOT A PERSONALITY TRAIT. IT'S A FEELING. A STATE. IT'S NOT FIXED.

Here's the challenge: turn your volume dial to where it feels right, and own it. What might feel like the wrong setting is exactly where your power lies because confidence is about being fully you, not trying to mimic someone else. As Susan Cain, author of *Quiet* and a leading voice on the power of introversion, puts it:

> *There's zero correlation between being the best talker and having the best ideas.*

Quiet confidence is the ability to hold space without filling it. It's steady eye contact. It's making others feel safe. It's listening deeply, leading calmly, setting boundaries without drama. Quiet confidence doesn't need to perform. It just is. And it's just as powerful as the loud kind.

Quiet Confidence in Action

Quiet is often mistaken for weakness. Softness for a lack of conviction. But some of the most powerful women in history have moved mountains, not with volume, but with quiet confidence.

Rosa Parks didn't shout, argue or raise her voice. On 1 December 1955, she simply said *no*. No to giving up her seat. No to injustice. That silent act of resistance ignited the Montgomery Bus Boycott and became a defining moment in the Civil Rights Movement. Her calm defiance was louder than any megaphone.

Greta Thunberg was 15 when she sat outside the Swedish Parliament with a handmade sign. She didn't storm stages or command attention with fiery speeches. But her quiet persistence sparked a global climate movement. When she stood before world leaders at the United Nations (UN), her words

QUIET
CONFIDENCE
DOESN'T NEED
TO PERFORM.
IT JUST IS. AND
IT'S JUST AS
POWERFUL AS
THE LOUD KIND.

were clipped, direct and charged with clarity: '*You have stolen my dreams and my childhood with your empty words*'. Greta shows us that quiet can be just as powerful as loud.

Malala Yousafzai, the youngest Nobel Peace Prize laureate, speaks with the grace of someone who has survived the unthinkable and still believes in the future. After being shot by the Taliban for advocating for girls' education, she addressed the UN on her 16th birthday not with rage, but with quiet resolve: '*One child, one teacher, one book, one pen can change the world*'. Her power lies not in how loudly she speaks, but in how deeply she believes.

These women didn't need to shout to be heard. They weren't interested in taking up space through noise. They stood firm. They spoke simply. They trusted the weight of their message. You can do the same.

Confidence at Your Level

One person who has learnt how to do this is Sanya Rajpal, CEO of AdagioVR. Sanya is also an international development expert and activist who has spoken at the UN. When we spoke on the *UPFRONT Moment* podcast she revealed that she's not a natural public speaker, describing herself as an introvert who often feels shy.[3]

> *I don't always love how I sound when I'm talking. I have a lot of that self-doubt in my head. That's my internal reality. But I also know the only way I can change anything in my life or in the world or anything I care about is if I change and develop myself. So I work really hard on developing the skill of being able to speak the way that people will listen but at my level. And this is still a journey I'm on.*

I think about it in terms of having the opportunity to communicate something that is important and that is of some value . . . I tell people their voice is of value. I'm very lucky that I was given that message consistently throughout my life. I didn't always believe it, but I try to live by that truth.

I love the way Sanya frames this. She pins her voice to the value of what she has to say. What would you say if you start with the perspective that you have something of value to say? Because you do. We all do. I promise.

Speaking Slowly

The number one thing you can do to increase your confidence when talking to others is to slow down. I have a theory that the reason women often speak fast is because we are so used to being interrupted. We've learned to rush our thoughts into the space before someone else jumps in. But speaking quickly can make us sound less confident and less certain, even when we know exactly what we're talking about.

Let's play a game. It's called 'The Full Stop Game'. Pick a short sentence you'd say in a meeting or conversation. Say it out loud. Then say it again, but this time, pause for a full second after every sentence. Literally count 'one' in your head before you speak the next line.

This will feel awkward at first, like you're being too slow. But it's not. That pause is powerful. It gives your words weight. It allows people to absorb what you're saying. Most importantly, it reminds your nervous system that you don't have to rush to be heard.

Practise it. Read this paragraph out loud or an email you're about to send. Pause at every full stop. You'll feel more grounded, more spacious, and so will the people listening to you.

When you slow down, something else starts to happen: you become more aware of how you speak. Not just the speed, but the shape and texture of your sentences. That's where filler words come in. You know the ones: *um, like, you know, so, just.* They sneak into the empty space. Often, we use them to soften what we're saying or to buy time while we think. But with a little more silence, the kind you've just practised in The Full Stop Game, you can start replacing those fillers with calm, confident pauses.

Like every habit, the first step is awareness. Many of our habitual fillers are a crutch we use when we're not 100% sure of what we're saying. They have become part of your speech pattern over the course of years, so don't expect to shed them overnight. You could even try filming yourself to spot your filler words, cringe forward remember! Some fillers to look out for:

- Hesitant noises: 'I . . . er . . . want to think about my . . . erm . . . habits around . . . er . . . fillers'.
- Non-verbal extras: clicking of lips, sudden inhales or exhales, clearing your throat.
- Extraneous additions: 'It's like so easy, you know, to just drop in like kinda extra words, and stuff'.
- Stumbly starts and clumsy endings: 'OK! So . . . I guess we should start and end our sentences cleanly, you know what I mean? Do you think? So . . . yeah'.
- Artificial adjectives: 'Great, so it's fantastic having such an awesome amount of brilliant adjectives to use, but there is a definite chance we could massively overdo it'.
- Unnecessary adverbs: 'I literally always use adverbs because I think it totally adds some real spice to my conversation, but essentially I'm actually just excellently filling time'.

Since you're filming yourself, you might notice your physical tics or movement patterns. Stillness is power, slow is power. But remember movement can also be part of your style, your personality or your body's natural way of being. For some of us, tics and movements are linked to disabilities, chronic conditions or neurodivergence, and they're nothing to 'fix'. Be careful with self-awareness, it can quickly tip into overthinking. There's nothing wrong with you. Everyone has their own ways of moving. You're brilliant, beautiful and unique exactly as you are. All you're doing here is exploring how you speak and present, not trying to be something or someone you're not.

These might sound like small shifts, but they can make a big difference to your confidence, as Angie found:

> *Even after week one the Bond gave me the courage and tips around changing and reducing what I call diminishing language, my pitches became snappier, my emails shorter and to the point and most importantly I finally priced my services appropriately. Since my Bond experience I have been firm and persistent in asking for what I am worth/due.*

Once you've slowed down and started noticing your words, the next layer of confidence work is to go deeper, beyond clarity and tone, into the source of your voice itself. Not just how you sound, but where your voice is coming from. Because confidence isn't only about pacing or polish. It's also about connection, to your thoughts, your feelings and your purpose. That's where your UPFRONT voice lives. And here's the good news: you don't have just one voice. You have three. Let me show you.

Three Voices, One You

We all have more than one voice, even though you might be thinking, *but I only have one voice* as you read this. Most of us use the same voice in every situation, but the reality is that we all have three different voices inside of us. When we can recognise these and tap into them, it's like rocket fuel for our confidence.

I want to encourage you to start playing with your voice based on where you feel it, rather than where you hear it. This has nothing to do with the volume you speak at. Caroline Goyder, vocal coach and author of *Gravitas*, teaches us there are three main places to feel your voice, which gives us our three voices: head voice, heart voice and gut voice. You can use these voices for different things in different ways. They are all inside of you, and all yours. We can see others using these differing voices across different media too. For example:

- HEAD VOICE is intellect, thoughtfulness and curiosity; think of someone like Judi Dench or Sandi Toksvig.
- HEART VOICE is love, passion, care, empathy and warmth; listen to Oprah Winfrey or Michelle Obama.
- GUT VOICE is power, drive and action; Nicola Sturgeon and Beyoncé Knowles both embody this voice.

When you tap into how you feel, your tone, pace and intonation all change. This allows you to tailor your voice to the situation you're in. This has nothing to do with how loudly or quietly you speak and everything to do with the way you present yourself.

Confidence doesn't always speak. It can look like writing a bold email, holding steady eye contact in a difficult conversation, saying '*no*' without padding it with excuses, or building something that speaks for you. A system, a piece of art, a boundary. One Bonder from the Bond, Amina, shared that she didn't say a single word in her first leadership team meeting after joining the Bond but she quietly deleted a chaotic, outdated process and replaced it with one clear, inclusive and efficient tool. No announcement. No applause. Just radical clarity. *That* was her confidence speaking. Confidence shows up in quiet conviction just as much as it does in powerful words. Your actions, your choices, your stillness—these all carry a voice of their own.

Back to the three voices Caroline Goyder teaches. Take a moment to tap into each of your three voices now.

- HEAD VOICE: Think of something that takes you into an analytical place in your head. Imagine filing receipts or doing your tax returns. Say the days of the week. Feel the voice in your head.
- HEART VOICE: Put a hand on your heart and think of someone you love. Imagine you are reading a child a bedtime story or talking to a tiny bird with a broken wing. Say the days of the week.
- GUT VOICE: Tap your stomach then perform a physical movement that has power. Imagine you are standing in front of a crowd demanding they listen to you about women's rights! Or imagine you are trying to inspire everyone in your neighbourhood to go and vote. Say the days of the week.

Notice how each one not only sounds different, but feels different in your body. These voices were always there, and will always be there, so use them. Now that you have this knowledge, you can think about what voice you want to use in different situations. Maybe you want to access your gut voice for a speech, or perhaps for a particular presentation you want to make sure you access your heart voice. Some of you will have a voice where you feel most comfortable and some of you will feel very uncomfortable in one or two of these voices. Reflect on this, notice what comes up for you and play with each voice. Practise all of them, but focus on the one that feels least comfortable, because this is where you'll gain the most confidence.

For me, my most comfortable voice is my gut voice. Combine that with a strong regional accent and I've been labelled 'scary' and 'intimidating'. For years, I thought that was something I had to fix. Now I know it's part of my gift and my brilliance. My gut voice has inspired thousands of people all over the world to take action. When I sing, I switch to my heart voice, and I've been told it melts my dad's heart.

Showing Up After Silence

Stacey joined the Bond to help her regain her confidence following illness.

> *In my past life, before the onset of a debilitating neurological condition, I spoke a lot. I was an educator, public speaker, teacher trainer and more. I represented the universities I worked for in promotional videos. When I lived overseas, I had my own TV programme and was co-host of a radio show. I was never daunted by speaking to people, or in front of them. One person. Hundreds. I didn't mind. But since relearning how to speak after my condition, regaining control over the mechanics of speech, relearning how to modulate my tone, learning how to make the words*

in my head come out of my mouth in something vaguely resembling a sense, I've shied away from speaking. To anyone. My beautiful speaking voice is gone. My clear articulation, often commented on by others, is gone. And so was my confidence. Until UPFRONT.

In the onboarding call for the Founders and Freelancers Bond, I found myself suddenly expected to introduce myself. Then I was placed in a break-out room with a few other women and was also expected to speak. Because I was familiar with Lauren's work (I'd completed her Domestika course over the Christmas holidays), because I trusted and because our host Daisy was so kind, I spoke. I believe I probably gabbled. I certainly know I felt embarrassed. But not only did I survive, I felt so supported, so listened to, so uplifted, that I left wanting more. Which is why I enrolled in UPFRONT in the first place. Because I cannot live the life I want to lead, cannot live true to my values, if I remain silent. I'm still scared that I'll jumble up my words. That I'll confuse others. That I'll gabble. But I face my fear knowing that I'm invisibly supported by a huge network of women. I know they want me to show up. That I must show up. And I will.

Stacey's story is a perfect example of someone who knows their voice is there and that they just need the confidence to use it. Stacey knew what she had to say was valuable and she knew she wanted to share her thoughts but she had lost the physical ability to do so, which in turn caused a mental shift that knocked her confidence. She practised her way through the physical part during her version of physiotherapy, and came to UPFRONT for the confidence needed to take her to the next step.

You were never meant to shout to be heard. You are here to speak, write, lead, make art, create change, with confidence at YOUR volume. That is more than enough. And the world needs exactly that.

UPFRONT Moment

Confidence isn't always loud but reflection does always require space. This is your space. By now, you've read 10 chapters. You've nodded in recognition. Maybe you've seen yourself in Stacey, in Sanya, in the slow power of a pause. But reading alone won't build your confidence muscle. Writing and doing will.

So I'm asking you, no scrap that, I'm daring you, to take this seriously. Your voice, at your volume, is asking to be heard. So make space and write it down. This isn't homework. It's healing. It's a rep for your confidence muscle. These prompts will help you stretch it.

Think about the last time you felt pressure to be louder, faster, more 'on'.

- Where were you?
- Who were you with?
- What did you do?
- What did your body want to do instead?

What might've happened if you'd honoured your own volume?

On a scale from whisper to megaphone, where does your confidence sit? Is that your natural setting or one you've learned to perform?

Write about a moment where you didn't speak but your confidence was still felt. What were you doing? What did your presence communicate?

Take a breath. Then say the days of the week aloud in your:

- **Head voice** (fact, analysis, logic)
- **Heart voice** (emotion, care, empathy)
- **Gut voice** (conviction, urgency, truth)

Which one feels most natural? Which one feels like a stretch? Which one would you like to grow?

We all carry old soundtracks:

- 'You're too quiet'.
- 'Speak up'.
- 'You talk too much'.
- 'You're too much'.

List the ones you've heard. Then rewrite them as truth. You might want to try:

- 'I don't need to shout to be clear'.
- 'Stillness doesn't mean I have nothing to say'.
- 'My presence speaks even when I don't'.

Finish these sentences:

- 'When I stop chasing volume, I find. . .'
- 'My quiet confidence sounds like. . .'

- 'My voice is powerful because. . .'
- 'I was never meant to shout. I was meant to. . .'

Let this be the chapter where you stop waiting to sound different and start honouring how you already sound. Let your voice stretch its legs, not to be louder, but to take up space in its own way. That space is yours. Take it.

Notes

1. Rudman, L.A. and Glick, P. (2001). Prescriptive gender stereotypes and backlash toward agentic women. *Journal of Social Issues* 57 (4): 743–762. https://doi.org/10.1111/0022-4537.00235.
2. Karpowitz, C.F., Mendelberg, T., and Shaker, L. (2012). Gender inequality in deliberative participation. *American Political Science Review* 106 (3): 533–547. https://doi.org/10.1017/s0003055412000329.
3. Virtual Reality—supercharging our confidence revolution, *UPFRONT Moment with Lauren Currie* [Podcast], 2023.

12

You Are Choosing Confidence Again and Again

Old Rule: Confidence is a fluke

New Rule: Confidence is a practice

It's 7:45 p.m. on 24th March 2017 and I'm backstage at a venue in central London, about to step into the spotlight. My hands are shaking, my heart is hammering and sweat is pooling in places I'd rather not discuss. This is unusual for me. I have a long-standing, borderline-flirtatious relationship with the spotlight. Put me on a stage and I light up like a Pinterest mood board. I get paid to speak, applauded for it, and I've built a reputation for excellence on stage. Big audiences don't scare me, they caffeinate me. So why, tonight, am I terrified? Because tonight, I'm not going on stage to educate, inspire or inform. Tonight, I'm going on stage to BE FUNNY.

I signed up for a stand-up comedy course because I refuse to build companies, deliver keynotes and write books about confidence without testing my own. If I was going to tell you that confidence is something you build, then I had to keep building mine! And what better way to put my own

149

confidence to the test than to step into a space where I have no confidence whatsoever?

The thing about stand-up is no amount of knowledge or preparation guarantees laughter. I could rehearse a speech until my voice was hoarse, but comedy is different. It's about timing, tone and risk. It's about failing publicly and then trying again. It's a craft, an art and more than that, it's a practice.

I used to believe that comedians were just naturally funny, born with a magical gift that made audiences roar with laughter. But as I sat in that comedy course, painstakingly rewriting punchlines and reworking my delivery, I realised the opposite is true.

Every pause, every expression, every perfectly timed joke you see on stage has been tested, rewritten and performed a hundred times. Comedians aren't naturally funny in the way we think they are. It's practice. They're practising all of the time.

And YES confidence works the exact same way! We love to tell ourselves that confident people were simply born that way. That they were lucky. That it just happened for them. But confidence isn't a fluke. It's built. Brick by brick, rep by rep, joke by joke.

Building a comedy sketch joke by joke was hard. At the time, I got angry. But not because I had a hard time knitting punch lines together but because I got feedback my stand-up script was too angry. And honestly that pissed me off. Because I was angry. My set tackled period poverty. I wanted the audience to laugh and leave ready to dismantle injustice. But I forgot something crucial: comedy invites, it doesn't demand. And I got it wrong.

Comedy thrives on truth, but comedians can't get away with raw anger. It makes people uncomfortable. It pushes them away. A seasoned comedian knows how to channel anger into something joyful, something that draws people in rather than shutting them down. I had to learn how to take a rage-fuelled message and deliver it with laughter, not lectures—this spun me right out of my comfort zone. I had to rewrite, again and again. One week, my classmates told me my set felt like a TED Talk with a few one-liners sprinkled in. Not the vibe. I had to learn to let go of control. So I let go. And I remembered my superpower: my face is my outside voice.

Once upon a time, my friend Kylie asked me what I thought about something and my colleague immediately said, 'It's all in her eyebrows. Watch her eyebrows'. It's in my eyebrows. My eyes. My mouth. My cheeks. You know how I feel and you know what I'm thinking. This used to keep me up at night. A weakness to be reversed. A flaw to get rid of. How the hell would I ever be able to be *strategic*? Ever tried googling '*How to learn to have a poker face?*' Don't. These days I'm proud of my outside-voice face and it turns out this is incredibly useful for stand-up.

Author David Deida says: '*Everything you do right now ripples outward and affects everyone. Your posture can shine your heart or transmit anxiety. Your breath can radiate love or muddy the room in depression. Your glance can awaken joy*'.

This is never more true than when you're standing on stage, mic in hand, waiting for that split-second reaction from an audience. I learned that I could manipulate the energy in the room not through force, but through my face, my voice and my breath.

I practised. I did what I've been telling you to do since Chapter 1, and will continue to tell you to do throughout this book. Repetition is the mother of learning. I practised a lot, most days. I recorded myself and watched it back. I listened to my delivery on repeat, tweaking my pacing and memorising my script. I rewrote it, and I even let my very funny younger brother (who is a comedic genius in his own right) roast my material and make it sharper. Then, one night, it all clicked.

Stepping onto that stage, I wasn't relying on luck. I wasn't crossing my fingers, hoping confidence would magically appear. I had built it, rep by rep, rewrite by rewrite, just like the comedians I once thought were naturally gifted. And then people laughed. They really laughed.

The fear, the self-doubt I danced with, the nerves, it all melted away in that moment. When it was over, I wasn't just relieved. I was hungry to do it again. Because confidence doesn't come from waiting until you feel ready, does it? It comes from doing the thing, scared, again and again, until one day you realise you aren't scared anymore.

I'm surprisingly going to mention Arnold Schwarzenegger now, briefly of course. You didn't see that coming did you? Look at the size of him when he was winning all of his medals for being muscular. His advice to young men and women wanting to follow in his footsteps is to gain weight for five years and then sculpt to win shows. And when you look at him winning on his stage, you can absolutely imagine that it takes five years to get that big. Now take that lens and look at confidence. There are many lessons in that thought. But the one I like best is this: you do not turn up at the gym with bulging muscles, just like you don't turn up in a new experience with all the confidence you need to perform well. We don't wait to feel strong before we start training. We train to become strong.

Confidence works the same way. It's not a fluke. It's not something other people just have. It's a muscle, a craft, a practice. It's something you can learn. And as with all learning, the more you practise, the more it becomes who you are.

Choosing Confidence

Practising confidence can feel scary so choose something small; don't go for the heavy weights on day one. Here's what Eli from the Bond did to help her feel more comfortable as she practised:

> *I was at a conference for a few days this week and took time on my journey to start scripting some ways to introduce myself and talk about my work without apologising or using 'just' and 'but'. And then I started to talk to people. I don't know if I could have spoken about myself in that more intentional way without having my pre-prepared comments, but I was able to do it and it did start to feel easier. Someone even complimented me on being confident enough to go to a networking reception on my own and start conversations. If only they knew!*
>
> *So, while I have a lot more to do before this is an embedded habit, I feel like I'm making progress and that my mindset is shifting. It also really helped that I could tell myself if anything goes wrong, I can share with the Bond and someone will tell me it's OK.*

Eli's practice is as real as it gets; it's not jumping on a stage nor is it joining a stand-up comedy club. But it is the very first step that is needed to get to those places. It's the lightest dumbbell in the gym, and that's perfect.

Eli didn't walk into that conference dripping in self-assurance; she scripted her sentences and practised her tone like a comedian rehearsing a punchline. That is confidence. It's intentional. It's a practice. And it's yours for the taking.

Start practising. Choose something small. Start with the lightest weight. Introduce yourself differently. Ask the question. Raise your hand. Rewrite the joke. Rehearse your delivery. Try again.

Because this is what confident people do.

They practise. They choose confidence.

Again.

And again.

And again.

So now it's your turn.

Choose confidence. Practise. Right here, right now.

UPFRONT Moment

You know what confidence is about. Yes, you got it. It's about practice and repetition. I know you already know this but unless you stop and write it down, that knowledge stays shallow.

I want it to get deeper for you. I want it to feel personal. Will you do the rep with me?

Let go of needing to sound wise or polished. This isn't about the perfect insight, it's about practice. Just like comedy. Just like lifting. Grab your notebook, your notes app, a scrap of paper and let's go again.

Think of a recent moment, maybe from the past week when you felt unsure, small or tempted to stay quiet.

Now finish this:

- 'If I could choose confidence in that moment again, I would have. . .'
- 'Next time, I will. . .'

I wonder what your smallest step is, what your version of the lightest weight is? What's a small, low-stakes action you could take today that builds your confidence muscle?

Maybe it looks like introducing yourself without qualifiers or sharing something you're proud of or saying 'no' without explanation.

Now finish these sentences:

- 'My light rep today will be. . .'
- 'Confidence, for me, looks like. . .'

Write down three areas of your life where you are currently *practising* confidence, even if you don't feel like an expert (for me this is parenting and making art!). Now consider what's getting stronger each time you show up? Where are you noticing growth, even if it's quiet?

Confidence isn't a one-time thing. It's a choice you'll make again tomorrow, and the next day. There's no shortcut or cheat code. Just reps and practice. Just you, choosing confidence again. And again. And again. That's not a fluke, it's being UPFRONT. Keep going.

CONFIDENCE ISN'T A ONE-TIME THING. IT'S A CHOICE YOU'LL MAKE AGAIN TOMORROW, AND THE NEXT DAY.

13

You Are Making Your Work Visible

Old Rule: Share to shine

New Rule: Share to learn

What if the bravest thing you did today wasn't a big, bold leap but two small words in the corner of a page?

My son has been signing his name on every single drawing since he first figured out how to hold a crayon. Scribbles of dinosaurs, flowers, rocket ships, rainbows with legs, each one, proudly stamped with his name. No negotiations. No exceptions. If you make it, you sign it.

It's not about ego. It's about ownership. I want him to know his work matters, even when it's messy. Especially when it's messy. That his voice deserves to be seen, not just heard. That the real power isn't just in the making, it's in the standing by what you've made. That's what I want for him. It's also what I want for you.

Visibility of your work matters just as much as the work itself. You are creatives and artists; you are entrepreneurs, managers and employees; you are employers, founders and freelancers. You are people in between, figuring it out. The thing you all have in common is that you are all women who care. You care about making things better for yourself, for your family, for each other, for your team and for your organisations. We are all women who care. That is what unites us in this conversation. You picked up this book because you want more confidence, not just for you, but for those you care about.

You also want to be recognised. You want your work to be rewarded. You want to be validated. You want to be paid. Which is all incredibly valid. But it feels scary being seen, so you're hiding. That hiding will look different for each of you—but that's why you're reading this book because, deep down, you know that there is a part of you that wants to stop hiding. There's a moment every woman faces: the choice to stay safely unseen, or to be fully visible and risk being misunderstood, judged or ignored but also to be respected, celebrated and rewarded. Visibility comes with risk. But it also comes with power.

My friend Camilla Walala chose to be visible. Today, her bold murals transform buildings around the world. Her art is celebrated in cities from Tokyo to New York. She's partnered with global brands like Armani and LEGO. But her journey didn't start with acclaim. It started with hiding.

> I used to do a lot of street art but never really signed my name. I'm not sure why. Perhaps I felt embarrassed. But this time I thought, f*** it, I'm just going to sign my name as big as possible, and it'll be really clear for all to see.

That mural, with her name right there on it, led Armani straight to her. This is what happens when you stop hiding and start owning your work. Visibility is not self-importance. It's economic power. It's leadership. It's how opportunities find you. It's how the right people recognise you.

Imagine a world where you're fully visible, in all the ways you dream of, and maybe a few you don't yet dare to. What do you see? Hear? Say? Do? The more detail you can paint into that picture, the more power you build. You don't need a personal brand, a logo, a press kit or permission. You need something to say and the confidence to say it. This chapter will show you how. It's time to sign your name.

What I Learned About Visibility at School

Lesson 1: Showing Your Work Helps Others Help You

Mrs McKenzie was the first person who asked me to work in the open. She was my maths teacher, and she called it '*show your working*'; it was a way for me to help her understand my process. Mrs McKenzie wanted a deeper insight into my thought process, so she could support me better. I vividly remember scribbling over my wrong answers and misspelled words so nobody could see my errors. But if nobody sees your work, nobody can help, nobody can hire you, nobody can learn from you, your career cannot progress. If you do not show your work, the only thing you are creating is a dead end.

Lesson 2: Showing Your Work Is a Creative Process That Helps You Learn

Mr Grant was the second person who asked me to work in the open. He was my art teacher, and he called it '*showing your process*'. He pushed the idea that the messier, bulkier and more colourful my process was, the better. The woman with the largest, heaviest sketchbook wins the race. I love this approach, it flips the narrative on its head. The mistakes are what you're there for, perfect.

Lesson 3: The Internet Is an Easy Way for You to Talk About Your Work

Fast forward to university, and I found myself registering a blog on my way out the door to the airport. I was on my way to Amsterdam to join Design Thinkers, a design-driven innovation agency, for my first-ever job. I decided I'd keep a blog to document my day-to day-work; a diary of sorts. Just for me. Redjotter.com was born. I didn't use my real name for another 15 years.

Now, working in the open is part of my daily routine. Like many of you, I've learned how to share my process in a way that helps me and the people who engage with my work. It's become second nature now, but I know that for many, the idea of working in the open still feels confusing, cringeworthy or like a luxury you don't have time for.

The three lessons I learned still stand: working in the open leads to opportunities, it makes me smarter and it makes me, and my work, findable. The people I admire most are those who are genuinely open about what they're building. They consistently share their ideas, opinions and process, not just their polished outcomes. The old motto *'If you build it, they will come'* doesn't work. Not now. And especially not for women. Visibility isn't guaranteed. Recognition isn't automatic. You can build something brilliant and still be overlooked if no one knows it exists. For many of us, it has felt safer to hide behind our work than to stand beside it.

But working in the open means choosing to be intentionally visible and that changes everything. Visibility is a confidence turbo boost. Beyond that, it's good for you.

It strengthens your thinking, sharpens your message and invites the opportunities your work deserves. Here are 10 reasons why shining a light on yourself and your work is a good idea:

1. **Transparency:** The more people understand your work, the more likely they will engage, support, buy or champion.
2. **Sharing learning:** If you share the mistakes you make and lessons you learn, it makes it easier for those a few steps behind you.
3. **Creating new networks:** Like-minded people will find you and your work, and this can lead to connections, opportunities and even friendships.
4. **Building trust through honesty and connection:** The more open you are about what's working and what's not, the more others will trust your intentions.
5. **Promoting accountability and openness:** When you write something down, you are more likely to do it. When you write something on the internet, you are even more likely to do it.
6. **Inhibiting spin:** Sharing your work in progress reduces temptation and opportunity for spin and fluff. All hail any process that does that!
7. **Bringing others along:** Making change happen with others is incredibly difficult. Sharing your thinking and process regularly and often makes it easier for people to join you for the ride.
8. **Building credibility and self-esteem:** Working in the open helps you become known for the things you are working on and the things you think. It also makes it easier for people to give you positive feedback (and yes it's nearly always positive and constructive—people aren't as mean as you may think).

9. **Helping with recruitment:** What's the first thing you do when you have a job interview? You google the company.
10. **Helping with learning, reframing and reflecting:** Building a habit of sharing your work encourages self-reflection. Self-reflection makes you smarter.

It's important we recognise what working in the open is and what it is not. Working in the open is sharing your journey, sharing the day-to-day lessons, thoughts, progress and setbacks. It is not a public performance or showing off. Let's take the most common objections I hear and plug in some quick fixes so we can move on in the open with no excuses.

Objection 1: 'I Really Struggle for Time'

There is no doubt about it, making yourself and your work visible does require time. But you need to realise that nobody is going to give you more time or take something off your plate, so you can prioritise it.

Try this: Put a recurring hold of 30 minutes every Wednesday morning (or whenever might work best for you) in your calendar and commit to making this time sacred. You have to decide being visible is worthy of your time, because it is, and then take it. In your 30 minutes, share one thing you've learned, post a quick update on LinkedIn, write a behind-the-scenes note or message your team about a recent win. Visibility doesn't need to be big or polished, just consistent. Try it for seven days and see what happens.

Objection 2: 'I Don't Feel Safe Enough'

It's really important we recognise that working in the open is riskier and practically more difficult the more disadvantages you face. For example, a white man in a senior role will find it easier to work in the open than a newly hired Asian woman in a junior position.

Try this: Design a working-in-the-open experiment that feels safe to try. This means it's something that isn't perfect but means you will start. It's safe to try because if it goes wrong, no irreversible harm will come to you. This might look like a three-sentence LinkedIn post every Friday evening with one thing you learned that week or writing down the three questions on the top of your mind every second Monday morning and sharing them with your team.

Objection 3: 'I Don't Have Permission'

You don't need permission to be visible. It's up to you to decide what's safe to share, and you're already more trusted and capable than you think.

If you're unsure, don't share confidential details. Share something else: a process, a challenge you overcame, a useful resource or a lesson you've learned.

Try this: Start small. Share a win from your week, a behind-the-scenes look at your process or an idea you're exploring. Focus on what's yours to tell and build from there. The more you practise, the easier it becomes to know where your line is and to confidently stand just beside it.

Objection 4: 'I Don't Think My Work Is Interesting Enough'

This is the most common objection I hear when I talk to women about working in the open. Sara Wachter-Boettcher, author, speaker and leadership coach who helps people build more inclusive, humane workplaces, captures this fear brilliantly and shares how to overcome it in her powerful article, 'Don't feel like an expert? Share anyway'.[1]

She reminds us that waiting until you feel like an expert is a trap, because that feeling might never come. The myth of needing to be interesting enough or expert enough often stops us from sharing what's already valuable. Sara explains that the people who need your perspective most aren't looking for polished thought leaders. They're looking for real, relatable insights from someone just a few steps ahead of them. That person could be you. She writes: '*When you feel like you have to be "an expert" to share your ideas, you miss opportunities to think out loud, to learn by doing, and to connect with others who are wrestling with the same stuff*'.

What you're experiencing right now, the messy middle of figuring something out, is useful. It's what people resonate with most. Sharing what you're working on, what you're learning or even what you're stuck on, creates space for others to reflect, respond and grow alongside you. That's community. That's visibility. That's leadership.

Try this: Show your work for the past you. You know, the person who didn't know a damn thing about the work you are doing now. The person who stared at a problem with no idea how to start solving it.

Objection 5: 'I'm Too Busy Doing the Real Work'

Putting your work out there and making it findable while doing good work is absolutely possible. In fact, I'd argue that working in the open will actually increase your impact, not dilute it. Visibility isn't a distraction from the work, it's an extension of it.

The book *How Women Rise* by leadership expert Sally Helgesen and executive coach Marshall Goldsmith dives deeply into this. It identifies 12 habits that hold women back in their careers, and one of the most common is '*the belief that hard work alone will get you noticed and rewarded*'.

Helgesen and Goldsmith explain that women are often conditioned to '*keep their heads down*' and let the results speak for themselves. Meanwhile, their male counterparts are more likely to build visibility and networks as part of their day-to-day work. This creates what some call a 'confidence gap' and a 'visibility gap'. The book makes the powerful case that if women want to rise, they must become comfortable being seen and heard, and that means making time to share what you're doing, how you think and what you stand for. '*Women often focus on delivering great work rather than on ensuring that their contributions are known and recognized. But being overly invested in expertise and results can limit your visibility and reduce your chances of advancement*'.

So, yes, you're busy. But being too busy to be visible is a trap. It keeps your talent hidden. It leaves your work up to interpretation. And it makes it easier for someone else, someone louder, more confident or more connected to take credit for it.

Try this: You must accept that good work does not speak for itself. You must help people find you and your work. Start here: what's the one question people ask you most often about what you do? Write down your answer. Make it simple, clear and human.

Then share it in an email, on Slack, on LinkedIn or in a team meeting. Use it as a springboard to talk about your work, your thinking or your why. It doesn't have to be polished or perfect, it just has to be you.

You're not bragging. You're building a bridge.

Still not convinced? Here's one more truth I can't let you leave without knowing.

It's called the PIE model, developed by Harvey J. Coleman, author of *Empowering Yourself: The Organizational Game Revealed*. Coleman spent years helping people understand what truly drives success at work, and his insight was this: success isn't just about how good you are at your job. In fact, performance, what you actually do, only accounts for about 10% of career progression. Yes, really!

The rest? Image, which is how you're perceived. Exposure, which is who sees you doing the work. That's right: 90% of what moves you forward at work is about how visible and valued your work is in the eyes of others.

Yet, you've been taught (directly or indirectly) that if you just keep your head down and work hard, the rewards will come. That's a myth. A comforting one, maybe, but a myth all the same. Sharing your work is not a side project. It's part of your work. You don't have to go viral. You don't have to be perfect. But you do have to show up. Even a whisper of your process could be the roar someone else needs to begin theirs. Here's your new mantra, one I learned from Dr Anne Laure Le Cunff, author of *Tiny Experiments* and founder of Nesslabs: I don't share to shine, I share to learn. To connect. To lead. To be seen, yes, but more importantly, to be findable by the people who need what only you can offer. Just like my son signs every rainbow-legged dinosaur, it's time you signed your work too. It matters. You matter. Now go. Make your work visible. Sign your name.

UPFRONT Moment

This isn't about showing off. It's about showing up. You've made the thing, done the work and put in the time. Now comes the hardest part, letting someone see it. This is where so many of us freeze. We tell ourselves it's not ready. Not impressive. Not important.

We wait for permission and perfection. For a version of ourselves that feels more 'qualified' to be visible. You get more confident by practising visibility, gently, consistently, on your own terms.

So this is your moment to stop hiding behind your work and to stop waiting to feel ready. And to make moves towards being seen. It starts right here, with your pen, your thoughts, your words.

What's something you've made, contributed to or led that no one really knows about?

- Why have you kept it quiet?
- What's the risk you feel in being seen?
- What might be possible if you shared it?

Now finish:

- 'This part of my work deserves to be seen because. . .'

Think of something you've done recently, big or small, that you *didn't* put your name on.

- Why not?
- What story did you tell yourself? Why it was better to stay invisible?

Now write:

- 'If I signed this work, I would feel. . .'
- 'The version of me who signs her work knows. . .'

Let's design a safe experiment together. What is one way you could practise working in the open *this week* that feels safe but still stretches you?

Try:

- Posting a one-sentence lesson you've learned
- Sending a behind-the-scenes email to your team
- Telling a trusted friend what you're working on

Then commit:

- 'My safe-to-try visibility experiment is. . .'
- 'I will share it by. . .'
- 'This matters because. . .'

Which of these objections feels most true for you right now?

- I don't have time
- I don't feel safe
- I don't have permission
- My work isn't interesting
- I'm too busy doing the real work

Pick one. Now reframe it with truth and possibility. Try:

- 'Even though I feel ____, I choose to share by. . .'
- 'Visibility isn't extra. It's part of my work because. . .'
- 'I will make time because____'

Imagine someone out there is looking for exactly what you've built, written, said or created. But they can't find it because it's hidden. Write to that person:

- 'Here's what I want you to know about what I'm creating. . .'

- 'If you're feeling stuck, I will help. . .'
- 'I'm sharing this because. . .'

This isn't about becoming a thought leader, even though I am here for women becoming thought leaders all day every day. This is about refusing to let your brilliance stay invisible. Visibility is how people find you.

Post the sketch. Share the draft. Say your idea out loud. And don't forget to sign your name. Spit spot.

Note

1. Wachter-Boettcher, S. (2022). Don't feel like an expert? Share anyway, *Medium*, 8 August. https://modus.medium.com/dont-feel-like-an-expert-share-anyway-661f2f8cd038.

14

You Are Making Yourself Visible

Old Rule: Your work speaks for itself

New Rule: You speak for your work

When I was 12, I made a poster for a school campaign. It had a red background, white letters, glitter everywhere. I was proud. I'd spent hours on it. But when I taped it up and walked away, I pretended it wasn't mine. Even when someone asked, 'Who made that one?' I just shrugged. The work was good. Owning it felt scary.

Fast forward a decade (or two), and that feeling still bubbles up. Sharing your work is one thing. Sharing yourself, your voice, your values, your face, your fears, that's a different kind of confidence. It's easier to tuck yourself behind the process. To say, *'Here's what I've made'* but never, *'Here's why I care about it'*. To hit publish on a thought, but blur out the part of yourself that sparked it.

In the last chapter, we talked about putting your work out into the world. This one's harder. This is about putting *yourself* out into the world. It's about the shift from being visible for what you do, to being visible for who you are. That kind of visibility can feel even more icky. Risky. Too much. Especially if you've spent years being told to be modest, humble or not too full of yourself. So, if you've ever said, 'I can get behind people seeing my work, but not me', I hear you.

Have you ever left a meeting feeling invisible, even though your work was praised? I have. I've been told I was 'impressive on paper' but 'not what they expected' in person. I've spent years learning how to show my work to the world. But learning how to show *myself*? That's been much harder. Showing your work is about process, ideas and progress. Showing yourself is about truth, identity, values and emotion. It's what happens when you stop hiding the parts of you that don't fit the script. This chapter is about being seen for who you are, not just for what you do.

It's important because people connect to people. Not just your words, your graphics or your slidedecks. You. Because that's what builds trust. That's what inspires me. That's what shifts culture. So let me ask you this: if someone followed you around for six months, online, in meetings, in passing, what would they learn about what matters to you? Would they know what makes you laugh? What makes you angry? What values you live by?

My Instagram feed is full of content hacks: how to show up every day videos, reels full of must-dos if you want to be visible and lists of tech and SEO (search engine optimisation) tips and tricks to get 'seen'. You know the ones: follow these 20 steps, join this 12-month programme. Something very simple has been turned into something so very complicated. Visibility is simply this: showing yourself and your work to the world before you feel ready. That's it. That's what visibility is.

So why is this simple act so damn hard? Here's a deeper definition: visibility is the deeply personal and courageous act of showing yourself and your work to the world despite fear and self-doubt. Visibility is emotional work. It's about overcoming fear of judgement and fear of rejection.

Now it would be easy for me to write a chapter of a hundred steps you can take to be more visible practically, but that's the easy bit, and that's readily available across the internet. The hard bit is the emotional work. Showing up when you're scared of showing up and when you don't feel ready. But let's move some things out of the way before we look closer. Let's be clear about what visibility is not. It is not being a content creator. It's not having to be online every day. It's not having to be active on social media. It's not chasing likes, follows and views. It's not about going viral. It's not about being loud or extroverted.

So what is it about, and why does it feel so hard to do? Visibility is learning to take up space despite judgement and despite rejection. It's building a muscle you can train and grow so that you become more and more comfortable with showing yourself and your work in any context. This could be a coffee with a friend where you open up your sketchbook. It could be sending your first novel draft to a bunch of peers for comment. It could be showing up on social media. But in all cases, it's overcoming the emotional barriers that produce fear. What you'll get back is not just recognition and feedback on your work which will improve it, but most importantly the next time you share you will feel less fear. You'll be learning how to show your work the more you do. As Dr Anne-Laure Le Cunff says, 'You're sharing to learn, not to shine'.

This isn't easy, simply because 90% of all people have a negativity bias towards women. I mentioned this before, and I will keep saying it until it changes. Ninety per cent of all people have a negativity bias towards women. Think about what this means. The scale of the beast. It also means that the problem isn't that women aren't confident. It's that confidence in women is not rewarded in the world. It means that the same world that's telling you to be visible and speak up more is also judging you the moment you do, because you're too quiet, or you're too confident, or you're too much, or you're not enough. This fact, the society we all live in, means that your visibility isn't a neutral act. Visibility is a risk, because you're operating in a system that was not designed to applaud you, it was designed for the opposite. The game is rigged, but you're going to play anyway.

I decided to play many years ago and I want you to decide now. I've taught thousands of women to play and they shine when they do. We're showing our work, we're wealthier, we're taking the mic, we're showing ourselves to the world, to our clients, to our customers, to our communities, to our peers. I don't want the game to be rigged, I was born into it, as were you. But that doesn't mean our daughters and sons have to be. I said I'll keep telling you about the 90% negativity bias towards women until it changes, because we all have to know what we're up against; we have to know the setting, the context of the rigged game and how it works. Only then can we change it.

This is where we are as a collective, as women. Now let's work on you and where you are. Ask yourself where you are in terms of your visibility. Are you:

Low visibility	You're unseen. Your work is flying under the radar, known only to a small circle, whether that's your immediate team, a handful of colleagues or a few loyal clients. The people who could open doors aren't seeing the full impact of what you do.
Medium visibility	You're seen. Your work is acknowledged by your manager, your team and a few colleagues beyond your immediate circle, or by your clients and a small network of peers. Your impact is starting to gain recognition but there's still room to expand your reach and influence.
High visibility	You're seen and heard. Your contributions are widely recognised by your manager, colleagues across teams or influential leaders or clients who can create opportunities for your growth and success in your industry.

THE GAME IS RIGGED, BUT YOU'RE GOING TO PLAY ANYWAY.

There will be areas in your life where you're either high, medium or low. I want you to hold that in mind as you read this chapter, because this is about you moving along that scale in different areas of your life. Now, you're not going to move from medium to high in half an hour, this takes time. But you are going to move along that scale, and you are going to keep moving along that scale until you get to a place where you are seen and heard. Here's how Dr Dupe Burgess, NHS doctor and founder of Bloomful, a digital women's health platform, describes her own journey of moving along this scale:

> *I used to be an introverted person who rarely engaged in the social media realm. No one believes that now, but if you look at my Instagram, you'd probably assume I had disappeared. I haven't used Facebook in years, and being visible online was never something that came naturally to me. I wasn't the kind of person to shout about my achievements, but deep down, I knew I was missing out on opportunities by staying in the shadows.*
>
> *A year ago, I decided to change that. I wanted to become more visible, but I had no idea where to start. Then, I won an award. That moment felt like the right entry point. I told myself, this is something worth sharing. So I posted about it on LinkedIn. That single post led to another, and soon I was sharing content twice a week. As my confidence grew, so did my engagement. I realised I was inspiring others who wanted to break into the same space, and from there, I started to understand how to use LinkedIn strategically, not just to showcase myself but to push my business forward. The journey hasn't been linear, but over the last six months, I've experienced outcomes beyond what I ever imagined.*

Not everyone will use LinkedIn like Dupe, and that's OK. There are countless ways to be visible, both online and offline. Visibility doesn't have to follow a prescriptive formula, it's about finding what works for you. Some people will share their journey on social media, while others might prefer speaking at events, networking, writing articles or short stories. The key is to take inspiration from different approaches and craft your own version of visibility.

Dupe also reflected on why it took her so long to show up:

For a long time, I was paralysed by the fear of being seen, especially by my ex-colleagues. The thought of them reading my content made me cringe, which we now know was the time to cringe forward. But when I really thought about it, I asked myself: Why am I doing this? Who am I doing this for?

The truth is, my ex-colleagues weren't paying my bills. They weren't paying my mortgage. They weren't the ones who would support me in a crisis. So why was I giving them so much power over my choices? Once I reframed my thinking, I was able to rip off the plaster and start.

Along with a perspective change, I found finding like-minded people who were also stepping into visibility powerful. In community, you can find accountability partners, people to cross-promote with, and a support system to keep pushing each other forward.

Visibility is easier and more rewarding when you do it together. Because the point isn't to please old colleagues or anonymous onlookers, it's to build a life and career that serves YOU. When you stop handing your power to the people who aren't paying your bills, and instead surround yourself with those who cheer you on, visibility shifts from something to fear into something that fuels you. That's the real lesson: visibility isn't about them, it's about you and us, doing it together.

The Ripple Effect of Visibility

Since showing myself and my work to the world, I've had opportunities I never could have predicted. I've built relationships, grown my business and opened doors that would have stayed closed had I remained invisible. But the most rewarding outcome has been seeing other women take the leap alongside me.

If you're still hiding, now is the time to challenge yourself. You have this book, there's a motivation behind you, there's just a fear in the way. Take your first step today. Whether it's a post, a conversation, sharing a draft with a bunch of beta readers or an event—put yourself out there.

I'm going to lead by example. Here's a vulnerable part of my visibility journey, which has been very different from Dr Dupe's. At the time of writing, I have been showing up online consistently for 17 years. But when I was putting this chapter together, I had a wow moment, because for 10 of those years my profile picture was of my fingernail (painted red of course).

I was afraid to show my face, sick to my stomach thinking about what my ex-boyfriend would say and what the girls I went to school with would be thinking. We all have those people who are holding us back in our minds. It took me 10 years of blogging under the pseudonym of Redjotter and only showing the tips of my fingers before I could show up as me. Ten years until a single question made me realise how much I was hiding, how much fear I was holding onto. It happened at a networking event in London. An industry leader from my field named Joe asked me, '*Do you follow Redjotter? Do you know her work?*' I didn't know what to say,

I stumbled on my words and dismissed Redjotter as someone I'd never heard about. I'd distanced myself from who I was so much that it had created a whole different being who I now professed I didn't even know. This was a pivotal moment in my own relationship with sharing my work.

From here and for the last seven years I have been using my name and using my face, which feels like such a small thing to say. But the ripple effect has been exponential. I have led an 8,000-person protest in London for Pregnant Then Screwed, I have had incredible leaders like Nicola Sturgeon, the ex-First Minister of Scotland, come and speak at our conference, UPFRONT and Centre, where I interviewed her. My newsletter subscribers, Instagram followers and LinkedIn followers are growing every day. But the best part is I show up as me, Lauren Currie. It's all me and I'm OK with that, better, I'm proud of the journey. I still have red nails but I no longer hide behind them.

Up until a few years ago, I never had a strategy other than loving the colour red. That was it. I wrote a story called 'Red Wellies' when I was nine and started sharing a blog called Redjotter when I was at university in my early twenties. For the first few months, my mum was the only person who read it.

My visibility now is an act of generosity with my younger self in mind. I am showing up to be the person that I wish I could have followed and learned from 10 years ago. The person who would encourage me to use my own name. I'm showing up to say the thing that I wish somebody would say, showing up to start the conversation that I wish I was involved in when I was hiding, having the conversation I want you to have with yourself and others. Are you hiding? How are you hiding? And what from? Only then can you truly start to share yourself and your work.

Before we dive into how to make yourself visible, we need to name and dismantle the unspoken beliefs that keep so many of you from doing it. These myths aren't just harmless stories, they're invisible fences that have been built around women for generations. Let's burn them to the ground.

Myth 1: 'Hard Work Will Speak for Itself'

This is one of the biggest lies women have been told.

Hard work does not speak for itself, unfortunately, and yes, it's infuriating, so yes, you should be angry, but it is the world we live in. It is reality. You cannot only do the work. You need to do the work of getting people to notice your work. That is different depending on what type of organisation you work in, what type of business you have or what type of mission you're on.

But regardless of what you do, you need to do the work of getting people to notice your work. We make the mistake of thinking that people will mention our name in rooms when we're not there. The only person you can trust to cheerlead you with the conviction and energy that you deserve is you. You are too precious and too important to leave this to chance. You need to take charge. Take the reins. Be in control. Make sure that people know who you are. They know what you do. They know how to promote you. They know how to pay you. They know how to hire you. So that when you're not in that room, your work is in the room for you.

Myth 2: 'Cringing Is Bad'

Yeah, maybe it feels like showing off. Probably makes you feel sick. We've all been there. We've all had the cringe. Cringing doesn't go away. Cringing is a sign of growth. You cannot progress and grow without cringe. So today, learn to love it. Nobody will die. Cringing is not fatal. Awkwardness is not fatal. Get over yourself. It's not that big a deal. The more you do it, the less cringe it will be, until it feels normal. Then you'll do something else that will feel cringy. There's no shortcut. It's necessary. Cringe forward, just like we learned in Chapter 10. Because what's the alternative?

Staying exactly where you are? Letting the status quo remain? What a tragedy.

Myth 3: 'You Can Do This Alone'

One of the biggest myths you need to let go of is the idea that you can do all of this on your own. Visibility needs community. You need a support network. If you can find others who are striving for the same goals, people willing to support you along the way, everything becomes easier. Less difficult. More achievable.

Community provides accountability. It amplifies your reach. It helps you cross-promote. Even if it's just one other person who also wants to be more visible, having that shared space to check in, support each other's posts and encourage one another makes a massive difference. When I was starting to build my presence on LinkedIn, I found my own small group of people doing the same. It changed everything.

Myth 4: 'I Don't Want to Add to the Noise'

I hear you. You're thinking 'There's so much noise out there, and I don't want to add to it'. Let's do a little thought experiment together. I want you to think of your favourite song, the one that fills your heart with joy, the one that always makes you want to dance in the kitchen. Imagine if the artist who wrote it had thought, 'There are already 158,464,880 songs. What's the point of writing another?' Or your favourite book, the one that changed your life. Imagine if the author had decided, 'There are already eight million books in the world. What's the point of adding another?'

It doesn't matter how many songs, books or ideas already exist. None of them are yours. That's where the opportunity lies.

NOBODY WANTS TO LEARN FROM PERFECT PEOPLE. PERFECT PEOPLE ARE BORING.

Myth 5: 'I'm Not Senior Enough. I Don't Know Enough. I Need More Qualifications'

Nobody wants to learn from perfect people. Perfect people are boring and more importantly they're not real, they're marketing and PR. We want to learn from people who are in the messy, scrappy beginnings, figuring things out, making mistakes, sharing what they're learning.

Think about the people you love to follow and learn from. Chances are, they're showing up exactly as they are, not waiting until they're ready. Some of the most influential people in the world right now are teenagers—Greta Thunberg, who started a solo climate strike at 15; Gitanjali Rao, named *Time*'s first 'Kid of the Year' at 15 for her inventions tackling water contamination and cyberbullying; and Malala Yousafzai, who began advocating for girls' education at 11. In pop culture, Billie Eilish was winning Grammys at 18 while rewriting the rules of what a global pop star can look and sound like. In sport, Coco Gauff won her first Grand Slam tennis title at 19, after years of playing and winning on the world stage as a teen. They didn't wait for seniority, a title or permission. They started. You don't need to wait either. You are ready now.

These myths aren't new, they've been shaping women's lives for centuries. And yet, history is full of women who defied them. Women who refused to wait for permission, who promoted themselves when no one else would, who made themselves visible in a world determined to overlook them. Their stories remind us that visibility is rarely easy but it's always powerful.

Beatrix Potter struggled to find a publisher. She self-published and delivered her books by hand. By the time of her death in 1943, Potter's books had sold more than forty million copies worldwide, making her one of the most successful self-published authors in history.

YOU DON'T NEED TO WAIT EITHER. YOU ARE READY NOW.

Sylvia Plath battled constant rejection and still personally followed up with every editor. By the time of her death in 1963, *Ariel* and *The Bell Jar* had forever altered the literary world, establishing Plath as one of the most influential writers of the twentieth century.

Frida Kahlo was a self-promoter long before social media. She wore traditional Mexican dresses to establish her personal brand and hosted exhibitions in her home. She is now considered one of the most influential artists of the twentieth century, with her paintings commanding high auction prices and her legacy continuing to inspire generations.

Zora Neale Hurston fiercely advocated for her work, self-publishing and challenging a predominantly white, male literary world despite immense barriers. She is now regarded as one of the most influential writers of the twentieth century. Her works are celebrated for their profound impact on African American literature and culture, continuing to inspire generations.

Madam C.J. Walker was the first female self-made millionaire in the United States, building her fortune in the early 1900s with haircare products for Black women. She made herself visible by putting her own image on every product, travelling the country to give demonstrations and training thousands of Black women as 'Walker Agents' to sell her products and build their own businesses. She turned self-promotion into a tool for both personal success and collective progress.

Visibility is economic power. Just like these women, you have the ability to shape your legacy. Your story deserves to be seen.

I'd like to introduce you to Beth. Her story deserves to be seen. She found the Bond in its early days, after attending one of my in-person workshops in 2018, where I handed out handmade badges from my very own badge machine.

When I found UPFRONT, my son was at nursery age and I was still suffering from post-natal depression. Like many others, I experienced a real setback in confidence when I went on maternity leave and then tried to go back to work.

I was gritting my teeth and white-knuckling through, hoping it would get better. Then I saw Lauren speak. That's when I started to question the assumptions I'd made, that I should be a completely present mother and an amazing employee at the same time. I started wondering: who gets to decide what 'perfect' looks like?

Beth describes this as a *'slow lightning bolt of an idea'* that planted a seed. At the UPFRONT workshop, she met women who were also starting to question the roles they'd been handed. *'We practised speaking and being listened to. It was the first time I'd paid attention to what we expect public speakers to sound and look like and why. It was also my first experience in a women-only space. I was working in the male-dominated energy sector, so it was eye-opening'.*

She joined our first-ever Bond during the COVID-19 lockdown in 2020, juggling work and homeschooling. *'The Bond gave me ideas and a community'*, she says. *'I started saying yes more, first to panels, then to keynotes. Each time, the world didn't end. I realised I could impact hundreds of decision makers in one room, instead of one person at a time'.*

That confidence paid off. When the UK's energy crisis hit, Beth became the press spokesperson for a campaign against unfair disconnections. *'I went on Radio 4's Today programme, BBC Breakfast, Sky News, live. It was terrifying, but we won'.*

Thanks to Beth and her team, the rules changed in the UK so that people who can't afford their energy bills, and especially those who are disabled or have young children, cannot be disconnected. *'We wanted to make sure people could stay safe'*, Beth explains. *'For me, one of the biggest impacts of UPFRONT is being able to say that I brought all my years of expertise to lead that change and partner with the media to make it happen'.*

Later, she brought her voice to her workplace, too.

I was diagnosed as neurodivergent at 30, but I didn't disclose it for a year. Through The Bond, I found the courage to share, and it led to training, adjustments, and a domino effect of others doing the same. Visibility helped me, and it helped others. I keep a DM from one woman who I supported: 'Your kindness may have saved my life'. That message stays on my phone as a reminder. Being UPFRONT. Trusting my voice and supporting others to do the same really can change the world.

Beth's journey shows what happens when we stop hiding. Her voice, her visibility and her leadership changed lives. Including her own.

Visibility isn't a marketing tactic. It's a way of being in the world. It's a decision to stop hiding, not just for yourself, but for the people who need to see what's possible. Just like Beth. Just like Dupe. Just like me. Whether you're speaking at a protest or sharing a sentence in a meeting, your presence matters. Visibility isn't the reward, it's the work. And the world shifts when you show up.

That's why I love what Arlan Hamilton says. She's the founder of Backstage Capital and author of *It's About Damn Time*, and she reminds us to: *'Be yourself so that the people looking for you can find you'*.

Because they are looking. They've been waiting. And now, they'll see you.

UPFRONT Moment

You've read this far because something in you knows it's time. So let's do the work, not just in your head, but on the page. Because journalling about your visibility *is* visibility. And it counts. Let's go.

Where are you still tucking yourself behind the scenes? Be honest.

- Is it in meetings?
- On social media?
- In your workplace?
- In your art?
- With your voice?

Write down the places, roles and relationships where you are hiding. Now answer:

- 'What am I afraid will happen if I'm seen there?'
- 'What opportunities might arise if I let myself be seen anyway?'

Think about the people who come to mind when you imagine being more visible. Who are you still performing for, protecting or trying to please?

Fill in the blanks below:

- 'I worry what _____ would think if I. . .'
- 'But _____ isn't paying my bills, living my life or holding my values'.
- 'So I choose to. . .'

Visibility isn't all or nothing. It's a scale. A muscle. A rhythm. Choose one small act of visibility you will try this week, something that makes you feel exposed, but not unsafe.

Options I like:

- Updating your LinkedIn profile
- Speaking up in one meeting
- Hosting a mini-event
- Sending a message you've been sitting on
- Sharing a part of your story
- Telling friends and colleagues about one thing you've learned from this book
  - Write me a note to tell me about one thing you've put into practice from this book (I read every message I get and your messages make me so happy! lauren@ wereupfront.com)

Who are you showing up for, besides yourself? What would it mean for someone younger, newer or braver-than-they-know to see you being visible? What would it mean for the other women and girls in your life?

Try:

- 'If I show up, maybe they'll. . .'
- 'If I stay hidden, they'll never know. . .'
- 'I want to be the kind of visible person who. . .'

Write this down. Then take a step. And let the world see you exactly as you are.

15

You Are Ready Now

Old Rule: I need to be an expert before I start

New Rule: I start now and learn as I go

UPFRONT was my side project for six years before I trusted myself to go all in. I spent 52,560 hours believing I wasn't ready; 52,560 hours convincing myself that I needed to know more, be more confident and do more before I could dare to take my dream seriously.

Here's an inexhaustible list of things I was waiting for:

- To have a higher-level qualification in the study of confidence.
- To have read every one of the 10,000 books written on confidence.
- To understand the ins and outs of the tech stack required to build an online education system.
- To take a coding course so I could fix any tech issue myself.
- To know exactly how to scale, price and market the programme.

- To feel 100% sure that nobody would criticise me.
- To research every possible competitor and analyse their strategies.
- To fully understand GDPR (General Data Protection Regulation) and every legal requirement for an online business.
- To identify and train key people who could deliver the work instead of me.

I owe everything to the version of me who finally got sick of herself and did the thing anyway. The version of me who stopped waiting for a green light and just walked forward. The version of me who decided that she would rather fail in motion than never try.

Now, UPFRONT is a global movement that upskills thousands of women, and I've written this book that you are holding in your hand this very second. I owe everything to that version of me, yet this story still breaks my heart. It breaks my heart because I know the chances are high you've got a story just like mine.

My heart breaks for the song I'll never get to dance to because the musician was brought up believing her ideas were never good enough. My heart breaks for the book I'll never read, the book that would change my life and make me cry, because the woman who carries the story in her bones is convinced that nobody cares about what she has to say. My heart breaks for the art I will never hang on my walls. The photographs that will never be taken. The restaurant I'll never dine in. The scent I'll never wear. The heels I'll never strut in. The soap I'll never bathe in. The knowledge I'll never have access to. The women with the power to bring these gifts to the world are living in a waiting room. They are waiting for their doorbell to ring, for someone (probably a man in a suit, right?) to say, '*It's time. You are good enough now*'. Deep down, I think most of us believe that if we are *really* meant to do something, someone with authority will let us know. So we wait forever and our art dies. This makes me weep.

Imagine how our world would change if every woman woke up tomorrow morning feeling ready, *knowing* she was good enough to share her ideas with the world. Economists have crunched the numbers: if women started and grew businesses, invented products and led projects at the same rate as men, it would add trillions to the global economy. Billions in new ideas, products, services and solutions that don't exist right now, simply because women are still waiting to be told they're ready. The joy it would deliver is priceless.

I don't want to learn from perfect people. I am bone-tired of hearing sugar-coated, over-edited, corporate-polished nonsense. I want to learn from the woman who started before she was ready. I want to learn from the woman who messed up, who doubted herself, who took action anyway. I want to learn from the woman who shares her knowledge while she's still in the messy middle, not from the one who only speaks once the ending is tied up in a bow.

Start now. Start before you're ready. The world needs you to begin. I need you to hear me and stop making excuses. The waiting room is full of excuses. Doesn't smell great in there either, little stuffy. I know, because I've sat in almost every seat. And the door doesn't open until you decide to walk out. Let's take each seat in turn.

Objection 1: 'I'm Not Qualified Enough'

I used to think that too. I believed I had to have some shiny certificate or perfect curriculum before anyone would take me seriously. But nobody feels fully qualified at the start. The most successful women I know didn't wait until they had certificates and titles, they started imperfectly and figured it out as they went. They learned more in the doing than in the waiting. Just look at Sanna Marin, who became the world's youngest prime minister of Finland at just 34. She didn't wait until she had decades of leadership titles behind her. She stepped forward, led through global crises and proved that the experience you need often comes from the act of doing.

Objection 2: 'I Need More Time to Prepare'

Time sounds safe but it's often just a way to stay stuck. I spent six years thinking I wasn't ready. But none of that waiting made me any more ready than I was the day I started. It just gave more space for self-doubt. The truth is you don't need more time. You need more action.

Look at Doechii, the Florida-born rapper. She started sharing her voice online after she was fired from her job, self-funded, rough around the edges, far from waiting-room ready, and within a few years, she was winning a Grammy for Best Rap Album. No waiting for perfect timing. She leaned into her art, her identity, her story and made it real. Her qualification didn't come from holding back, it came from stepping forward.

Objection 3: 'I Don't know Enough Yet'

The best teachers are often the ones who are learning right alongside you. It's not about knowing everything before you start; it's about learning through the process. I didn't know half of what I know now when I started UPFRONT. But you know what? Every step I took taught me something new. The knowledge you think you're missing shows up as you go. You can't access it until you start.

Think about Allyson Felix, the most decorated track and field Olympian in US history. She wasn't a business expert when she left her Nike sponsorship over their treatment of pregnant athletes—she was an athlete. But she launched her own shoe company, Saysh, anyway. She learned manufacturing, marketing and retail on the fly. Today, Saysh is thriving, and Allyson has shifted an entire industry's conversation about motherhood and sport. She didn't wait to 'know enough'. She started, and the knowledge came.

Objection 4: 'I Might Fail'

This is a big one. Pay attention. I refuse to think of myself as a failure. I don't do that. I've never failed, I've just learned. Every setback or mistake is simply a lesson in disguise and it's something that's helped me evolve. I've had moments where I've felt uncertain, vulnerable or faced criticism, but I've always tried to turn those moments into opportunities to grow and understand myself better.

Look at Viola Davis, one of the most acclaimed actors of our time. Early in her career, she faced years of rejection, typecasting and being told there weren't roles for dark-skinned Black women in Hollywood. She's spoken openly about auditions that went nowhere and performances she felt didn't land. But she treated each 'failure' as data, something to refine her craft and deepen her resilience. Today she's one of the few performers to achieve the EGOT (Emmy, Grammy, Oscar and Tony Awards)—proof that what some might label as failure can be the exact soil where mastery grows.

Objection 5: 'What If People Criticise Me?'

They will. If people are criticising you, congratulations! It means you are being UPFRONT. I worried about this for years, afraid of what people would think. If you're doing something meaningful, the criticism won't matter. It's just noise. Look at Greta Thunberg. Since she first sat outside the Swedish Parliament aged 15 with her School Strike for Climate sign, she's been mocked, dismissed and attacked by world leaders, media outlets and strangers online. She's been called 'too young', 'too angry' and 'too naive', and she keeps showing up anyway. Greta has spoken at the United Nations, inspired millions of young people to take climate action and shifted the global conversation about the climate crisis. The criticism didn't stop her; it was proof she was being heard.

Objection 6: 'I Don't Have Everything Figured Out Yet'

I still don't have everything figured out. If I'd waited until I had it all together, UPFRONT would never exist. If I'd waited until I felt ready to write a book, this book would never exist. Perfection is a trap and it's making your life worse. Start before you're ready. Get messy, then get sharp.

Look at Amanda Gorman. When she was asked to perform at President Joe Biden's inauguration in 2021, she didn't have months to prepare the perfect poem, nor did she have every line mapped out when she accepted. She's spoken about feeling the weight of the moment and the doubt that crept in about whether she was 'ready enough'. But she said yes anyway and delivered *The Hill We Climb*, a performance that electrified millions and made her the youngest inaugural poet in US history. She didn't wait until she had it all figured out. She started, and the sharpness came in the doing.

Objection 7: 'I Need More Confidence First'

Sneaky! That's why we are here having this conversation isn't it? I spent years thinking I'd only take the leap when I was more confident. That day never came. Confidence is built in the doing, not in the waiting. The more you act, the more confidence you build. Start now, and the confidence will follow.

Tina Fey puts it perfectly in her book *Bossypants*: '*You can't be that kid standing at the top of the water slide, overthinking it. You have to go down the chute*'. She didn't become one of the most influential comedians in the world by waiting to feel confident—she took the stage, wrote the sketches, made the calls and figured it out as she went. Confidence wasn't her ticket to start; starting was her ticket to confidence.

Objection 8: 'I Don't Have Enough Money'

Don't let money be an excuse. There are free tools, resources and communities out there waiting for you. The only thing standing in your way is the belief that you need more than what you have right now.

Consider Malala Yousafzai. Long before she was a Nobel Peace Prize laureate, she began as a teenager writing an anonymous blog about life under Taliban rule for the BBC. She had no funding and no formal resources, just her voice, a borrowed pseudonym and a belief that her story mattered. That small, unpaid act of visibility sparked global attention, led to activism on an international scale and eventually to the founding of the Malala Fund, which has invested millions in girls' education. She didn't start with money, she started with what she had.

Objection 9: 'I'm Too Old/Too Young'

I've heard this one in every waiting room. Women are never the right age. It's exhausting. The only thing that matters is your drive. The world is waiting for you regardless of what age you are.

At 64, Diana Nyad became the first person to swim from Cuba to Florida without a shark cage, a 110-mile journey she'd attempted (and 'failed') four times before. People told her she was too old, that it was impossible, that her moment had passed. She didn't listen. She prepared, she tried again and she made history.

Objection 10: 'Someone Else Is Already Doing It'

Good. I'm thrilled for you. That means there's a market and you know it's possible. But nobody else will do it like you. They can't. Your perspective, your voice, your style, that is what sets you apart.

Like I said, there are hundreds of books for women about confidence. I've read some of them, learned from them and loved many of them. And still, I wrote this one. Not because the world 'needed another' confidence book in a generic sense, but because no one else could tell *my* stories, share *my* tools or connect with *my* community in the way I can. The world needs *my* book about confidence. I believe that with all my heart. That's true for you, too. Even if there are 100 people, 1,000 people or 10,000 people in your field already, none of them are you. The fact that someone else is already doing it isn't a stop sign. It's a green light.

Let's hear from an expert, meet Kat Vellos.

Kat Vellos didn't wait until she felt like an expert. She didn't wait for a book deal or an institution to validate her ideas. She started where she was, with the skills she had, in the community she was part of, and took consistent, visible action. Today, she's a speaker, experience designer, connection coach and the author of *We Should Get Together: The Secret to Cultivating Better Friendships*.

When Kat came on the *UPFRONT Moment* podcast, she revealed that one of the most common questions she gets asked is, '*How did you know you could write a book?*' And I loved her response.[1] You don't need permission to begin.

Kat's first job out of college was working as a designer on an independently owned newsweekly in Florida:

> *I was designing the cover and doing the editorial layouts, and every seven days we published a book between 80 and 120 pages long.*
>
> *It was a really significant experience to realise that if you get your act together you can put out a book very quickly. We did this every single week and I worked there for four years. For about two hundred weeks straight, I was in the process of releasing a piece of editorial content. That experience showed me you don't have to ask for permission to share your writing with the world.*

She also set up a literary community in her town, where people could come together and share their creative writing and poetry. Kat shared content regularly, not just through her work, but also through this community that she built. She practised. She developed her confidence muscle.

> *It never occurred to me later on when I was writing my book, We Should Get Together, that I had to ask for someone's permission to share it with the world. I had already been sharing my writing and my design in multiple ways for years. That gave me the confidence to know that I could do it.*

Imagine all the things you could do and all that you could achieve if you started *right now*.

Stepping Up

These aren't just my lessons. They belong to hundreds of women in our Bond community who stopped waiting and started acting. Women who moved before they felt ready, scared, imperfect, uncertain and did the thing anyway. Like Susan. Like Laura.

Susan said:

> *Speaking in public has always made me very anxious and has been something I have tried to avoid. The Bond changed my mindset about my confidence and gave me practical steps to take to feel calmer about the idea of speaking in public. After the Bond I volunteered to co-present a slot at an industry conference, which ended up being standing room only! The tips I gained from the Bond let me actually enjoy the experience, presuming that the audience wanted me to succeed rather than fail. I actually put forward a proposal for the same conference the following year to speak by myself and was put on the main stage this time. Old me would have been freaked out by this with weeks of anxiety beforehand, but I returned to my Bond notes to refresh my mindset and it went really well! Already planning my proposal for next year's conference. . .*

Laura shared that the Bond helped her move forward with her podcast:

> *In January I decided to do something that I've been putting off for about a year: I started a podcast. I checked the stats earlier and so far there have been 67 downloads. I've also had people reach out and say how much it has helped them. I am taking*

these little wins as a massive confidence boost and
motivation to keep going.

These women didn't wait to feel ready. They didn't wait
for perfect conditions or perfect confidence. They started and
now they're in motion. Motion builds momentum. Momentum builds confidence. And some women don't just make
moves, they disrupt. They take that motion and use it to
break every rule, burn every waiting room and build a whole
new blueprint. Cindy Gallop is one of those women.

Cindy Gallop is the founder and CEO of Make Love Not
Porn, a revolutionary platform built to change the world's
relationship with sex. In a world that constantly tells women
to stay quiet, to wait until they're 'ready' or to polish themselves into perfection before stepping forward, Cindy chose a
different path. She chose visibility. She chose action. From the
start, Cindy's mission was clear: do good and make money
simultaneously. Not as an afterthought. Not apologetically.
She stands for building businesses that centre justice, confidence and radical honesty and she demands that they be
wildly profitable too.

But building a business in sex tech wasn't easy. Since
launching at TED in 2009, Cindy has faced brutal barriers.
Every business infrastructure you take for granted—banking,
advertising, hosting—slammed the door in her face. Payment processors wouldn't touch her. Investors ran. She spent
14 years fighting daily systemic battles, keeping Make Love
Not Porn alive on just $3 million of angel investment. Most
founders would have given up. Cindy didn't. Instead, she
changed the world around her. *'If you have a truly world-changing idea'*, she says, *'you have to change the world to fit
it, not the other way around'*.

She also redefined how to raise capital. Traditional
investors weren't an option so Cindy worked in the open. She
posted relentlessly on LinkedIn (her now-favourite platform),

talked openly about her mission, her funding needs, her vision. Her goal is to be her own filter; attracting the right people and repelling the wrong people.

Visibility wasn't just about marketing, it was about attracting her people. Investors who *already got it*, so she wouldn't waste time convincing those who never would.

It worked. Incoming interest began landing in her inbox. Investors sought her out. Not because she softened her message but because she amplified it.

Cindy's strategy is a masterclass in leadership. Show up. Be UPFRONT. Share what you believe, how you work and what you value. Stand for something. Let people opt in or opt out. Be unapologetic about making money. As Cindy says, when women make a shit-ton of money, we fund and uplift other women too. Get very, very angry. Anger is not something to be feared or suppressed. It's rocket fuel for action and change. This is the single biggest unlock to personal and professional freedom.

Her advice is crystal clear:

Life becomes infinitely simpler when you know exactly what you stand for. Then you can live and work in a way that's true to you. That's the secret to happiness, and to not giving a damn what others think.

She also urges women to start their own industries. Because when you work for yourself, you control your schedule. You design your culture. You build the kind of world you want to see. You stop asking for permission and you start building new rules. Cindy is passionate about how AI and digital tools are opening up entrepreneurship to more women, even those with no money and no safety net. As she points out, '*You only need two things: your brain and your network*'. You don't need a business plan, a fancy website, a logo or investors to start. You need a voice. A point of view. A willingness to act despite fear.[2]

If you're waiting to feel like an expert, Cindy says, you'll wait forever. If you're worried about who might not like you, you'll stay stuck.

And remember: every single woman you admire still feels fear. Still doubts herself. The only difference is she acts anyway.

Fear doesn't mean stop. Fear means go.

Cindy didn't wait for credentials. She didn't wait for permission. She didn't wait to feel ready. She did the scary thing and she made change happen. And so can you. This chapter is not asking you to fake confidence (as if I'd *ever* suggest that, have we met?). It's asking you to start. To stop rehearsing readiness and begin. To trust that you are ready enough. Because you are. You are ready now. It's time to get out of the waiting room.

The Invitation You're Waiting for Isn't Coming

The waiting room is full of world-class art, hit songs, brilliant business ideas and dreams that will never see the light of day. But here you are, waiting. Waiting to be asked, waiting for permission, waiting to be seen. You believe that if you work hard enough, someone will notice. But let's be honest, they simply won't. Because life isn't a waiting room, nobody will call your name and ask you for what you need. No, life's waiting room is where your ideas go to die.

You've been taught to wait your turn, to avoid bragging, to stay quiet and deep down, you're afraid. Afraid of criticism, afraid of being too much, afraid of not knowing enough.

So you wait, you wait for permission and you wait for someone else to decide you are now good enough to be invited. The waiting is eternal. Meanwhile, others—who know less than you but invite themselves—are taking the lead.

This isn't just about you missing out on a chance to progress. Waiting to be asked, waiting for permission, waiting to be seen and invited adds up to a lifetime of regret. This next sentence is a concluding statement from bestselling author Bronnie Ware's, *The Top Five Regrets of the Dying*: '*I wish I'd had the courage to live a life true to myself, not the life others expected of me*'.[3] I think it speaks for itself.

Inviting Yourself Is the Only Way Forward

Beyond sharing my work online every day, even when it's not perfect as we've discussed in Chapter 13, I pitch myself for speaking gigs when I think I have zero chance of a reply. I invite myself by creating my own stage with events, webinars and opportunities. I decide what I want to do and then I invite others.

I learned this skill and now it's your turn to learn. It's time for you to stop waiting and start inviting yourself, to get out of the waiting room; it's time to relearn your relationship with where you show up and where you actually want to show up.

Inviting Yourself

Let me tell you a story about Emma, Charity Bond graduate, who had always waited for formal recognition to step into leadership at her company. She worked as a mid-level manager and believed leadership was reserved for senior executives. But during the UPFRONT Bond, she realised leadership comes from taking action, regardless of your title. When her team was struggling with unclear direction during a major project, Emma took the initiative. She organised a meeting, clarified the objectives and created a plan to ensure everyone knew their role. Her approach boosted team morale and delivered the project on time, earning her respect and visibility within the company.

Emma didn't wait for a promotion to lead. She chose her work herself and made a lasting impact on her team and organisation. I'm very sure the promotion will come next but Emma invited herself by leading.

But inviting yourself isn't just about stepping into leadership positions. Often it's about accessing new opportunities. Nita, from the Bond, had been considering voiceover work for a few months, asked the marketing department at the company she worked at whether they produce videos that required voiceovers. They did and they had a project she could get involved in. Sometimes it's as simple as that.

Imagine if she had waited for someone to ask her though. Imagine if she hadn't invited herself. *'I'm glad I found the courage to ask, otherwise I would never have known the opportunity was there'*, were Nita's words. How many opportunities have you, me and all the other women in this world lost out on because we were waiting to be asked?

Reflect, then act.

Start by reflecting on the things you want but haven't yet made space for. Maybe it's a hobby you've always been curious about, a project you'd love to start or a conversation you've been putting off. Think of the people you admire, perhaps someone in your workplace, community or online, who you've thought about reaching out to but never have. What story do you tell yourself that holds you back? And then flip it: what's the best thing that could happen if you took that step?

UPFRONT Moment

The waiting room is full. And I've just called you to the front. Yes, you! This is the part where you stop underlining sentences and start getting damn serious. Because reading this chapter without writing yourself into it is another way to hide. And we're done with hiding. You are not missing knowledge or credentials. You are missing motion.

Writing these reflections will not magically make you confident, but they will build your confidence muscle. And from there everything changes.

Pick up the pen and get honest.

Write a list of all the things you've been putting off because you 'aren't ready yet'. Keep writing until you can't think of anymore, when you think you're done, keep going, you're not done.

Now write what you're *really* waiting for.

- 'I'll do it when. . .'
- 'I need to feel. . .'
- 'I'm scared that. . .'

Next, circle one thing on the list and write the *smallest* possible next step. Then, schedule it. Today. This week. Not later.

List three places, conversations or opportunities where you are currently waiting to be invited. Now flip it:

- 'What does inviting yourself look like in this context?'
- 'What would you do if you weren't waiting for permission?'
- 'How will you remind yourself that you belong here, now?'

Think of a woman you admire who *started before she was ready*. Write about what her choice made possible, for her, for others, for you. Now ask:

- 'What could *my* starting make possible for someone else?'
- 'Who needs me to go first?'

This is the part where you commit. Name one thing you will do in the next 48 hours to move out of the waiting room. It can be teeny tiny but it must be real and you must do it.

- 'I will. . .'
- 'I expect to feel. . .'
- 'But I'll do it anyway, because. . .'

Then, seal it with this:

- 'I am not waiting anymore. I am moving. I am ready now'.

You are now in motion and that's the only place confidence lives. No more waiting. No more permission slips. No more what-ifs. You are ready. Right now. And before you get to work, let me leave you with a wee something from my roots: 'Gie it laldy'.

It's a Scots phrase that means: Give it your all. Go full tilt. No half-measures. Say it out loud if you need to. Stick it on a Post-it. Whisper it to yourself before that big meeting, pitch or leap.

Because this is your moment. And laldy is the only way forward.

Notes

1. We should get together, *UPFRONT Moment with Lauren Currie* [Podcast], 2023.
2. Women challenge the status quo because we never are it, *UPFRONT Moment with Lauren Currie* [Podcast], 2023.
3. Ware, B. (2012). *The Top Five Regrets of the Dying: A Life Transformed by the Dearly Departing.* Hay House, Inc.

16

You Are Demanding More

Old Rule: Be grateful

New Rule: Be grateful and demand more

I am grateful, and I demand more. Both of these things are true. I have a secret and I want to tell you, but I'm scared. I think you might judge me and I'm worried that you won't quite understand. I want to tell you because there's a chance you'll celebrate my win and what it represents. That you'll share it with another woman. That it will inspire you to raise your prices, to push beyond the limits you thought were set. To remember that you can do good in the world and make money at the same time.

I want to tell you because I want you to be grateful, and I want you to demand more. I want to tell you because women talking about money is a radical act. Women building successful, impactful, profitable companies is still rare. Only 13% of women-led businesses reach a turnover of £1 million to £50 million, compared to 29% of male-led businesses. But what about the what-ifs? What about the cost-of-living crisis? What about global layoffs? What if it upsets you? What if it makes you feel uncomfortable?

Yes, and what about women in leadership? What about women having power? What about women building wealth? What about women talking about money and profit so often that it becomes ordinary, instead of a conversation that makes everyone uneasy?

So here it is. In 23 months, my mission-led, profitable company went from zero to one million pounds in revenue. No funding. No investment. No loan. No grant. One million pounds.

There, I said it. Now, on to the next million. Because I am grateful, and I demand more. You've been taught to be grateful. We all have. From the moment you were born, the message came through loud and clear: be grateful for what you have. Be thankful for the small things. Don't ask for too much, don't be too bold. Stay humble.

Women are socialised to be grateful for the crumbs. To accept what is given, to make do and never demand more than what's in front of us. I can't count the number of times I've heard, 'be happy with what you've got' or 'you're so lucky, don't complain'.

There's this quiet but constant pressure that when you've hit a milestone, like a revenue target, you're supposed to stop and feel content. You've made it, so don't ask for more. Don't be greedy. There's only so much to go around. You should be happy with what you have and stop reaching for more.

I am grateful. Grateful for every woman who joined me, every team member who believed, every challenge that forced me to grow. Yet still, I demand more. More revenue. More impact. More women leading companies. More women building wealth. More women taking up space. Gratitude and ambition are not opposites; they fuel each other.

When I wrote about this financial milestone on the internet, there were horses in my tummy. I was terrified. Terrified of being seen as wanting more, of being too bold, too brash, too hungry. The backlash came, as I knew it would. All of the criticism came from other women. Women who decided I had become too successful and they didn't like it. They tried to force me into silence. They told me that talking about money like this was crass, unfeminist and selfish.

But that was their insecurities talking, that was their insecurities projected onto me, and I don't want them, no thank you. Money is a resource and my ambitions need fuel. Money is freedom and I will never apologise for wanting freedom for myself and the people I care about. I will never apologise for wanting the resources and freedom to support you and many women like you. Wanting more isn't greed. Wanting more is necessary, for me, for my team and for the causes I believe in. The more I have, the more I can fund other women.

I see it everywhere, this quiet message to women. Be grateful for what you have and don't ask for more. Whether it's the expectation that women in leadership should smile and stay humble or the idea that talking about money is rude, unfeminist or even selfish. Studies show most women avoid money conversations even with close friends, reinforcing the belief that asking for what you deserve is rude or selfish.[1]

This is what holds women back. This is one of many systemic barriers that keep us poor. This is why so many of us undercharge for our work, stay quiet about our successes and suppress the ambition that could take us, and the world, further. Ask yourself, who gains from you being grateful and not demanding more? Imagine, for a moment, if we could change the narrative. If we could love gratitude and ambition together. If we could build a world where women are encouraged to make money and still be good, to be profitable and still care deeply about the world around them. Imagine if you, right now, could give yourself permission to be grateful and demand more. Do it!

Success is not just about the number in my bank account. It's about a large number of women raising their prices after watching me do it. It's about the long list of charities who can now benefit from our work. It's about the companies that now prioritise confidence in the women in their leadership teams, their decisions and their culture. It's about my son watching me build a bigger life.

But it's also about individual messages I get from women who say:

- *'I doubled my rates'.*
- *'I applied for the job and now earn three times more'.*
- *'I didn't know it was possible for me until I saw you do it'.*

That's why I'll keep talking about money. I'll keep demanding more. Because when I do, another woman gives herself permission to do the same. She gets paid, she is seen and society values her and her daughter more. So here's to gratitude, and here's to demanding more. The world is waiting.

What If They Say Yes?

One of the reasons women tell me they don't ask for more is because they worry they'll be told 'No'. But what if they say yes? What if you get what you've asked for and more? There are many women in the Bond who have asked for more and seen incredible results.

Take Jess, who shared that she turned down a freelance job because it paid too little for the work required. *'This ter-rified me as I am not getting much work as a freelancer at the moment and this client is my most consistent and generally well-paying. The outcome: they responded by offering to pay me more for the job!'* What's even better is that Jess didn't stop there. A week later she posted this: *'Second week in a row when I have requested more money for a freelance job and had my request accepted. Getting the hang of this now'.*

Then there's Milly, who shared her ambitions with her manager:

> *I've fairly recently started a new role, and am really loving it. I can see how my skills and experience can add value to the company and am excited to have found such a good fit. Today I shared with my manager that I'm aiming for a promotion by the end of the year, by proving myself with an upcoming project that I've been tasked with. I've found it really hard to share my ambitions before, for fear of being 'shot down' or told I'm not ready. But it felt really good to be transparent!*

Demanding more doesn't only benefit you. It has a positive ripple effect that leads to change in more dramatic and far-reaching ways. Milly is motivated to deliver on her project because she has been clear about what she wants, her expectations are on the table so she can strive forward with a clear motivation to do good work. Dalma's story is a stellar example of how others benefit when you ask for more. She took a job in a public sector organisation assuming that it offered decent maternity pay as 'enhanced maternity pay' was listed on the job description. However, a chance comment from a colleague about choosing not to have children because of the poor maternity pay led her to dig deeper.

> *I got a copy of the maternity and family policies from the HR department and it was just as bad as my colleague had said. I started to do research on other comparative sector maternity pay, got a list of evidence together and took it to my manager at the time and my directors. They both told me it wasn't in their power to change it and advised I should join the union if I was frustrated.*

I joined the union, only to realise it was led by middle-aged men who were counting down their years before retirement. But something simmered underneath; a women's working group started to form both within the union and within the organisation.

Dalma explained that, at the same time, there was widespread frustration around a lack of pay rises, which led to strike action being called. However, the organisation refused to negotiate on maternity pay, saying they only negotiated on salaries. Dalma wasn't about to give up though. The Bond had taught her how to have uncomfortable conversations and how to advocate for herself.

I published the company's maternity policy and comparative research internally, comparing it to what other companies pay as I got frustrated that the men in the union downplayed the importance of better maternity pay. By then I had got a fair few women together who encouraged me both privately and publicly to share my comparative research more broadly and take an active part in the union. I decided to go to the top on the eve of the strikes. I emailed the evidence of how poor the maternity pay was compared to other organisations to our managing director, people director, group chief executive and our city's mayor. I told them that by sustaining the poor maternity policy, they were not attracting women to work in our sector, hurting local families and driving women into poverty while on maternity leave.

The strike action now had two key focuses; better pay and family policies. The strike action took place over two days. I even gave a short speech during the march outside the mayor's office with shaky kneecaps. Then we sent the facts to be published in the local media. More strikes were planned but were called off based on a promise of better pay and better family friendly policies four months later.

Dalma hadn't quite finished. She then joined the negotiating team, by which point her organisation had a strong offer aligned with best practice.

Through the negotiations, we achieved better paternity leave for fathers and partners, five weeks full pay for paternity leave. The new family-friendly policy for mothers included twenty-six weeks full pay, thirteen weeks fifty percent pay, and thirteen weeks twenty-five percent pay, which is higher than many other public sector organisations. Overall it's been a huge success and our combined local authority has even matched our policy, so even more women and families benefit from our work.

Dalma and her colleagues had in effect bettered their own lives and those around them simply by demanding more.

Dalma's story is one of huge change for her organisation and the women in her everyday life, and now beyond. And where did Dalma gain her strength to challenge the larger system around her? You guessed it, the idea of wanting more for herself and other women. Here's what she had to say about that:

Without taking part in the Bond, I probably would have taken the first 'no' from my manager and my director and wouldn't have spoken out, or would have left the job. But with UPFRONT, I learnt

*to speak up and create change from within. I
was driven by the care for other women and by
the encouragement of the younger women in my
organisation, many of whom were afraid to speak
up but were also upset they couldn't afford to have
children. They loved their jobs and felt torn about
having to change jobs if they wanted to afford kids.
I don't know if I will have children but now I know
the financials decided by someone else will not be
a key deciding factor in that decision any longer.*

To practise gratitude while also naming your desires is
not a contradiction, it is a reclamation. They are not opposing
forces; they are partners in you being UPFRONT.

The stories you've read in this chapter from Dalma's
transformative fight for maternity rights to Jess's quiet revolution in freelance negotiations are not outliers. They are
evidence. They show us what becomes possible when women
demand more, when they choose to make noise about the
things that matter: money, equity, visibility and care. These
stories remind us that asking for more isn't about greed or
ego. It's about creating conditions that support dignity, choice
and change not just for yourself but for the women around
you and the women who come after you.

This is the kind of confidence we are here to practise
together. Not the kind that dominates but the kind that liberates. The kind that knows every time a woman raises her
voice to ask for better pay, more recognition or stronger policies, she is not just serving herself—she is tilting the ground
beneath all of us, just a little more in our favour.

You don't need to justify your ambition. You don't need
to soften your needs to make others comfortable. You are
allowed to want more, and you are capable of holding that
desire with integrity, courage and clarity. So stand in your
gratitude. Let it steady you. Then speak the words that push

your future closer. You are not too much. You are not ungrateful. You are ready. And the world is better when you demand more from it.

UPFRONT Moment

There are no chapters to simply nod along to in this book, this certainly isn't one. Reading about gratitude and ambition is not the same as practising them side by side. And the practice starts with what you ask for next. Because we're socialised to be grateful and quiet, asking for more feels wrong but now you know it isn't. It's powerful. It's generous. It's necessary.

Pick up the pen. Let these words stretch your ambition. You can be grateful. You can be generous. And you can want more. All at once. All in. Right now.

Write three things you are deeply grateful for in your work or life right now.

Now write three things you want next.

- 'I am proud of_____'
- 'I am ready for_____'
- 'Even though I'm grateful, I also want_____'

Let these truths live beside each other.

Think of a time you held back from asking for more. More money, recognition, support, because you didn't want to seem ungrateful. Write about what it cost you. Maybe it was like the Bonder who stayed in the same role for five years without a raise, even though her male colleague, hired at the same time, asked every year and got one. By the time she finally spoke up, she'd missed out on over £25,000. Bonus points if you can put a financial figure on your own loss.

Now write the version of that story where you ask anyway.

- 'When I didn't ask, I. . .'
- 'If I had asked, I might have. . .'
- 'Next time, I will. . .'

What's one belief you inherited about money, success or ambition that keeps you playing small? Write it down. Then write the truth you're choosing instead. I used to quietly accept the speaking slots and panel seats I was offered, even when I knew I could deliver the keynote. The first time I asked to be the keynote speaker instead of just a panellist, they said yes and it became one of the most impactful talks of my career. Your turn.

- 'Old belief: If I ask for too much, they'll think I'm. . .'
- 'New truth: When I ask for more, I. . .'

Think of a woman who talked about money, leadership or power in a way that stirred something in you. Write about what her boldness made possible for you. I'll go first.

For me, the way Cindy Gallop talks about business with unapologetic clarity, refusing to dilute her opinions to be more 'palatable' taught me that my directness is not arrogance, it's power. Author of *We Need You, Art*, Aimee McNee talks about ambition like it's an act of love for your work, stripping away the shame and guilt that so often clings to women's goals. She taught me that wanting more is not greed, it's devotion to myself and my potential. Rachel Rodgers, author of *We Should All Be Millionaires*, talking about wealth as a tool for change, not just personal comfort, made me reframe my entire relationship with earning.

Your turn. Think of a woman who talked about money, leadership or power in a way that stirred something in you. What did she teach you? Bonus points if you tell her!

Now ask yourself:

- 'Who might feel more UPFRONT because I choose to demand more?'

This is the part where you start doing. Name one conversation, email or boundary where you will ask for more in the next 48 hours. It doesn't have to be perfect. It has to be honest.

- 'I will ask for. . .'
- 'I expect to feel. . .'
- 'But I'll do it anyway, because. . .'

Then, finish with this:

'I am grateful. I am powerful. And I am demanding more'. Mic drop.

Guan yersel.

Note

1. Money and Pensions Service (2025). Women and money: Talking about finances. Opinium Research. https://www.moneyandpensions service.org.uk.

17

You Are a Big Deal

Old Rule: Don't make a big deal out of it

New Rule: Make it a big deal

Celebrating yourself is hard. It's really hard. And it's not just about popping champagne after a win or getting a pat on the back. It's about truly internalising and honouring your success, something many of us struggle with. I want to live in a world where women make huge deals of themselves and their own success. Let me walk you through one of my first solo trips to Lisbon, which taught me a whole lot about how I view success and what I mean when I talk about celebrating yourself.

Forty-eight hours into my five-day trip, I text my coach from my hotel room '*This trip is f***ing with my head, can we chat?*' I was surrounded by luxury that felt foreign to me, confronted with a sense of discomfort that I wasn't expecting. The marble floors echoed. A waiter in crisp white offered me champagne I didn't want. The velvet chairs, the silence of the hallways, the weight of the price tag—I felt like an imposter walking through someone else's success. It wasn't just the price tag of the room or the fancy meals. It was the sudden weight of being in a space that I never thought I deserved. The grandness felt suffocating, almost like I wasn't allowed to enjoy it. The thoughts that crept in were sharp and harsh, reminding me that I didn't *need* any of this, and that everything I had achieved so far had been, in some twisted way, luck. My mind, usually caught up in work and pushing ahead, had no way to busy itself during this celebratory pause. Every corner I turned, I faced myself and my success head on, and for the first time, it felt like a burden rather than a gift. It was an emotional reckoning with my worth, my confidence and how hard I find it to celebrate myself.

I was staying in a hotel that cost per night what I used to pay for one month's rent. I was experiencing luxury that no other woman in my family had ever experienced. The purpose of this trip was simple: to celebrate hitting a revenue milestone and to take time to rest after the hard work getting there. I wanted to create space to accept my new reality and figure out how I felt about it. In just two years, growing my team and my business had changed my life dramatically. But in trying to celebrate myself I came face to face with how uncomfortable doing that is. I needed time to stabilise, consolidate and catch up with myself. But I realised that was going to take more than five days. The trip was a reminder that this process of acceptance and celebration takes time, and it won't always feel smooth or easy.

I've been taught to pop champagne (prosecco—who am I kidding?) and move on to the next thing, never pausing, always pushing forward. 'Keep going and keep pushing or it'll all disappear', I believed. So, I never stopped. I've spent most of my career operating in sixth gear, always striving for the next thing. When you live like that for so long, slowing down feels like a betrayal of the momentum you've worked so hard to build. But when you actually stop, when you hit the brakes, you see where you are. That can be hard too.

Going on this trip, leaving behind my little boy, my partner and my business broke a lot of social norms. When I stepped outside those norms, I started hearing doubt, I started hearing deprecating self-talk. They had always been there, but I'd been too busy to notice.

You don't deserve this, it wasn't even that hard.

You are a white, able-bodied woman, your privilege made it easier to get here.

You feel lonely, that's what you deserve.

You're a bad mum, who leaves their child for five days?

Your family is fine without you, they don't even need you.

You know this won't last, it'll all be taken from you.

We're collectively primed to slip into questioning our very worth when we celebrate ourselves. The root of this questioning is a society that judges women incredibly harshly and holds us to impossible standards. Therefore it's easy to see how this societal judgement becomes your own. The opposite of judgement is acceptance. This is what I want you to take away from this chapter. Practising acceptance of what is, accepting both the success and the discomfort that comes with it.

Learn to hold two things at once; learn to hold celebrating success and self-judgement separately. Yes, I am experiencing success. Yes, I have worked hard for it and I deserve it. At the same time, I am allowed to struggle with this success. I am allowed to feel lonely and still feel proud. I can celebrate this luxury and acknowledge my privilege without guilt or shame. This is mine and I've earned it. When we practise the idea that they are two separate thoughts, two separate perceptions, we can accept our successes when they come. We can work on our self-judgement without one ruining the other.

One of the thought processes that helped me get better at celebrating myself was imagining myself as a Russian doll. There's the outer, expanded shell; the bigger version of me who's growing and becoming better. This represents all of the parts of me that have high confidence. Then there's the little doll in the middle; the one who still feels small, scared and uncertain. That little doll is still part of me and I'm not going to shame her for struggling with this new experience. I'm not going to rush her to catch up with the rest of me. She's still here, and that's OK.

The Russian doll metaphor has become an anchor for me in my confidence journey. It wasn't just about seeing myself as a bigger, expanded version of who I was; it was about understanding that the little doll inside me—the one who still feels unsure, scared and small—also plays a role in my success. That little doll is still a part of me and it's OK that she hasn't fully caught up with the new version of me yet. I can't force that little doll to feel the same sense of accomplishment or pride that I do now, but I can hold space for her. She's not something to be pushed away or rushed. In fact, I'm learning to love and care for her very much. What I won't do is let my little doll pull down my bigger doll.

Celebrating yourself is not only necessary, it's fundamental to the practice of building confidence. Learning to celebrate myself has been a challenge but it's one I have faced. It's easier to celebrate others than it is to celebrate your own wins, especially when society tells you not to. I'm not interested in somebody else's idea of when and how I celebrate myself, and neither should you be.

The final act in fully celebrating myself was permission. As I sat in that beautiful hotel room in Lisbon, I realised that part of me still felt like I wasn't allowed to fully appreciate the journey I'd been on. It was almost as if I needed permission from someone, permission for me to say 'Yes, I worked hard, and yes, I deserve this' to myself for my own work. I hope by now you are shouting at the pages, 'It's you who needs to do that, you need to give yourself permission', because you'd be right, and I did. I started to reflect on the work I had put in, the sacrifices I had made, the challenges I had overcome and the ways in which I had grown. Instead of suppressing that, I chose to honour it. I made it a big deal. In doing so, I'm learning that the more you celebrate yourself, the more you give others permission to do the same. I can't say it to you—the permission to celebrate yourself is not mine to give, it's yours. Give yourself permission.

Celebrating yourself in a world that tells women not to is an act of revolutionary confidence. By celebrating our success, we not only acknowledge the hard work that got us here, but we also signal to other women that they too can be successful and proud of it. The more we do this, the more we shift the narrative from *don't make a big deal out of it* to *make it a big deal*, because celebrating yourself is one of the most powerful acts of self-love and confidence you can give yourself.

When I talk about making your success a big deal, I'm not suggesting you stand on a pedestal or shout about it from the rooftops. Although this is also highly encouraged and very valuable use of your time! It's not about arrogance or inflating your ego; it's about honouring the work, sacrifices and challenges that got you to this point. It's a rational, controlled, calm inner act of self-appreciation and love. It's a deliberate acknowledgement, celebrating what you've achieved and a recognition of your effort. It's a powerful act of self-love that shifts the narrative from being ashamed of your success to embracing it. When you make your success a big deal, you're not only validating your own worth, you're also validating the worth of other women; you're inviting them to give themselves permission, to shift their narrative.

I want you to picture the women in your life who are celebrating themselves, who are making themselves a big deal. Now, picture a world where every woman, including you, gets to be a big deal. That's the world we're building. That's the world we all deserve.

Bonders Learning to Celebrate Themselves

Here are three stories from Bonders who have changed their perception of celebrating themselves. Let's start with Louise from the Government Bond.

> *Before The Bond I was always very negative and critical of my own actions. Receiving praise didn't feel comfortable or right. It felt undeserved while receiving negative feedback felt deserved. The Bond helped me to change the way I think about myself. I consciously took steps to change my mindset. Internalised misogyny made me believe that nothing less than perfection was acceptable. I hated feedback and used even the slightest of improvement points as a way to punish myself for not being good enough. I now have the mantra: Be kind to yourself. At my latest appraisal meeting, my manager gave me feedback around something I could do differently to deal with a particular situation. Previously, this would have led to a spiral of negativity for not being good enough, for failing. This time, using my changed mindset, the feedback became opportunities to improve. There was no negativity spiral, no blaming myself for not being good enough, no hours of anxiety of being a failure. The things I had achieved were separated from the things I could improve upon. I am good enough. I am not a failure. I am me and I can make mistakes while still being amazing.*

We don't know the details of Louise's story, but we don't need the details to recognise where she is in her journey. Louise has changed a crucial aspect of the way she sees herself.

The places where she needs to improve are now accepted in a constructive way because she has given herself permission to accept the ways in which she is amazing. The two go hand in hand. If you are only looking at the ways in which you need to improve and not also separately looking at your wins and moments of celebration, confidence dives and progress becomes incredibly hard, plus you are doing yourself a disservice. Now, let's hear from Meenal who we met in Chapter 4.

> *Taking part in the Bond was truly a transformative experience. I gained a deeper understanding of what it means to be confident, not just in the obvious moments, but in everyday life, whether at home, at work, or in my social interactions. One of the most empowering lessons was learning that I didn't have to downplay my skills or knowledge, I can celebrate them. I discovered that it's not only OK to show up as an expert, but also necessary in order to fully step into my own power and contribute meaningfully in all areas of my life. The impact of the course rippled into every corner of my daily routine. Professionally, I found myself making clearer, more decisive choices without second-guessing. Personally, I grew more comfortable asserting boundaries and stepping away from relationships that no longer served me. I started to surround myself with people who genuinely support and uplift me. Perhaps the most profound effect has been within my role as a mother. I now have the tools to model confidence for my three young daughters, showing them by example what it means to speak up, stand tall, celebrate, and value themselves. I truly believe this experience will not only shape their lives, but echo through future generations. It's more than a course; the Bond is a gift that keeps on giving.*

Meenal raises the question of downplaying our achievements and expertise and the generational ripple effect this has. How many times have you downplayed your input, whether at work, home or socialising with friends to then later punish yourself for doing so? I want you to celebrate yourself and start seeing yourself as a big deal because this is how you change this behaviour. Start today.

Meenal's story reminds us that the impact of celebrating ourselves goes beyond the individual, it shapes what's possible for others, especially our children and the women around us. But not every celebration has to be bold or visible to matter. Sometimes, the most powerful acts of self-honouring are quiet and deeply personal. While Meenal stepped into her power by showing up as an expert, others began by reclaiming something much smaller, but just as significant, just like Julie shared:

> *After the Bond, I celebrated saying no to a work request that pushed my boundaries. It felt tiny but it was massive for me. I made tea, lit a candle, and let myself feel proud.*

Make It a Big Deal: UPFRONT Celebration Ideas

Let's reimagine what it looks like to celebrate ourselves, not just for typical milestones, but for existing, surviving and growing. So often we wait for someone else to throw the party, to validate our joy, to name our moment as worthy. But what if *you* are the one you've been waiting for?

Celebrate your new business launch like a wedding. Get dressed up, gather your friends, make toasts, dance in the kitchen. Hang fairy lights in your lounge. Let people bring cake. Let them tell you how proud they are.

Host your own birthday like you're the guest of honour, because you are. No more downplaying or shrugging when someone asks what you're doing. Organise the long lunch. Send the invites. Make the playlist. You're allowed to *love your life out loud*.

Create your own rituals of celebration. Made it through a hard season? Buy yourself flowers.

Set a boundary for the first time? Light a candle and whisper 'well done'. Left a toxic relationship or finally rested after burnout? Write yourself a love note.

Why do we go big for weddings and babies, but stay small for finishing degrees, starting businesses, writing books, moving house, healing trauma, asking for more or just *making it through*?

The world is full of outdated markers of success, markers women didn't choose, but inherited. What if your version of success is quieter, deeper, more internal, more meaningful? What if it looks like letting yourself be *seen*?

This is your permission slip to celebrate *everything*—the loud wins, the tiny shifts, the days you just kept going.

Make it a big deal. Because it is.

Because *you* are.

UPFRONT Moment

This chapter opened the door to a truth many of us were never taught: that celebrating ourselves is not indulgent but necessary. This work isn't about waiting until someone else tells you your moment matters, it's about deciding that *you* matter enough to mark it.

So now is the time to pause. You do not need a podium or a confetti cannon to take yourself seriously. Although I do believe every household should have a confetti drawer. But you *do* need a practice, a ritual of recognition, built by you, for you. Without this pause, your confidence can't land and your success will feel distant. Let's practise what at UPFRONT we call 'The Big Deal Practice':

1. Name your win (big or small).
2. Say out loud: *I did this. I am proud.*
3. Note what it cost you to get there.
4. Choose one way to honour it: tell a friend, light a candle, write it down, throw confetti, take a solo walk. . .
5. No guilt, just acknowledgement.

Close your eyes and visualise your inner Russian dolls.

- Who is the outermost version of you today?
- What does she believe about success, pride and celebration?
- Now meet the smallest doll inside. What does she need to hear from you?

Write a note to your smallest doll, offering reassurance, compassion and permission.

For me, the smallest version of me is very worried about being too big for my boots, for building a life that's so far away from the life I grew up with that I alienate the people I love, that I will die a lonely old woman on the top of my ambition. I have to remind her, in my gentlest voice, she is safe and loved. I have a picture of five-year-old me on my fridge to remind myself every day to be kind and gentle to her.

Tell your little doll that she hasn't been left behind and she's being carried. Tell her that success doesn't mean isolation and celebration definitely doesn't mean arrogance. Let her know that she's not being abandoned, she's being taken great care of.

And when the celebration feels too much, too loud, too far from where you started, come back to this practice. Come back to her. Wrap her in kindness. Tell her what she needs to hear: Some words you can borrow.

You're not too much.

You're not alone.

You're not a fraud.

You are allowed to be proud.

You are allowed to be seen.

You are allowed to be a very big deal.

Think of something you've achieved recently, big or small, that you didn't celebrate.

- Why didn't you mark it?
- What story stopped you?
- Now, plan one small act of celebration. Something symbolic. Something just for you.

Describe how you'll honour that win this week.

Think of a woman in your life who deserves to be celebrated right now.

- Write her a note or message. Tell her why you want to celebrate her.
- Then reflect: What would it look like to speak those same words to yourself?

Seal this practice with your own mantra. My favourite way to do this is to record a voice note to myself that I can listen to whenever I wish.

'I am learning to celebrate myself, not because I'm perfect, but because I'm here. I've worked for this. I'm a big deal. And I'm allowed to feel proud'.

Celebrating ourselves isn't just a nice-to-have. It's a non-negotiable part of rewriting the narrative we inherited, a narrative that taught us to be humble, often to the point of invisibility. Celebration is how we integrate our progress and it's how we build the muscle of self-trust.

And you don't need anyone's permission. Not mine. Not your boss's. Not your mother's. Just your own.

One of my favourite rituals is to scroll LinkedIn every morning and find posts where women are sharing progress. A new job. A book launch. A big pitch. A public win. And you'll always see me in the comments asking the same thing: *How will you celebrate?* It's my way of saying, 'Make this a big deal. You deserve to take up space in your own story'. I want you to join me in that question, not just for others, but for yourself.

So next time something good happens whether it's loud and public or quiet and just for you I want you to ask that same question. Ask it like a ritual. Ask it like a declaration with your head held high. *How will I celebrate?*

You already are a big deal. Your work, your growth, your courage to show up in the world as you are, these things matter deeply. Don't let them pass by unnoticed. The more you celebrate yourself, the more you remind every woman watching that she can too. And that's how we shift the world, one UPFRONT celebration at a time.

18

You Were Never Meant to Be Humble

Old Rule: Women should be humble

New Rule: We will never be humble

When Kamala Harris said, *'There are a whole lot of women not aspiring to be humble',* I didn't just nod, I wanted it on a T-shirt, a tattoo and a billboard in every city.

Women are told to be humble because it's a way of controlling us, making us smaller and keeping us quiet. Why should we be humble? For who? For what? Who wins when we are humble? The patriarchy wins. Those who gain from our humility are often the very people who create systems that depend on us doubting ourselves.

If we're not being told to be humble, we are being told to be modest. Which sounds more palatable, but let's not make the mistake of assuming these are different demands, they are not. They share the same root, the same message, the quiet erasure of us. Humble is defined as: 'having or showing a low estimate of one's own importance'. Ugh. And modest is defined as: 'unassuming or moderate in the estimation of one's abilities or achievements'. Double ugh, and no thank you.

Both are telling you to shrink, to downplay your confidence for the comfort of others. Choose not to. And tell others to do the same. I choose not to from the core of who I am and where I come from. When there is a hint in the room, when there is a sniff in the air of someone somewhere telling me to be humble or be modest, my reply is always the same. A very Glaswegian reply, '*On yer bike!*'

I celebrate my wins like I shared in Chapter 17, and I shout about them from the rooftops. At the time of writing, over 15,000 women and counting supported and upskilled. Over £10 million donated to the charity sector. Thousands of women are earning more, thriving and excited about their future. You're damn right I'll shout. I'll also shout about my little boy being kind and caring because they are my wins to celebrate how I like.

I'm unapologetically proud of my work and I want the world to know it. This is a radical act for me because where I grew up being called a show-off was the ultimate insult. I spent my childhood, my teens and my twenties terrified of being called a show off. It makes me weep to think of the lost joy and opportunity. I now understand this is not a personal localised case, it's a silent gendered global pandemic sucking the life out of women. Even those at the very top. Not anymore.

Let's get uncomfortable, now we know that's where growth lives. Think of the humbleness on display by the women at the top of their careers, those in public view. The interview with your favourite female celebrity. Ready? The humbleness you see in those interviews isn't real, it's strategy. Do you think Beyoncé, a woman who's built a multimillion dollar career from nothing, who rides into rooms on a horse wearing a crown, has a low opinion of herself? It doesn't add up. She's played the game her way and won, and that's ok, except it fuels the expectations placed on us. Oprah often presents herself with humility in interviews, attributing her success to luck, hard work and the influence of others. She frequently downplays her power and impact with phrases like *'I'm just a girl from Mississippi'* or *'I never imagined this would happen to me'*. Oprah is one of the most powerful and influential women in the world. She built an empire through sheer vision, determination and confidence. You don't become a billionaire and a global icon by having a low opinion of yourself!

Oprah's public persona of humility is strategic. Her strategy has been to be more relatable and likeable, but behind closed doors, she knows exactly what she's worth. She negotiates multimillion dollar deals, runs massive enterprises and commands rooms full of powerful people without hesitation. Humility isn't what got her there; confidence, audacity and a clear sense of her own value did. She was forced to play by their rules and, like Beyoncé, she has won despite having to.

Meryl Streep, widely regarded as one of the greatest actresses of all time, often downplays her extraordinary talent in interviews. She regularly speaks about how she's just *'lucky'* to get roles and emphasises the importance of the ensemble cast, rather than owning her central role in the success of a project. She is known for being self-deprecating, often making jokes about not feeling like a *'star'* and referring to herself as just *'doing her job'*. You can feel its seductive power right? That's the patriarchy, not Meryl.

Meryl's career speaks for itself. She has won numerous Academy Awards and nominations, made bold choices in her career and consistently pushed the boundaries of her craft. The success she's achieved has been the result of immense skill, dedication and belief in her own abilities. In reality, her accomplishments are anything but humble.

We see women like Oprah, Beyoncé and Meryl appear humble in interviews, but humility in public is a strategic choice playing for the patriarchy, not a reality of who they are. It's worked for a handful of women and honestly I'm glad they've got the success they have, always. But we should not replicate this if we want to show up on our own terms. Fake or strategic humility is a barrier to us all. Why are we, as women, taught that we have to downplay our greatness to be likeable? It's unfair that we've been socialised to believe we need to pretend to be modest or humble to be accepted. The world needs your full presence, not a watered-down version of you.

The dictionary tells us that humility and humbleness is defined as 'a modest or low view of one's own importance', yet we run around praising women for being humble and obsessing over how we stay humble when we achieve something great. No thank you.

And then there is Serena and Venus Williams—two women who have never pretended to be anything less than extraordinary. From the moment they stepped onto the court, they brought not just skill, but pride, power and presence. Serena famously said, *'I'm the best tennis player in the world'*. And she wasn't wrong. She knew it. We knew it. She didn't couch it in niceties or cloak it in humility.

The media often criticised them for being 'too confident' or 'too aggressive', words never used to describe equally dominant male athletes. But the Williams sisters refused to apologise for their excellence. They wore bold colours, celebrated their wins unapologetically and built empires in the process. They didn't just win, they changed the definition of what a winner looks like. Serena and Venus didn't pretend to have a low opinion of themselves. And neither should you.

There's a viral interview clip that I think about often. CNN anchor Christina Macfarlane sits down with American rugby union player, Ilona Maher. She asks Ilona how she overcomes imposter syndrome. Ilona blinks for a second and replies simply, *'I don't have that'*.[1]

The clip garnered over three million views in just one day. Sit with that for a minute.

Maher continues to say, *'No, I don't know what that is'*. Macfarlane asks in response: *'How is that possible? I feel like imposter syndrome ruins my life sometimes'*.

Ilona says she feels like she deserves what she's gotten because she has worked hard for it. *'People are told sometimes to feel like they have that imposter syndrome'*, she said. *'But it's OK to be proud of what you've done. It's OK to believe you deserve something because you've put in the work for it'*.

The confidence. The clarity. The refusal to even entertain the idea that she doesn't belong. It's a breath of fresh air. We've been taught to expect women to minimise themselves, to pretend they're surprised to be good at what they do. But Maher models something else. UPFRONT confidence. Normalised self-belief. The absence of apology. And it's revolutionary.

Ilona's clarity isn't common, but it should be. Because studies show just how rare this kind of self-assurance really is. Research shows this pattern runs deep, right into boardrooms, interviews and performance reviews. One study found that when business leaders are asked about the reason for their success, men are far more likely to credit their own ability, vision and hard work. Women are more likely to say they were *'lucky'*, *'in the right place at the right time'*, or that it was a *'team effort'*.[2] These aren't throwaway comments. They're cultural scripts, deeply ingrained habits of humility we've been trained to perform.

I've seen it play out in my own life. There was a time, many years ago, when my business partner and I were shortlisted for a major award. I said, *'Let's write a speech, just in case'*. She looked at me like I'd grown two heads. *'We won't win. Let's not get ahead of ourselves'*. I knew we would win. Of course we would win! But I didn't push it, I didn't want to seem cocky. So we didn't write a speech.

And then. . . we won. There we were, on stage, in front of a room full of people, hearts pounding, completely unprepared. We mumbled our way through something half-coherent, smiled too wide, and I walked off wondering why we didn't back ourselves. That moment stayed with me. Not because we won, but because I didn't own it. We let doubt decide how ready we were allowed to be. I let her learned modesty cloud my own confidence. That's what learned modesty does. It makes us underestimate not just ourselves, but each other. I've never made that mistake again and I never will.

The Humility Trap

Research shows that women who are modest and not seen to be bragging about their achievements are considered more likeable, but less competent, than their peers who self-promote.[3] And the women who self-promote? They're considered more competent, but not as likeable. It's a lose-lose.

This double bind is often particularly noticeable for women in leadership. We're expected to be assertive and authoritative, to lead effectively, but also be warm, nurturing and likeable. No matter what we do, we're criticised. This societal pressure is real, and it's holding us back. Research shows that women leaders are often judged by a 'masculine' standard of leadership, which limits our options and makes us feel stuck.[4] We have been conditioned to be modest, to minimise our achievements and our strengths.

Ask yourself the following questions:

- What makes me extraordinary?
- What am I great at?
- What do I need to work on?
- What am I bad at?

Which of those questions was easier to answer? I'm going to guess you found the last two questions a hell of a lot easier than the first two. Women feeling discomfort with their brilliance is a global problem. Its severity can change depending on where you grew up, cultural groups you belong to and identities you hold, but the discomfort is always there. This is one reason you find the idea of being confident, talking in front of others, putting your work out there, asking for help, believing in yourself and so on, incredibly uncomfortable. So let's get to changing that.

Write Your 'I Am Extraordinary' List

Talking about your accomplishments is a skill. Over time, I promise you will find your own natural voice and get more comfortable. The first step—you're going to write your 'I Am Extraordinary' list.

This exercise is transformative and beautiful, which means it can also be uncomfortable and emotional. It's inspired by Google's I am Remarkable project. Find a quiet space, focus on your breath and remember why you are here. It's time for you to stop hiding your talents in the name of humility. You owe it to yourself to show the world what you can do.

- Think about everything you have experienced in life, both personal and professional. I want to write down what makes you extraordinary. You have plenty to be proud about, so let loose! Don't hold back.
- Write about things that you either do or did over attributes; for example: 'I did something extraordinary' over 'I am extraordinary because I am x, y, z'.
- This is like a journalling exercise, where your pen should keep going on the page, and you shouldn't filter what you're writing.

- When you start doing this exercise, you'll have a voice in your head telling you '*that's not really* extraordinary *enough*'. The goal is to ignore that voice and write it anyway.
- This is *difficult*, don't tap out. Stay in the game.
- Put your I Am Extraordinary paper on your fridge or somewhere you will see it every day.

Letting Go of Learned Modesty

As Stefanie Sword-Williams, author of *F*ck Being Humble*, put it when we spoke on the *UPFRONT Moment* podcast, '*The core of my message is making sure that you never miss out on an opportunity because you were being too modest*'.[5]

Stefanie shared a specific example that I'm sure will be familiar to you. She was working her ass off, being given more and more work, while being told she was a high-performer and that doing all this extra work would lead to a promotion and a pay rise. But none of that happened. It turned out that the business she was working for didn't have the finances to give her the promotion they kept dangling like a carrot. '*Instead of being honest with me, they put it back on me and made it seem like I hadn't done enough*'. Stefanie chose to leave the company and is very honest about the fact that she moved jobs six times in seven years because she didn't want to be overlooked again.

> I didn't ever sit around in places where I didn't feel appreciated. But on the flip side I also really wanted to be challenged and to be in environments where I felt like I was growing and learning.
> I think the reason my message has resonated with so many people is because I'm not just one

of few, I'm one of many. As soon as you say, 'F*ck being humble', someone somewhere is saying, 'God yeah, I've been too humble' or 'I've been too modest', or 'I've let myself be conditioned to think that this is the only way'.

Stefanie's story is far from rare. This isn't just about one company or one career path, it's a pattern so many of us recognise. We've been taught to keep our heads down, wait to be noticed and trust that hard work will speak for itself. It rarely does. That's why conversations like this matter—the realisation that modesty is never a virtue and that owning your value out loud can change everything, especially the numbers in your bank account. Many of the women who go through the Bond talk about how they change their relationship by accepting positive feedback and how this shifts their internal voice, in turn changing how they show up.

Here's how Natasha from the Charity Bond felt after changing her relationship with positive feedback: '*I was prepared as usual but the conversation flowed differently this time. Because I slowed down and paused, I was able to reflect coherently and not stumble over my words. I was completely present and felt confident. I was given positive feedback which I really listened to, said thank you and didn't brush off like I used to! I am loving the new confidence the Bond has given me*'.

And Yvette from the Bond, gaining paid work after pushing humbleness to the side and having the confidence to speak up about herself: '*I answered the dreaded question "What do you do?" without diminishing myself and I said yes when they asked if I wanted some paid work, even though my internal voice was telling me "I'm not ready", "I don't have time", "You'll be too stressed", "You'll mess it up", "You don't know enough yet"... Thank you UPFRONT*'.

So let go of your modesty. Let go of your fake humility. You were never meant to be humble, you were meant to be UPFRONT.

If you feel a little angry reading this, good. That anger is your signal. You were never meant to be humble.

This world doesn't need more women who have a low opinion of themselves. It needs women who walk into rooms like Serena Williams, answer like Ilona Maher, and write their brilliance on the fridge in permanent marker.

You're done being humble.

UPFRONT Moment

If I've done my job well, this chapter will have lit a fire in you. Good. Let it burn.

You are not here to be quiet about your excellence. You are not here to apologise for your brilliance. You are here to practise radical self-recognition. Your fear of being perceived as arrogant is the exact lever the patriarchy pulls to keep you out of the room or, worse, still in the room but silent. Not on my watch.

Reflect on a time someone praised you and you brushed it off. Rewrite that moment. What could you have said instead?

- 'Thank you. That matters to me'.
- 'Yes, I'm proud of that'.
- 'I worked hard for it'.

Now, make it real. Text someone who's praised you before and simply say, 'I've been thinking about what you said, and I want you to know, it meant a lot. I'm owning it now'.

List the names, phrases or rules that taught you humility was the safest path. Whose voices are you carrying? Write them down. Then beneath each one, write the new truth you've learned in this chapter. Here's some from my own practice:

- 'You're being too much'. → 'There's no such thing'.
- 'No one likes a show-off'. → 'I do. I want my son to grow up in a world where women show off'.
- 'Don't get ahead of yourself'. → 'If I'm not ahead of myself, I'm not trying hard enough'.

And if you're feeling particularly UPFRONT today, say these words out loud. Twice. Heck, shout them out your window, startle a pigeon, confuse a neighbour and make it weird in the best way:

I am done being humble. I am done being small. I am big, bold and UPFRONT.

I AM DONE BEING HUMBLE. I AM DONE BEING SMALL. I AM BIG, BOLD AND UPFRONT.

Notes

1. CNN. (2025). *YouTube.* https://www.youtube.com/shorts/hBntZGgaZls.
2. Frontiers in Psychology. (2022). *Ability or luck: A systemic review of interpersonal attributions of success.*
3. Rudman, L.A. (1998). Self-promotion as a risk factor for women: The costs and benefits of counterstereotypical impression management. *Journal of Personality and Social Psychology* 74 (3): 629–645. https://doi.org/10.1037/0022-3514.74.3.629.
4. Catalyst. (2018). *The double-bind dilemma for women in leadership.*
5. F*ck being humble, it's time to be confident, *UPFRONT Moment with Lauren Currie* [Podcast], 2023.

19

You Were Never Meant to Do This Alone

Old Rule: Confidence comes from within

New Rule: Confidence grows in community

It's March 2023, I'm standing on the edge of a freezing lake in Stockholm, Sweden. My heart is pounding and there are horses in my tummy. The water is 11°C, and my friends are hyped, ready to jump in. I am not. I feel sick and embarrassed. I feel like I don't belong.

At this point, I was planning my excuses, imagining how I'd busy myself while they swam and had a lovely time. I didn't know what to wear. I didn't know where to go. I didn't know what to do. But at the same time, I wanted to do it. I wanted to be the kind of person who does things like this. I wanted my wee boy to see me swimming in cold, deep water, joy on my face. I wanted to walk the talk I share with thousands of women in the Bond.

So I took a step. Then another. My friend Pippa held my hand. My friend Kate cheered me on. My community was physically right there in the water with me. Their words, their presence, their belief in me made the impossible feel . . . possible.

The first time, I made it to the third step, the water just below my belly button. I didn't dare go further. The second time, I went a little deeper, the fifth step. My friends were there the whole time, saying all the right things, making me feel safe, reminding me that I *was* safe. Each time I went in, my confidence grew, little by little. Each time, my fears got smaller. The water didn't change. I did. I changed. And on my fifth attempt, after 45 minutes of trying, I let go and swam.

So why am I telling you this story?

Two reasons.

One, because I don't want you to ever think that I don't have to work on my confidence too. Of course I do, there are situations that make me feel icky, scared or embarrassed. I am still discovering new and amazing ways to activate my own confidence. This was one of them. I immersed myself in fear. I trusted myself. I pushed myself outside my comfort zone and stayed there. I trusted my friends. I trusted my body. And yes, I even trusted the water.

Second, because I want you to ask yourself: What do I need to do to take that step? Who are the friends who will say the right things? Hold your hand? Remind you that you're safe? I want you to think about your community as you are building your confidence. Lean on your community. Ask them for help. You don't have to do this alone.

Confidence is often painted as a solo pursuit, something hidden away deep inside yourself. But that's a fallacy. I didn't find my confidence deep down inside whilst I was standing at the edge of that lake, I was too busy overthinking my fear and panicking. I found my confidence in my people, my community. The ones who reminded me I was safe. The ones who believed in me, even when I didn't believe in myself.

This is the new rule: Confidence doesn't happen in isolation. Confidence happens in community.

The old rule says: Go it alone. The new rule says: Grow it together.

So, ask yourself, what's your version of the cold lake? And who's standing beside you, ready to help you take the first step?

You don't have to do this alone.

For too long, we've been sold the glorification of the lone wolf, the self-made success, the myth of the fearless individual who just decides to be confident one day and never looks back. That's nonsense. If we're being factual, wolves don't even do s**t alone either. Don't listen to the propaganda of the solo winner, it's ego boosting for the ignorant. Confidence doesn't happen in isolation. Nothing much at all happens in isolation. It all happens in community.

Think of the old rule like this: You've got to do it all yourself. Pull yourself up by your bootstraps. If you want to be confident, you need to grit your teeth, push through the discomfort and just be better. No help, no support, just you against the world. It's the same rugged individualism that tells us that asking for help is weak and that the strongest leaders never need guidance.

Nobody, not even the most confident people you admire, are alone. They have mentors, networks, communities who hold them up when they doubt themselves. They have people who saw their potential before they did. Confidence is a team sport.

Seth Godin, author, speaker and entrepreneur, would call the old rule *'industrial-era thinking'*, the idea that we're all just cogs in a machine, expected to figure things out alone, to compete rather than collaborate. It's the same thinking that tells artists to wait for a gallery, writers to wait for the permission of a publisher, employees to wait for a promotion.

It's the lie that says: You must prove yourself first, and then you'll be invited in.

The new rule calls this out and flips it. Confidence doesn't come before the invitation, before the art, before community; hear this loudly, it comes because of community. This is why community is an integral part of the Bond. The Bond is a growing global community where people don't wait to be chosen, they choose themselves and find others who are on the same journey as they are. Real confidence is built in rooms where people remind you of who you are when you stumble. It's built in the small moments when someone gives you feedback kindly, that makes you better, when a friend sends a message saying '*Keep going*'. When a mentor nudges you forward before you feel ready because you are in fact ready. The old rule isolates us. The new rule brings us together.

The Power of Community

One of the messages we share with Bonders is to build brave spaces for yourself and others. There is power in sharing your struggles with trusted friends while also celebrating your wins. What is a brave space? It's somewhere that you and other women in your life feel comfortable to share your challenges and your successes. It's a place you can go to for a pick-me-up on a tough day. It's somewhere you can laugh and cry together. It's another way we can lift each other up. These spaces are where we build ladders. These spaces are where we grow our confidence.

If you don't already have those kinds of brave spaces, this is your nudge to build one. Pull your friends into a WhatsApp group and tell them you want it to be a brave space for each other. Share what you're experiencing with your friends. If they aren't proactively sharing, then encourage them to. None of us have to do this alone, and we can go much further together.

Having a community around you doesn't just improve your confidence and help you to grow, it also helps you live a healthier life. When I spoke to Kat Vellos, author of *We Should Get Together,* on the *UPFRONT Moment* podcast, she shared some shocking statistics around loneliness in the United States and how that impacts us in a multitude of ways.[1]

In 2021, 61% of people in the United States said they felt lonely on a regular basis, either some or all of the time. In the United Kingdom, the data paints a similar picture. A 2022 survey found that almost half of adults in the UK feel lonely occasionally, sometimes, often or always.[2] Kat pointed out that feeling lonely isn't only an emotional challenge, it also affects our physical health. '*What we see is that the people who have the strongest social bonds tend to live the longest, have fewer health problems and lead healthier, happier lives*'. That's the power of building a community and creating strong bonds with other people who can lift you up, champion you and support you.

Here are some words from Bonders about the power of our UPFRONT community. Rochelle, from the Government Bond, shared her experience:

I attended my first Huddle & Bond with an amazing group of women. We all expressed how uncomfortable we felt talking about ourselves, so we each practised introducing ourselves and explaining our job roles. We smashed it! It was so inspiring and supportive, a real confidence boost. We also coined a new phrase 'Be an Ambassador of your work'. Can't wait for the follow up meeting next week. Thank you Bonders!

Sandra leaned on the Bond when she was out of work for a year.

My main reason for joining the Bond was due to being out of work for approx a year. (This is a long time for me.) I felt depleted and a loss of confidence. I had an interview in January and I left the in-person interview feeling very small, disheartened and completely questioning myself and my capabilities. I pushed myself to do as much as possible in the Bond. It has been such an introspective and positive experience. I had an interview this week and because of the Bond I have picked myself up off of the floor, made up my face and took a whole new attitude into the virtual room. By the end of the interview I knew I smashed it! Not because of the actual job, because I felt that my mojo was back in a format that I know I had previously lost. I actually left the room feeling like I could skip down the road because I had nailed the best job in the world! (It wasn't the best job in the world I might add.) I'm proud of showing up for myself and believing! As a result I've been invited back for round two.

That's why I call it a Bond. Not a club. Not a course. A Bond. The word matters. A Bond is a collective noun for a group of women. It means to fasten securely. To hold tight. This word has become a movement and now you are part of it! Because when women come together inside the Bond, something happens. Collective unlearning. A shared knowing. A collective exhale. A decision to stop doing this alone.

And when Eddie, from our very first ever Bond, put pen to paper to describe it, she didn't just write a poem. She wrote a mirror. What she wrote captures what confidence in community looks like when it's real, messy and alive. This is what it means to be in a Bond. She didn't write it for this chapter. She wrote it to process what was happening in real time. And when I read it, I knew: this is what confidence in community looks like.

This is why we call it a Bond. Here's Eddie's poem:

What Is a Bond?

Bond: a collective noun for a group of women.

Bond: to securely fasten.

Bond: a strong connection.

Something magical happens.

No wait – it's not magic, which implies unseen or mystical.

Or a cauldron, a wand, a hat and a cat.

(And these are good things. But this is not that.)

It's consciously stepping into connection.

It's saying: I'm here for me, and I'm here for you.

It's kettle on, sleeves up.

All the things that women do when there's work to be done on our worlds – for our worlds.

It's hard work.

It's deadlifting dumbbells and gym ropes.

It's heart work.

Life-lifting smart minds and new hopes.

It's women trusting women with their laughter, and their fears.

It's holding space, making it safe for tears to be brought out – Unexploded landmines that we step around.

All those danger lines on your map of:

> *'I can't do this.'*
> *'No way.'*
> *'Never.'*
> *'Not me.'*
> *'I'm not ready.'*
> *'I don't think I could ever.'*

But your Bond gets to work.

Explosives are neutralised with the delicate skill of a bomb squad whose operatives work from kitchens, bedrooms, and sitting rooms in between a busy day of Zooms, before school runs, in coffee shops, at bus stops.

All bonded to this bold belief in better.

But how can this be?

I don't know them, and they don't know me.

'In real life.'

Wait, what does that even mean?

Are they real?

Are you?

Is this life?

Yes.

You hear your Bond's voices as you step through your day, trying on the new clothes of new ideas with each lesson you learn.

Their hands type messages into your phone.

Their pens write words in your notebooks.

They upload files to your inner cloud and their playlists sing in your ears:

> *'Well done.'*
> *'What about this?'*
> *''Gosh that sounds hard.'*
> *''Wait, did you just apologise?''*

Like.

Like.

Like.

Love.

As you hold your place in Bond, the Bond holds your place.

So you are safe as you start running at a whole new pace to the spaces you take up, to the spaces you will make.

Hear the sound of the ground as your ideas land.

Soak up the silence where your sorries once spoke.

Because your Bond is your word.

Your words are your voice.

Your voice has so much it has to say.

*And the world awaits – to hear **You.***

—Eddie

This is why confidence doesn't only live inside you. It lives between us. In the spaces we create, in the hands we hold out, in the voices that say, 'Go on, we've got you'. This is how we build confidence. Together.

UPFRONT Moment

I'll be honest with you. Writing the prompts for this chapter was the hardest so far. Not because I didn't believe in them. But because I am constantly working to unlearn the idea that leadership means loneliness. These prompts might bring up resistance in you like they did for me. Maybe they will poke at your pride or your disappointment. They might feel 'too much' or 'too tender'. That's OK, in fact it's a sign that these are the questions you need to look at. Do them anyway. This is your place to stop performing independence and start practising connection.

Let's go together.

What's your version of the lake? The moment that makes the horses arrive in your tummy and your excuses get loud? Write about something you *want* to do but are currently talking yourself out of.

- Who are your Pippas and Kates? What are their names?
- What would it look like to let them help you in?

Write a letter (or voice note) to someone who's held you through an UPFRONT confidence moment. Perhaps a boss, a friend, a coach or a colleague. Tell them what they did. Why did their support matter and how did it help you? You don't have to send it. . . but maybe you will.

Eddie gave us a whole poem. You just need one word. In 2024 my word of the year was SECURE. I wrote on my Instagram 'Even in the wildest of storms, I'll be safe and secure. Surrounded by the mountains of my family and friends.

When I'm rooted and secure I can do BIGGER things. It'll sound like my dad playing the piano in the house I grew up in. It'll feel like every single person who knows and loves and supports me standing beside me—their hands resting on my shoulders. It'll taste like a mug of English breakfast tea, made just the way I like it'.

What word describes what it feels like when you're feel supported?

Write it on a Post-it. Put it by your desk, on your mirror, next to your kettle. Let it remind you that you are backed and you are not doing this alone. Bonus points if you go into the detail of what it sounds, feels and tastes like. I'm with you.

Notes

1. We should get together, *UPFRONT Moment with Lauren Currie* [Podcast], 2023.
2. Campaign to End Loneliness. (2024). *Facts and statistics—Campaign to end loneliness*.

20

You Are Allowed to Be Bigger

Old Rule: Don't take up too much space

New Rule: You're allowed to be bigger

In the summer of 2023, I made a decision that challenged every belief I had about how much space I was allowed to take up. It was terrifying. A few months before, my friend Yanni signed us up for a five kilometre run. The first few attempts were brutal. I felt sore, tired and frustrated. My legs ached, and all I could do during the run was whine and ask, 'How much longer?' and 'Is it nearly over?'

Nobody in my family is a runner. I didn't buy my first pair of trainers until I was 25, and I knew maybe one person who had run a marathon. The internet seemed flooded with people obsessed with running, offering tips, strategies and life-changing marathon stories. At first, it all felt too much. But then something shifted.

As cliché as it sounds, I fell in love with running. The forests, the lakes and the sense of pride after each run gave me a new energy. I loved how strong and alive I felt, and yes, I did get excited about the idea of running a marathon. But it wasn't just the physical act of running that intimidated me, it was what the decision represented.

The decision to run a marathon was about prioritising my health and movement in ways I never had before. It was about committing to training for hours, reshaping my business to allow time for it and even adjusting how I parent to make room for this. Training required me to run for 10 entire days over a period of 20 weeks. That's 240 hours away from my family, my business and my home.

As I've made room for running, I've realised it's not easy but it is possible. Swimming in the lake, running in the forest, it felt otherworldly at times. Every run, every swim has been a step towards seeing myself as a strong, fit human. But I also recognise the privilege that has made all of this possible. Moving to Sweden, feeling safe outdoors alone and building a business that allows me to control my time and routine.

I'm telling you this story because I want you to allow yourself to take up room, without guilt or self-doubt, allowing yourself to be bigger both physically and emotionally. By running a marathon, I stepped into a bigger version of myself. Being small won't lead to the transformation you're hungry for. Have the power to say, 'I am allowed to be bigger', even when it scares you. This new rule is about standing tall, both physically and metaphorically. Because taking up space isn't just limited to the miles run or the strength I've built in my legs; it's also about the way I show up every day, in every room, in every conversation.

This next bit is difficult for me to write, and I'm consciously trying to be kind to myself whilst doing it. I'm five foot nine inches tall, and for most of my teenage years I tried desperately to be five foot five inches, literally smaller. I wasn't just trying to blend in, I was trying to shrink, cross my legs, slouch and avoid taking up too much space.

I was tall before most of my tall friends were. I desperately wanted to be smaller than the boys. I tried not to be 'lanky'. Tactics ranged from severe shoulder slouching to my head being down at all times and to my personal favourite, standing with crossed legs at all kinds of angles just to shave off an inch or two.

I didn't know I was doing this until a friend pointed it out in the only way he could. I worked in a bar pulling pints. We'd all hang around the back of the bar texting, playing snake and stealing sips of Smirnoff Ice until a customer needed serving. I'd make my way to the bar, I'd start to twist and distort in shape, squirm in the most unorthodox way up to and around the beer taps. I was showing up as quite literally a smaller, more dishevelled version of myself. My friend said, '*You walk like you need the toilet mate, what're you playin' at?*'

I didn't think about this again until years later when I was being observed facilitating a workshop for a client, and my colleague Louise told me that my leg-crossing stance made me look nervous, weak and unsure of myself. She said it was giving a very confusing message, as my delivery was very strong, and my voice was clear and powerful.

This is when I began to notice the role confidence played in how I showed up physically. This is when I decided to stop crossing my legs for good. Here's where it stops being just about me. Let's talk about you. What does taking up more space look like in your world?

Everywhere you go, you will see this behaviour. The more self-conscious or exposed we are, the more we do it; when we have to address a group, stand on a train platform amidst a sea of men in suits or introduce ourselves at an event. Women everywhere are physically making themselves smaller and lowering their status by doing so. Now, I know it can feel comfortable because it's something some of us have been doing for years. But, and it's a big but, I'm here to tell you it's taking away your power! It makes you look nervous and small when you are not and it's creating a physical barrier between you and your audience, between you and your confidence.

Imagine Michelle Obama, Meryl Streep or Viola Davis making themselves look smaller. You can't, because they don't do it, they refuse to. They have realised that leg crossing not only decreases their height, it destabilises them, it weakens the rest of their body, particularly the muscles in their legs and back. This restricts their breathing, which, of course, influences the sound of their voice and the breath they have to speak with. It literally takes away their voice, their power.

I hear from women every day who want to understand how to be taken seriously, how to be heard and how to demand respect. The first way to achieve all of these things is to find a stable position—standing, seated, or supported—that works for your body, with your legs about shoulder-width apart and your hips square.

This can feel odd at first. Some women have told me they feel like they are standing like a superhero. I only have one answer for that: yes you are. This is what you need to get used to! To an audience, you look competent and confident. Yes, it is more culturally acceptable for men to adopt this stance. Firstly, this is often due to necessity, but it is also culturally ingrained. This stance is also associated with alpha behaviour, which is another reason why some women often avoid it.

Not any longer. Here's exactly where to start: stand up, yes right now where you are. If you're in bed, get out. Root yourself through your toes as if you're preparing for action, as indeed you are. Be careful not to lock your knees, your knees should feel spongy, a solid spring in them. Bounce up and down a little to find what feels comfortable. Place your feet shoulder width apart, square your hips and relax your shoulders. At the end of this paragraph, take your eyes off the words and fix them dead ahead. Don't be distracted by anything around you. You are now a force to be reckoned with. You are in control. This is who you are. Notice how it feels.

PRACTICE MAKES CONFIDENCE. PRACTISE EVERYWHERE. PRACTISE UNTIL YOU FORGET HOW IT USED TO BE.

Practice makes confidence, so practise when you're brushing your teeth. Practise in front of the mirror. Tell your friends and colleagues about your new commitment so they can hold you accountable. Practise on the train, on the bus. Practise everywhere. Practise until you forget how it used to be.

I love nothing more than standing tall, with my legs slightly apart, in silver cowboy boots. It's time for us to stop lowering our status before we've even begun to speak.

Both my journey with running and my decision to stop crossing my legs have one thing in common: they're about refusing to physically make myself smaller. They're about stepping into my power, whether in the forest or in front of an audience. Confidence isn't just something we feel, it's something we build in our bodies, something we practise every single day by taking up space, standing tall and allowing ourselves to be big.

Becoming Bigger

Meet Faye, a Bonder who has become bigger in a multitude of ways since her Bond experience. One of Faye's biggest takeaways has been the idea that she is in control of her own growth, who she is and how she shows up in her professional world. Faye joined the Bond because she wanted to be taken more seriously and be on non-executive boards. Here's her story:

> *A lot of work around my growth stems from building a writing habit, which doesn't just mean publishing online. It's also about journalling, reflecting on challenging questions and thinking about what I want to achieve, as well as what I have achieved. One of the decisions alongside this has been whether to publish my writing somewhere. I decided I would, so I've been writing weekly online, on LinkedIn primarily, alongside building*

CONFIDENCE ISN'T JUST SOMETHING WE FEEL, IT'S SOMETHING WE PRACTISE EVERY SINGLE DAY.

my own website. I write about leadership, financial services, career transitions and well-being.

Financial services is very male-dominated and it's also over complicated. One of my big takeaways from the Bond was to share generously because someone reading will appreciate it, and that has absolutely been the case. Other people would perhaps have said I was active online before, but I agonised over those posts. I'd spend time worrying about what some guy I worked with in 2005 might think! What changed was thinking about who I was writing for. Who is looking up to me rather than potentially down. Sometimes I write for myself to process my thoughts, but often I have someone specific in mind, and weirdly often that person contacts me after I post.

Since I've been writing online, my network is stronger. By that I don't mean I've got a following of thousands, but that the people who know me professionally have got to know me as a person a lot better, I'm not just 'Faye from the third floor'. The people I work with are more interested in spending time with me because they've seen a fuller version of who I am and what I'm working on. It's not that I'm any more interesting now than I was two years ago, I've just shown them more of me. To the world I am bigger.

Faye choosing to be bigger has led to new opportunities, among them the board roles which she had always wanted to build into her career. In 12 months, Faye has landed two board roles, been invited to speak on two panels and been a guest on a podcast.

I got my first board role because of the work I was doing around showing up. Sharing my skill set gave me the confidence to contact a charity CEO who I know quite well and ask if she knew of a charity looking for my skills as a board member. The way I framed the question was, 'Do you know anywhere that's a good fit?' and her reply was, 'We're a good fit'. From there, there was an interview process with the CEO and the Chair and I became a board member.

Through that board membership, Faye met the CEO of a social enterprise who had found her writing valuable.

One of the other things I took from the Bond was the importance of sharing your expertise. That nudged me to start writing about my financial knowledge and the process I follow when I assess lending requests from businesses and charities. This prompted the CEO of a social enterprise to reach out and ask for my support. I told her I'd be happy to share what I know and help with their financial strategy. Through that spirit of saying, 'I'll share what I know. . .' and working with her over a period of months, she asked if I'd join their board. I'm now part of a talented non-executive board supporting the growth of a social enterprise. It's incredibly energising and brings me a lot of joy.

What I love about Faye's story is that she didn't wait for opportunities to come to her, she actively sought them out. She reflected on who she wanted to be and stepped into those shoes.

Taking action even when it's uncomfortable has been a big step for me, through being more action orientated, things come your way. If I'm honest, I still want to say no, but I also know I've got to take action and I force myself to say yes. I'm aware that if I told the friends I've met through the Bond that I'd said no to certain opportunities, they'd be furious with me! So that's an additional motivation, and accountability network.

When I think about where I was 12 months ago, before I started showing up as a bigger version of myself, in person and online, to where I am now, I can see a huge difference and I definitely have a more engaged network of people to call on. I'm also just about to start a new job, which will be a stretching role for me. I remember when I first looked at the job profile, I thought, 'Is this a bit much? Could I do this?' It felt scary, in a good way, and I applied and I got the job.

I went to an investor meeting for this new role recently, where someone asked, 'Why are you the right organisation to do X, Y and Z?' My boss turned to me and said, 'Do you want to take this Faye?' I had to answer this question in front of a group of people I'd never met before, some of whom were very senior. I shared my experience, told them what I'm good at and what I currently manage and then said, 'So when you're looking at that expertise in our team, it comes from me and my background'. Then I stopped talking. A year ago I would never have answered like that. After the meeting the Chief Executive of one of our senior partners approached me and told me that in his words, 'It was a mic drop moment'. I was very proud.

Let this be your reminder: bigness isn't something you earn. It's something you decide to be. Whether it's saying yes to the marathon, no to the leg cross or hell yes to the board seat, you are allowed to grow beyond the version of yourself the world has learned to expect. Incredible things happen when you do.

So here's the new rule I want you to carry: You are allowed to be bigger. Not only taller and louder, but bigger in vision, in value, in voice.

And you don't need permission.

Stand tall. Take the seat. Say the thing.

Big ideas. Big impact. Big presence.

So take up your space.

There's more than enough room for all of us.

UPFRONT Moment

You've just read about the daily decisions that build big, confident UPFRONT lives. This moment is for you to turn that reflection inward and ask: what does being bigger look like for me?

Think of a time when you physically or metaphorically made yourself smaller. Maybe you said less than you meant to in a meeting. Maybe you let someone else take the credit. Maybe you twisted your legs, lowered your voice or slouched to shrink your presence.

Now ask yourself:

- What would 'bigger' have looked like?
- What would you have said if you had taken up more space?
- How would you have stood, spoken or responded if you had given yourself permission to fully show up?

- Whose gaze or opinion made you feel you were safer being small?
- What belief are you ready to let go of in order to stand taller?

Today, I want you to take up *more* space on purpose.

- If you're walking, walk like you belong.
- If you're speaking, speak with a clear voice.
- If you're sharing online, write like someone needs to hear it.
- If you're sitting in a meeting, keep your legs uncrossed and your spine tall.

Where in your life do you feel the urge to shrink? Where are you ready to be bigger? Write your thoughts down.

This is where it begins. A decision you make to take up space, on the page, in the room, in your body and in your voice. Stand taller than your fear.

You're allowed to be bigger. I promise.

Part III

Be UPFRONT

21

You Are Learning to Love Mistakes

Old Rule: Fake it till you make it

New Rule: Mistake it till you make it

I much prefer 'mistake it till you make it'. Don't you?

Mistakes aren't failures, they're messages. They're lessons. They're inevitable and necessary. Want proof? Spend five minutes with a toddler. Children make mistakes freely, grinning wildly as they try again. They haven't learned to be ashamed yet. No one has told them the most damaging lie of all, that mistakes define us.

But somewhere along the way, you were taught that very lesson. Maybe you stopped experimenting. Maybe you started playing it safe. Maybe you've been so conditioned to avoid mistakes that you've put your confidence on hold. You overthink, overanalyse and hold yourself back, afraid of looking incompetent. Avoiding mistakes is robbing you of confidence.

Confident people collect mistakes. Innovators, leaders, entrepreneurs and athletes all know that progress comes from trial and error. Every mistake is an experiment that gives you valuable data. Instead of seeing them as setbacks, treat mistakes as experiments that give you insight. As stepping stones of growth.

Ask yourself what did I learn from this? And what will I do differently next time?

One example of this is my relationship with busyness. Early in my career, I wore busyness like a badge of honour. I equated being constantly booked, speaking everywhere and working late nights with being valuable. But what I didn't realise was that I was edging into burnout.

I dismissed the signs—exhaustion, snappiness, brain fog—telling myself I could push through, because that's what successful women do, right? Keep going. Don't let anyone see the cracks.

Eventually, I couldn't ignore it. I crashed. I ended up being rushed into hospital. And at the time, it felt like a failure. Like I'd let myself down, let others down. But it was the wake-up call I needed to rebuild my definition of success.

That burnout became a line in the sand. It taught me boundaries, rest and to stop proving my worth through constant doing. The word busy has not been in my vocabulary since 2017. I will never see this as a failure; it was a mistake. I learned my lesson.

Mistakes are an inevitable part of learning, growth and confidence-building. Yet most of us are conditioned to avoid any sort of failure at all costs, afraid of what it says about us or who might be watching. Mistakes are not proof that you're stupid or not worthy, they're proof that you're trying, stretching and building something new.

Part of why we fear mistakes so much is because of internalised voices, what artist and musician Amanda Palmer calls 'The Fraud Police' in her book *The Art of Asking*. She describes them as imaginary critics waiting to expose us as impostors. For many women, systemic injustices and patriarchal messaging have only deepened this fear, reinforcing the idea that making mistakes means we're not good enough.

> *The Fraud Police are the imaginary, terrifying force of 'real' grown-ups who you believe—at some subconscious level—are going to come knocking on your door in the middle of the night, saying:*
> *We've been watching you, and we have evidence that you have NO IDEA WHAT YOU'RE DOING. You stand accused of the crime of completely winging it, you are guilty of making shit up as you go along, you do not actually deserve your job, we are taking everything away and we are TELLING EVERYBODY.*

If we carry that fear with us into the workplace, it doesn't just limit individuals, it shapes entire cultures. That's why some of the most progressive organisations are deliberately rewriting the script around mistakes. Instead of punishing failure, they treat it as data. Instead of hiding errors, they surface them and learn in public. Companies like Etsy and Spotify have shown us that when mistakes are normalised, teams become more confident, more innovative and ultimately more human.

Etsy's 'Three-Armed Sweater' Award

At Etsy, they do something brilliant: they give out an award for the best mistake. Yes, really. It's called the Three-Armed Sweater award, named after a hilariously wrong product that somehow made it onto their site. One year, a senior engineer made a change that accidentally crashed the whole platform. Total chaos. But instead of pointing fingers, the team pulled together, fixed it and then celebrated her with this award. She even got a standing ovation.

This isn't just a quirky tradition, it's part of a deliberate culture. Etsy runs blameless post-mortems, where anyone who makes a mistake sends a company-wide 'public service announcement' explaining what happened, what they thought would happen and what they learned. The aim is never to shame, but to understand the root causes and share the lessons, so the same thing doesn't happen again. To this day, if you click on a broken link on Etsy.com you'll see a three-armed sweater.

It's a beautiful reminder that mistakes aren't shameful, they're part of the job. At Etsy, mistakes become community knowledge, not private shame. And when people know they can admit to getting it wrong without fear, they get braver, more creative and more willing to take the kinds of risks that lead to real innovation.

Spotify's 'Skateboard' Methodology

At streaming music service Spotify, engineering teams sprint to develop new features that they hope their users will love. As they begin each new project, they use the framework of the 'Minimum Loveable Product' to make sure they're learning as quickly as they can without frustrating their users or wasting resources. The analogy is simple: if you need a means of transportation, a car provides the greatest benefit, but it takes the longest to make and, worse, it's hard to learn as you go. A skateboard, meanwhile, lacks a lot of features, but it's better than nothing and gets you where you need to go. More importantly, it's quick to build and delivers immediate feedback. Spotify Agile coach Henrik Kniberg explains further:

> *The squad needs to figure out the smallest possible thing they can build to fulfill the basic narrative and delight the users. We need it to be narrative-complete, not feature-complete. Perhaps a better term is Minimum Loveable Product. A bicycle is a loveable and useful product for somebody with no better means of transport, but is still very far from the motorcycle that it will evolve into.*

It's such a helpful way to think about progress. Small, useful steps that get better with feedback. The skateboard of this book was an A4 page with twenty-four old rules and new rules written into a two-column table. What if instead of trying to build the perfect product (or life, or plan) from scratch, you started with a skateboard?

Both Etsy's celebration of mistakes and Spotify's Skateboard approach are rooted in the same truth that mistakes are an inevitable part of progress. You don't wait until it's flawless to share it, you put the skateboard out there, see how it rides and let what you learn shape the next version. That's what working in the open looks like.

I choose to work in the open, sharing my mistakes so we can all learn and grow together. At the end of each month I share three things that went wrong and what they taught me. It's not always easy, but it's a practice that helps normalise mistakes as a daily, inevitable and necessary part of meaningful work and life.

Mistakes aren't failures of character. They are milestones of progress. When we view mistakes as part of the process, as the dirt under the fingernails of growth, we free ourselves from the paralysis of perfectionism. We build confidence not by avoiding failure, but by moving through it, using it. There is no right. There is no wrong. There is only trying. I hope you will make new mistakes. Make bold, brilliant, messy mistakes. And most importantly: share what they teach you with others.

The Science Bit

Embracing mistakes and learning from them is far more valuable than you might think. One study found that more than 40% of people have a fear of failure and making mistakes between 20 and 40% of the time. What's more, that same study found one in two people believe they would perform better at work if they weren't worried about making mistakes.[1]

When the researchers split those figures down between men and women, they found 46% of women worry about making mistakes, compared to 33% of men. That means almost half of us are underperforming at work because we are scared of making mistakes. And that's just at work.

Think of all the things you aren't doing in your personal life too because you're afraid of failing. Maybe signing up for a pottery class, speaking up in a book club, learning a new language, posting your writing online, asking someone out, trying a new sport, learning to dance, singing at karaoke or finally starting that business you've been talking about for years. What would your life look and feel like if you learned to love mistakes?

Creating Confidence from Mistakes

The relationship you have with mistakes has a huge impact on your confidence. How you think about yourself and the story you tell yourself about confidence, public speaking and power is a big part of what can make it feel doable, accessible and safe. It's also what can make it feel like the scariest thing in the world. If you beat yourself up every time you get it wrong, you'll shy away from trying new things.

A crucial part of how you can help yourself learn confidence is by learning to be kinder to yourself when you make mistakes. Most of us feel rubbish when we make a mistake. We talk to ourselves in such a cruel voice that it makes us scared to try new things in the future. We focus on our mistakes and by default ignore achievements and positive thoughts. Behavioural psychologists call this negative reinforcement.

It's time to flip the script. Let me introduce you to one of my all-time favourite tools in UPFRONT's toolkit: the Woohoo. At first, you'll probably cringe, maybe even hide behind your hands, convinced this is ridiculous. I'm totally fine with that but you have to try it at least three times, and you'll feel its strength. It's tiny, it's joyful and it has the power to change your whole day (and maybe your whole life).

Next time you mess up, whether it's something small like spilling coffee on your shirt or something big like botching an important meeting, throw your hands in the air and yell 'Woohoo!' Praise yourself for noticing, learning and moving on. This small, joyful act isn't just about feeling good, it literally rewires your brain.

I must admit when I learned about Woohoo I had a dry smile and was very sceptical but I am now feeling like I need to eat humble pie as Woohoo really does work and I will continue to use it.

(Samantha, Bond graduate)

Woohoo Meets Neuroscience: Why Celebration Changes Your Brain

When you make a mistake, your brain's default setting, especially if you were raised in environments where perfectionism was rewarded, is to trigger the threat response: shame, fear, embarrassment. This activates your amygdala, the part of your brain responsible for processing fear and danger, which floods your body with stress hormones like cortisol. Over time, repeated cycles of shame around mistakes can wire your brain to avoid risk, fear failure and make it very difficult to build your confidence muscle.

When you respond to a mistake with celebration instead of shame, even if you have to fake joy at first, you interrupt your brain's automatic fear response. You switch on its reward system instead, especially areas like the ventral striatum, which lights up when we get positive reinforcement. Pairing mistakes with joy and humour triggers a hit of dopamine (and—say it with me—we *love* dopamine). This feel-good chemical boosts learning, creativity and confidence. And because your brain can rewire itself, the more you Woohoo when you make a mistake, the more natural it becomes to meet setbacks with curiosity and courage, instead of fear and judgement.

And here's my favourite part: when you teach this technique to others, your friends, family, teammates, you create what scientists call social reinforcement loops. We're wired for social learning through a process called emotional contagion. This means your emotions and behaviours can spread to others just like a smile or a laugh can. When you cheer yourself (or someone else) for a stumble, you make it safer for everyone around you to take risks, try new things and recover faster from mistakes.

> *I had my first Woohoo moment this week. Usually, when I make a mistake it clouds my mind and looms over me for the rest of the day. Instead, I said 'Woohoo', considered what I could do next time to prevent the same mistake, and carried on with the rest of my day. Reminder to self: your mistakes do not define you, nor do colleagues view you any differently.*
>
> (Hannah, Bond graduate)

Before you know it, mistakes become a source of smiles and learning rather than a source of anxiety and shame. You don't even have to shout it out loud at first. You can start by whispering 'Woohoo!' inside your own head whenever something goes sideways, a small internal high-five that says: '*Look at me, learning. Look at me, trying*'.

I learned this 'Woohoo!' technique from facilitator Belina Raffy, an improvisation expert and founder of Maffick, who told me about a senior leader who froze on stage in front of a huge audience. Instead of panicking, she threw her hands in the air and shouted 'Woohoo!' The audience laughed, she laughed and she carried on with confidence and power.

This is one of my all-time favourite 'Woohoo' moments— I'm running ridiculously late, hair half-dried, sweating like I've just climbed ten flights of stairs (spoiler: I hadn't), and frantically searching for my shoes. You know that kind of morning, right? And then, snap. My bra gives up on life. Just completely surrenders. Suddenly, I'm standing there, holding a cup in each hand like I'm about to take part in some weird Olympic event. For a split second, I wanted to cry. I was late! This bra made the outfit! But instead, I took a deep breath, threw my hands in the air and yelled, 'Woohoo!' Let me tell you, it's pretty hard to stay grumpy when you're standing in your bedroom, half-dressed, sweating, shouting Woohoo at your own reflection. I ended up laughing instead of stressing and, honestly, it was the best thing that happened that morning.

I've taught the 'Woohoo' technique to thousands of women in the Bond, and now families around the world are 'Woohooing' at their dinner tables, teams are 'Woohooing' in boardrooms, and children and teachers are 'Woohooing' in classrooms.

Now it's your turn.

What mistake will you celebrate today? Throw your hands up and say 'Woohoo!' because every mistake is a step towards confidence. Here are some Woohoo moments from Bonders to inspire you:

I lost my bank card this week. When I realised I shouted 'Woohoo' in the middle of the street. I've since cancelled and ordered a new one. All is well.

—Charlotte

I did a 'Woohoo' in my head when I dropped the chopping board on the kitchen floor at 7am this morning. I had a little smile to myself.

—Sarah

I attended a great spin class at my gym last night and after one of my favourite tracks I actually voiced my (formerly internal) 'Woohoo' inspired by my fellow Bonders. A positive change for introverted me and no-one looked at me as if to say 'showoff' or 'OMG she's loud' which my inner voice always told me would happen.

—Ceri

You can literally Woohoo anywhere, as I proved to myself by Woohoo'ing on the loo last week. I caught myself overthinking about a conversation and this was my impromptu solution. It worked. The overthinking turned to giggles, which enabled me to stop, be kinder to my inner thoughts and move on.

—Natasha

I made a mistake at the beginning of my presentation by talking out loud about whether the hundred-plus people had joined thinking I was in a small group, but the hundred-plus people were already there listening to me. . .so I did a mental WOOHOO and decided to learn that Teams meetings don't have waiting rooms like Zoom meetings do. Or not to assume I am in a waiting room online unless I clearly see I'm in a waiting room.

Or something. Anyway, Woohoo and some useful things came from being there so it is winning all round.
—Natalie

Learning by Failing

Here's another reason to change your relationship with mistakes: research has shown that deliberately making mistakes when you're learning something new helps you to learn that material more effectively. In one study, researchers got students to deliberately write wrong answers to questions and then correct their answers themselves. This improved their meaningful learning, memory and test performance.[2]

I'm not suggesting that you deliberately make mistakes at work, but this study shows the value of correcting mistakes. We've all heard business leaders talk about how they have learnt more from their failures than they have from their successes. You don't have to be running a business for that to be true.

Think back to a time when you made a mistake. A really howling error. I bet you promised yourself you'd never do that again. I also bet you haven't. But learning from those mistakes is often linked to painful emotions. This is why Woohoo! is so powerful, because it turns a negative into a positive. Not only do you learn from your mistake, but you feel good too. And speaking of turning failure into charm, let me tell you about a place that took a mistake and turned it into a national inside joke.

Did you know Vienna International Airport in Austria (the small, landlocked country in Europe, not Australia with kangaroos and beaches) has become famous for how it responds to mistakes? Every year, a surprising number of people mistakenly book flights to Austria thinking they're heading to Australia. To lean into the humour, Vienna Airport set up a 'No kangaroos in Austria' sign at the arrivals gate. You can even find airport staff wearing shirts that say 'No kangaroos in Austria'. The confusion is so famous that souvenir shops across Austria sell T-shirts, mugs and posters with the slogan. What a glorious, light-hearted way for Austrians to gently correct the mistake, and over time, it's become part of the country's tourism charm. I loved that Austria turned confusion into a charming moment and it reminded me of a more digital, but equally daft, moment I had.

I left last week's copy at the bottom of my newsletter. I sent it to 4,699 people. Actual shambles. You know that feeling when you confidently wave back at someone who wasn't waving at you? That. But digital. Was it lazy? Unprofessional? A bit clumsy? Maybe. Yes. Also yes. Did anyone care? Nope. Did anyone even notice? Also nope.

Turns out, nobody's got the time to zoom in on my tiny slip-ups or yours. We're all just trying to get the laundry done and remember where we left the remote.

We hold ourselves to impossible standards. We think a single mistake is our downfall. But the world is not watching you closely (with all the love in my heart you just aren't that important). So here's to pressing send anyway and to showing up, flaws 'n all. And when you make a mistake, now you know EXACTLY what to do.

Mistakes aren't signs of failure; they're signs of movement. Of momentum. Of trying. Whether it's your bra snapping before a big meeting or your name sitting awkwardly at the bottom of last week's newsletter—if you can laugh, learn and say 'Woohoo' anyway, you're not falling behind, you're practising confidence. One mistake at a time.

So here's your final reminder: perfect is a lie. Progress is necessary, clumsy, brave and human. And it often starts with a mistake.

You were never meant to be mistake-free. You were meant to try, like toddlers do, wobbly, wild and wide-eyed. Confidence isn't the absence of mistakes. It's the decision to keep going, arms in the air, laughing at the chaos and saying with pride: *Woohoo!*

UPFRONT Moment

This is your call to the front. Reading this chapter without picking up a pen is another form of self-protection. And you, my friend, are done with armour.

You know that confidence doesn't come from being flawless. I know you are with me on that. We've been together for 21 chapters now and you know confidence comes from taking action. Let's write.

Think back to the first time you felt making a mistake was something to be ashamed of. What happened? How did you respond? Where has that story still got its grip on you?

What's one recent mistake that you can now look at with curiosity instead of self-judgement? What did it teach you? What is the insight, the gold, the pattern?

Where in your life right now are you holding back because you're afraid of making a mistake? What would be possible if you let yourself do it badly, and grow anyway?

Write about a mistake you made this week. Tiny or titanic counts. For me, I wore new shoes for too long and got a blister *and* sent an email to 40,000 people with the wrong date on it. Brutal. 'Woohoo!'

Now throw your hands in the air and shout: 'Woohoo!' Yes, out loud. Yes, even in your head. How did it feel to treat that moment as a celebration instead of a shame spiral? You are smiling. I can see it. Cringe forward, remember!

Write down the words your inner critic says when you mess up. Be as honest as you can be. I'll go first; here are some words my inner critic has said to me recently: 'you never learn' 'why are you so upset about this, it doesn't even matter' 'when will you get your shit together?' Now: rewrite them. What would you say to a child? To your best friend? To yourself, if you were being tender? When you read how mean my critic is to me, how would you rewrite those words? Write those words down.

Where could you start being more open about your mistakes? At work? At home? Online? How would that honesty change your confidence and the confidence of those around you?

List three things you would try this month if you knew, without question, that making a mistake would be met with celebration, not criticism. Write them down. Circle one. Schedule it. You know what to do.

Now your job is to Woohoo. Go make a mistake. I dare you. It'll be fun.

Notes

1. Franklin, N. (2019). *Fear of failure holds people back at work*. https://workplaceinsight.net/fear-of-failure-holds-people-back-at-work/.
2. Emamzadeh, A. (2022). New findings suggest deliberately making and correcting errors boosts learning. *Psychology Today*, 26 March. https://www.psychologytoday.com/gb/blog/finding-a-new-home/202203/to-learn-better-make-mistakes.

22

You Are a Mirror

Old Rule: Confident women are threats

New Rule: Confident women are mirrors

I hated Taylor Swift for years. And one of my biggest joys of 2024 was falling in love with her music and her as an artist after realising that internalised misogyny had taught me to hate her. I thought she was rich, whiny, very beautiful and very thin—enough for me to decide I didn't like her. Writing those words now I feel ashamed.

The penny dropped the night I watched Miss Americana in 2020. I saw, very clearly, that my decisions, judgements and feelings towards Taylor Swift came from two things: internalised misogyny and subconsciously absorbing all the negative media trying to tear a successful woman down.

Taylor Swift is a force. A masterful businesswoman. A phenomenon. And the many failed attempts to take her down is part of a much larger pattern. In many societies, we are taught to celebrate the underdog but not the woman who dares to be great. This is where the concept of Tall Poppy Syndrome comes in.

In Chapter 9, we talked about Tall Poppy Syndrome, when people try to cut down anyone who stands out, anyone who achieves success or rises above the norm. It's this cultural tendency that teaches us to see confident, successful women as a threat, someone to be judged, criticised or even resented.

I let myself fall into that trap, and maybe you did too? We are conditioned to feel threatened by women who confidently take up space, who aren't afraid to be ambitious or claim their worth. We have all been exposed to a world that teaches us that when women succeed, they must somehow be doing something wrong or not living up to the right standards.

I believe something different.

Confident women are mirrors. When we see a confident woman, we're not seeing someone who threatens our space or our worth. Instead, we're seeing a reflection of what's possible for us. When we look at them, we're looking at our own potential, our own strength and, yes, even our own insecurities. The discomfort we feel isn't about them, it's about facing what we've been taught to suppress our fear in ourselves.

This statement hits my inbox every other week: '*I feel the most judgement from other women*'. Thousands of women come to the Bond every single year, confidence crushed by other women—a boss, a mum, a sister, a friend. Let's be honest with each other. Blaming men is too easy. Women are in this too. Let's face the ugly truth. We do not talk about the ways in which we are rewarded for bringing each other down, by judging, gossiping, labelling. By rejecting women who don't play by the old rules.

We have to talk about the hold internalised misogyny has on us. It's time to cut it out. For good. Teach your kids—no gossip. No body or choice comments. No double standards. I have written a children's book called *Taylor Meets The Trick*,[1] which will help you have these conversations.

There is no tidy answer, and I know we're all guilty. I am. But it has to end. We have to stop pretending that internalised misogyny doesn't affect us or that tearing other women down doesn't hurt us all. It's time to rewrite the script and stop rewarding behaviour that harms us, whether we're doing it knowingly or not. Like in medicine, doing no harm to each other must be our oath. We don't have to like each other, but we have to back each other.

Confronting Internalised Misogyny

Before we can tackle internalised misogyny, we need to know what it is. Internalised misogyny is what happens when you've absorbed the sexist messages the world has fed you, often without even realising it. It's believing, consciously or not, that women are less capable, trustworthy or worthy of respect.

It might sound like 'I don't really get on with other women' or 'I'd rather work with men, they're less drama'. It might show up as judging another woman's choices, clothes or ambition. It's us holding ourselves and each other to impossible standards that we never agreed to in the first place.

What's wild is how deep this runs. It often shows up in close female friendships, especially through Tall Poppy Syndrome. It's that instinctive drive to cut down women who stand out or succeed, the conditioning to believe her success means less space for our own. It's heartbreaking, but it's also fixable. Once we name it, we can challenge it and unlearn it. That's the work.

Research shows us time and again that women who actively support each other are far more likely to advance together. One study found that female MBA graduates who had a strong inner circle of women supporting them alongside a broader professional network achieved leadership positions that were two-and-a-half times higher in authority and pay than their female counterparts who lacked this combination.[2]

Stepping Out of Line and into Change

Remember when Pamela Anderson stepped onto the red carpet at the Golden Globes wearing no makeup at the start of 2025? I do. The reactions were equal parts uplifting and disheartening. For every person who described her choice as empowering there was at least another one (if not more) who said things like 'She could have at least worn a bit of lip gloss. . .'.

When we judge other women's choices, especially around appearance, it's rarely about the other woman, and it's usually about *us*. Our discomfort, our conditioning, our unhealed stuff. We've grown up in a culture that's trained us to believe there's a right way to be a woman. That your worth is tied to how you look. That beauty is a currency, and you better play the game if you want to stay in the room. So when someone like Pamela Anderson steps out and refuses to play, especially at 58 years old, which is code for 'how dare she', it rattles people. It breaks the rules we were told to follow.

When women police other women, it's often because we're used to policing ourselves. That lip gloss comment is a mirror. That's someone saying, 'I've spent decades making sure I'm polished and presentable and palatable . . . and now you're telling me I didn't have to?'

It's not just jealousy, it's grief, it's resentment. It's internalised misogyny in action. But when one woman steps out of line, it creates space for the rest of us to question the line itself. And *that's* where change lives. That's the opportunity we need to see and act upon. When you catch yourself rolling your eyes or making that comment, see it for what it is: fear dressed up as feedback. Then decide, be brave and follow her instead of cutting her down.

Breaking Our Own Barriers

I started UPFRONT in 2015. Back then, the world looked very different. The #MeToo movement hadn't happened. Trump was just an unrealistic reality TV host. Black Lives Matter wasn't a global movement. The words intersectionality and gender equity weren't part of mainstream conversations. Yet, for all the progress we've made in language, policies and awareness, the power structures that hold women back remain shockingly intact. Women are still underpaid, underestimated and our rights in many cases are being reversed.

If I were launching UPFRONT today, internalised misogyny would be at the forefront of that work.

Here's why:

1. **We're still talking about women versus men instead of acknowledging that women are no more equal as a group than men and women are.**

   The gender pay gap for white women in the UK is just over 8%, but for Black African women, it's 26%.[3] Yet mainstream feminism often ignores race, class and disability. The 'girlboss' era pushed the idea that if one woman can make it, we all can, ignoring that the systems holding us back don't impact all women equally, at all.

2. **Women are blaming men instead of looking at how we uphold the very barriers we're trying to break.**

   Studies show that women who self-promote are judged most harshly by other women.[4] Research has found that while confidence and ambition are celebrated in men, women who advocate for themselves are often seen as less likeable, especially by other women. This bias reinforces the unspoken rule that women should be modest, agreeable and self-sacrificing. Instead of lifting each other up, we unconsciously police behaviours that challenge norms.

3. **The feminist/women's development space is toxic and full of women tearing each other down.**

Look at the backlash against prominent feminist figures like author Chimamanda Ngozi Adichie and actor Jameela Jamil, women cancelling other women for not being 'perfect' enough. Instead of difficult and nuanced conversations, we see public pile-ons, where one misstep leads to being exiled. I want to see progress through discussion.

4. **We celebrate women breaking barriers while ignoring that most of them are just playing by the same old rules.**

The first female prime minister of a country isn't always a win for women. Margaret Thatcher broke barriers, but she did little to advance gender equality. She famously said, '*I owe nothing to women's lib*'. During the 2024 Conservative leadership race in the UK, Kemi Badenoch sparked widespread criticism when she described statutory maternity pay as 'excessive', calling it a 'function of tax' and criticising the redistribution from taxpayers to recipients. Her remarks underscored how even women in power can reinforce harmful norms rather than challenge them. Simply putting women in leadership doesn't automatically change the system if they uphold the same oppressive structures. True progress isn't just about women getting power. It's about redefining power itself.

5. **We've confused empowerment with actual power.**

The billion dollar self-care industry tells women to buy candles, do face masks and empower themselves through consumption. But where's the push for economic empowerment? Owning assets, running companies, building financial independence—that's power. Don't buy into the marketing campaigns; instead I want you to focus on building wealth.

6. **Women in leadership are still expected to behave like men, or else they're punished.**

Jacinda Ardern, a New Zealand politician and activist who was the 40th prime minister of New Zealand and leader of the Labour Party from 2017 to 2023, was praised for her kindness until she wasn't. Nicola Sturgeon, a Scottish politician who served as First Minister of Scotland and leader of the Scottish National Party (SNP) from 2014 to 2023, was seen as too controlling when it was her actual job to take control. The same qualities men are admired for—decisiveness, ambition—are still seen by women as negatives when displayed by women.

7. **We're still policing women's ambition.**

When Beyoncé called herself a businesswoman, the internet erupted with criticism. Meanwhile, Elon Musk is praised for sleeping in his office. Women who seek wealth and power are labelled greedy, out of touch or too much. But ambition isn't the problem, our discomfort with women having it is.

8. **Motherhood is still weaponised against women.**

Serena Williams won a Grand Slam while pregnant, yet after giving birth, she was asked when she'd retire. Meanwhile, male athletes have kids and no one even mentions 'work-life balance'. Women are constantly forced to justify their choices and other women are often the ones leading the judgement.

9. **Women are tearing each other down online, leaving no room for nuance, courage or real conversation.**
    When Taylor Swift was named *Time's* Person of the Year, the online discourse wasn't about her impact, it was women arguing over whether she was the perfect feminist icon. Meanwhile, tech entrepreneurs like Jeff Bezos and Mark Zuckerberg build destructive empires and are only ever thought of as representing themselves and their companies.

10. **We still struggle to celebrate other women's success without comparison or resentment.**
    One study found that women in male-dominated fields are more likely to compete against each other than support one another, because the system makes them feel like there's only room for one.[5] This is sometimes called the 'queen bee' effect, when women distance themselves from other women to maintain their own standing in a male-dominated environment. It's not because women are naturally competitive with each other; it's because the structure rewards scarcity and pits us against one another.
    You can see this play out in politics, for example. When Kamala Harris was chosen as Joe Biden's running mate in 2020, much of the media coverage immediately compared her to other high-profile women, questioning whether she was 'the right one' rather than focusing on her track record and vision. Instead of celebrating a historic moment for women of colour in US politics, public discourse often turned into a competition narrative, as if one woman's success meant fewer opportunities for the rest.

Time to Unlearn

From our earliest memories, the media teaches us what it means to be a good woman—thin but not too thin, ambitious but not bossy, sexy but not asking for it, successful but always humble. These stories don't just entertain us, they shape us.

We see women punished for ageing, gaining weight, being assertive, not smiling. We're told we're too much and not enough, often in the same sentence. Over time, we turn that judgement inward, then outward.

Think about reality TV. Tabloid headlines. Celebrity makeover stories. The obsession with what women wear, who we date, how we mother. The media rewards us for falling in line and punishes us for stepping out, and that reinforces the idea that other women are threats, not allies. That if *she* wins, you lose. For more on this idea, I'd highly recommend Sophie Gilbert's book *Girl on Girl: How Pop Culture Turned a Generation of Women Against Themselves*.

Internalised misogyny doesn't come from nowhere. It's taught by the stories we're told, then the ones we tell ourselves. The media plants the seed. We end up watering it. But we can unlearn it. And we are unlearning it, by questioning the narrative, calling it out and building new stories that centre truth, complexity and connection. I want us to be known as the generation of women and girls who refused to hate on each other.

Flip Your Internal Narrative

I'm sure every one of you reading this has, at some point, looked at another woman and thought: *who does she think she is?* The honest answer might just be: she's who you'd be if you weren't afraid. Instead I urge you to ask a better question: *who taught you to be afraid of her?*

'Who does she think she is?' was a phrase that followed me around school. Girls hated me for being confident. For having opinions. For raising my hand. They scribbled my name on the toilet walls. I carried that message for years. It shaped how loud I allowed myself to be. It still shows up sometimes, when I see a woman being incredibly herself. It's been a huge driver for me in building UPFRONT. But now I catch it, I talk back to it. Because I know better.

I now know it's not just a passing thought, it's internalised misogyny. And now it has a name and reason to be there, I can ask myself: *where did that come from? Who taught me that? Is it actually true?* This is the hard work, not being perfectly feminist or bias-free, but catching yourself in the moment and asking better questions.

Start with language. Am I calling her 'too emotional' when I'd call a man 'passionate'? Am I describing a woman as 'difficult' when she's just being clear?

Then **check your actions.** Am I lifting women up publicly, and privately? Am I mentoring, sponsoring, backing women or am I shrinking away because part of me still believes there's only room for one?

Finally: say it out loud. Talk about internalised misogyny with your team, your friends, your family. Buy them a copy of this book. Name the patterns. Share the discomfort. Make unlearning part of the culture around you, not just something you do in private. Because the more we talk about this stuff, the less power it holds.

When another woman makes you uncomfortable, it's an invitation. When you see a confident woman, don't look away. Look closer. She's not a threat. She's a mirror and an opportunity.

UPFRONT Moment

This one's different. Because *you* are different now. We're nearing the end of this book. You've peeled back layers. Faced hard truths. Practised standing taller, speaking louder, loving mistakes. Now we turn the mirror not just on ourselves but towards each other.

This moment isn't just for journalling. It's for *gathering*. For speaking aloud. For being witnessed. You don't need the perfect setting or lighting. You just need one or two women you trust, a little bit of time and a willingness to go there.

Take a picture of this page. Save it to your phone. Bring it to dinner, your next walk, your next phone call. Let this be your script for truth-telling and unlearning.

Mirror Talk: A Conversation to Have with a Woman You Love

Take turns asking each other these six questions. You don't need to solve anything. You just need to be honest, and listen.

1. **'What woman have you judged unfairly?'**
   Tell the truth. Was it her confidence? Her appearance? Her ambition? Her softness? Where did that judgement come from and what might it be reflecting back at you?

2. **'When have you felt judged by other women?'**
   Share a time you were made to feel small, too loud, too much or not enough by another woman. How did it shape how you show up today?

3. **'What were you taught about what a "good woman" looks like?'**
   Unpack the rules you grew up with, around bodies, ambition, emotions, success. How have those rules shaped how you see yourself and other women?

4. **'Who have you been afraid to support because of comparison?'**
   Talk about the woman you scroll past with envy. The colleague you can't quite compliment. What would change if you celebrated her instead?

5. 'Who in your life models confidence in a way you admire?'
   Name her. Celebrate her. What does she reflect back to you about who *you* can be?
6. 'What's one old belief about women you're ready to unlearn?'
   Say it. Claim it. Bury it.

After everyone has shared, ask each other:

- 'What did you hear me say that stayed with you?'
- 'What do you see in me that I might be afraid to see in myself?'
- 'What are you proud of me for?'

Now, speak this together—eyes up, voices steady.

'I will no longer shrink at the sight of a confident woman'.
'I will look at her, learn from her and celebrate her'.
'I will call out internalised misogyny in myself and others'.
'I will lift other women up, even when it's uncomfortable'.
'I will remember: she's not a threat, she's a mirror'.

This is the part where we rewrite the script. Together. The part where you become the woman who names it, shifts it and holds others to better. Because every time you celebrate another woman's power, you reclaim your own.

So go pour a glass of something delicious, grab your friends and have the conversation that patriarchy is counting on us not having!

You are not each other's rivals. You are each other's reminders.

She's not a threat. She's your mirror.

Notes

1. Currie, L. (2025). Taylor Meets The Trick. Self-published. Available via Amazon and IngramSpark. www.the-trick.co.
2. Uzzi, B. (2019). Harvard Business Review, *Research: Men and women need different kinds of networks to succeed.* https://hbr.org/2019/02/research-men-and-women-need-different-kinds-of-networks-to-succeed.
3. Fawcett Society in collaboration with the Global Institute for Women's Leadership at Kings College London (2020). *The Gender Pay Gap by Ethnicity in Britain.*
4. Harvard Business Review (2019). Why assertive women get called bossy. *Harvard Business Review.* https://hbr.org.
5. Ryan, M.K. and Haslam, A. (2015). Do women who succeed in male-dominated domains help other women? The moderating role of gender identification. *European Journal of Social Psychology* 45 (5): 599–608.

23

You Are Choosing Yourself

Old Rule: Putting yourself first is selfish

New Rule: Putting yourself first is confidence

When we think of the term 'self-centred', most of us flinch. We associate it with selfishness, arrogance, even cruelty. But Calypso Barnum-Bobb, leadership coach, speaker and founder of People Like Us, invites us to imagine something radically different. What if putting yourself first isn't selfish at all? What if it's the deepest form of confidence?

Growing up, Calypso was the eldest of four siblings, a caretaker, a 'good girl' shaped by expectations from every direction, family, culture, religion. She learned early how to abandon herself for others, shape-shifting to fit whatever space needed her: too Black for her white friends, too white for her Black friends. Like many women, she became fluent in people-pleasing, shrinking her needs and sidelining her dreams. Outwardly, she was thriving. Inwardly, she felt lost. It wasn't until her late twenties, burnt out from a demanding career and unhappy in a crumbling relationship that she began to question the old rule she had lived by: 'Everyone else comes first' and putting yourself first is selfish.

Through what she calls her self-discovery journey, Calypso realised that her life was built around external validation, not internal truth. She had spent years abandoning herself, and it was costing her everything: her energy, her joy, her voice. The breakthrough came with a deep, defiant knowing: the answers she was searching for were already inside her. She didn't need another job title, another relationship, another gold star. She needed to choose herself. To become, unapologetically, self-centred.

Calypso redefined the word. To be self-centred was not to be selfish. It was to place herself at the centre of her own life, to trust her needs, her voice, her dreams. It was to believe that nourishing herself first would allow her to show up stronger, more present and more loving for others. Today, through her coaching, speaking and retreat company, People Like Us, Calypso teaches that confidence is built not from sacrifice, but from sovereignty. She urges her clients to start small: Say yes to the quiet desire to host a new event, even if no one else comes. Protect five minutes a day for yourself without apology. Listen to the tiny voice inside that whispers more is possible. And she reminds them confidence doesn't grow from abandoning yourself. It grows from choosing yourself, again and again, especially when it feels uncomfortable.

As Calypso says: *If you don't take time for yourself, you become a selfish arsehole. You can't pour love into others from an empty cup'.* Her story is a powerful reminder: putting yourself first isn't a betrayal, it's a revolution. It's a profound act of self-respect. And it's the foundation for building a kinder, stronger, more confident world for ourselves and for everyone around us.

Calypso teaches us the power of choosing yourself before anyone else does. But what about the moments when you don't have a choice? When your body, your grief or your circumstances force you to stop? That's exactly what happened to Suzy, whose journey reveals why self-care is not selfish, but essential.

When Suzy Reading became a mother and simultaneously lost her father to motor neurone disease, she found herself in what she describes as 'energetic bankruptcy'. She wasn't just tired, she was utterly depleted. She was acutely aware of everything that was required of her—caring for her newborn, supporting her grieving mother, coping with loss—but she had no energy reserves left to meet those demands.

Suzy, trained as a psychologist and a yoga teacher, realised something staggering: despite all her professional training, no one had ever taught her how to take care of herself. In six years of studying psychology, the concept of self-care had never once been mentioned.

Her personal crisis led her to build a self-nourishment toolkit from scratch, not based on luxury or escapism but on survival. At first, self-care looked like lying down on her yoga mat and simply resting. Nothing more. As her energy returned, her practices evolved. But that early experience taught Suzy true self-care is not a luxury. It's a necessity. And practising it is not selfish, it's essential for survival, healing and growth.

Over the years, Suzy has supported thousands of women through her books, workshops and talks. Through it all, one profound barrier kept surfacing again and again: guilt. Even when women understood how to care for themselves, even when the practices were simple, tiny, manageable, many still didn't do them. Why?

Because somewhere deep inside, they believed putting themselves first was deeply wrong. They believed that to be valuable, to be good, they had to be selfless. Suzy challenges this toxic narrative head-on. She teaches that self-care is not selfish, it's boundaried. It's the act of honouring your own humanity. It's a commitment to replenishing yourself so that you can show up fully, for your family, your work, your community and yourself. She reframes confidence too:

Confidence isn't just a thought in your head. It's a feeling of being safe enough in your body, strong enough in your values, and kind enough to yourself to take up space.

In Suzy's philosophy, confidence is a whole-body experience, shaped by how we breathe, how we move, how we treat ourselves and how we allow ourselves to rest. She speaks candidly about the societal myths that trap women in endless cycles of exhaustion and comparison: the glorification of resilience as 'being unaffected by life'. The false expectation that we should always be improving, striving, becoming 'better'. The deeply ingrained belief that exhaustion equals virtue. Instead, Suzy teaches a radical new truth: Rest is a right, not a reward. Boundaries are kindness in action. Taking care of yourself is an act of courage and the ultimate foundation for UPFRONT confidence.

When you dare to choose yourself, when you stop waiting until burnout or collapse forces your hand, you unlock a kind of power that ripples outward. You model self-respect to your children. You strengthen your communities. You lead with compassion.

As Suzy puts it:

Your depletion serves no one. Your replenishment serves everyone.

How do we find the confidence to make space for ourselves when others are always demanding so much of us? This question sits at the very heart of what it means to be UPFRONT. It's at the core of the problem we exist to tackle together. It's at the centre of the old rules we are here to dismantle. Because the truth is women are taught, over and over again, that prioritising ourselves is selfish. We are taught that looking after ourselves is indulgent, unnecessary, even shameful. We are taught that our needs must always come second, to our children, our partners, our workplaces, our families. We are taught that our happiness will come only once everyone around us is happy first. A survey found that women typically reserve just 30 minutes a week for themselves and nearly one in five women said they never commit any time to something they enjoy—with guilt and responsibility being the reason why.[1]

This conditioning runs deep. It plays out in every corner of society. In workplaces, women carry the burden of emotional labour, often without recognition or compensation. It's women who remember birthdays, organise collections and make extra cups of tea. In homes, especially in heterosexual partnerships, women often carry the invisible load—the mental lists, the emotional caregiving, the 'project management' of family life. In parenting, women are told they must be tireless, selfless, endlessly giving. This is what we need to unlearn. And as always, unlearning begins with noticing.

Start to notice the moments where you are putting your needs last without even realising it. Start to notice the conversations where you automatically take on responsibility that isn't yours. Start to notice when you ignore your own discomfort to make others more comfortable. Because you cannot change what you are not willing to see.

If you want to live in a world where these outdated gender roles and expectations no longer define us, you must practise noticing. You must choose yourself, even when it feels uncomfortable. Especially when it feels uncomfortable. You are a match for your discomfort, as we learned in Chapter 4.

I was reminded of this in a brilliant conversation with a friend of mine. She shared a story that perfectly captures the power of choosing yourself. She was speaking at a conference. She had prepared carefully: brilliant slides, rehearsed words, a clear, powerful message. During her talk, she played a video as part of her presentation. But as she stood on stage, the tech failed. The audio distorted. The images broke apart. The audience shifted uncomfortably in their seats. My friend could have done what so many women are conditioned to do: push on, shrink back, endure the discomfort so nobody else had to feel it.

Instead, she chose herself. She chose to pause. She chose discomfort. She asked for the video to be played again properly, even though it made the audience squirm and the tech team flustered. She chose to deliver her speech in the way she deserved to deliver it. And because she chose herself, she gave the speech she wanted to give.

Your day is full of hundreds of micro-moments like this. Confidence is a practice of small moments, as described in Chapter 3. Here's inspiration from the Bond:

> *I prioritised a nap before the school run because a run of recent broken sleep left me exhausted today. I could have powered through as the 'conditioned me' really wanted to, but I said f*ck that and slept instead!*
>
> (Laura, Bond graduate)

> *I'm working to reclaim my mornings for me. Instead of going right to my work email I'm taking time to do a quick meditation and get myself mentally ready for the day.*
>
> (Katie, Bond graduate)

These are the moments where you can choose to stay small or choose yourself. Moments where you can prioritise everyone else's comfort or prioritise your own integrity. Moments where you can move out of default patterns and into something more powerful.

It starts by noticing. It grows by practising and it strengthens every time you choose you.

The next time the moment comes, I want you to ask yourself: What would it look like to choose myself right now? And then I want you to do it.

UPFRONT Moment

Choose yourself in real time. Don't rush this or skip it. Give yourself the same attention you give to your to-do list. Where are you in this very moment? Sit back. Unclench your jaw. Drop your shoulders. Feel your breath arrive.

Now begin.

I know this can feel tricky, it certainly does for me. But it's necessary. You can't serve from depletion, and you can't lead from a place that's simmering with quiet resentment. And you absolutely, no-way-around-it cannot build confidence by ghosting yourself every time someone else needs something.

And here's a wee reminder why this matters: studies in neuroscience and psychology show that writing things down especially when you're reflecting on past choices or imagining new ones helps rewire your brain. It's called self-directed neuroplasticity. You're not just journalling for the vibes. You're literally creating new neural pathways that make it easier for you to live in an UPFRONT life.

So this is your moment to pause, notice and begin again. With intention and kindness. With you, right there in the centre where you belong. Not later. And definitely not once everyone else is 'finally sorted' (come on now, when has that ever happened?). If you wait for that, you'll be waiting forever. Like, till your inbox hits zero. Or everyone in the group chat agrees on a restaurant. Ok, let's go.

List three small moments this week where you didn't choose yourself. They might feel ordinary. Maybe you replied 'no worries at all!' when it absolutely was a worry. Maybe you skipped lunch to finish someone else's urgent request. Maybe you said yes to plans when what you really needed was your sofa and silence.

Now rewrite one of those moments, this time, as if you had chosen you.

- 'Instead of ____, I would have ____'.
- 'That might have felt ____, but I would have gained ____'.
- 'Next time, I will. . .'

Think back to what you were taught growing up about selflessness.

- 'I learned that putting myself first meant. . .'
- 'Today, I know the truth is. . .'

Name three tiny ways you will choose yourself this week. They don't have to be loud. They just have to be doable.

- 'I will say no to. . .'
- 'I will protect time for. . .'
- 'I will listen when my body tells me. . .'

Now find the discomfort. What's one situation coming up that you know will challenge your ability to choose yourself? Write about it honestly.

- 'The part of me that wants to please everyone says. . .'
- 'The part of me that's learning how to Be UPFRONT says. . .'

Write one sentence you can return to in that moment of tension. You can keep coming back to it, as many times as you wish. 'Choosing myself is not selfish. It's the most generous thing I can do'.

I'm proud of you. Are you proud of you?

Note

1. Glamour UK. (2024). Survey on women's self-care and personal time commissioned by G Spot (wellness drinks brand). https://www.glamourmagazine.co.uk/article/gillian-anderson-wellness-survey-women-me-time.

24

Your Confidence Will Upset Them

Old Rule: Don't be difficult

New Rule: Be UPFRONT

onfidence doesn't make you likeable. It makes you powerful, and that's not always welcome. We've been told our whole lives to be agreeable. To not make a fuss. To smile more. To be easy to work with, easy to promote, easy to like. Confident women make people uncomfortable. Not because we're doing anything wrong, but because our confidence disrupts the status quo.

You've already met this truth in Chapter 9, where we explored the unlikeability tax. Now, we're going back there. Not because you didn't get it the first time, but because living it is different. You will upset people with your confidence. You just will.

And in this final chapter, I want to show you what that looked like for me. What it felt like before I believed I deserved to be UPFRONT. Before I learned to stop apologising for my ambition.

While writing this book, I found an old file from 2018. A list of everything I was afraid of. It was buried in a folder I hadn't opened in years. And dear reader, when I say my shoulders went up to my ears . . . here it is. Word for word. Cringe forward!

1. Nobody who succeeds has to think this deeply about it, you are forcing it.
2. You are being greedy.
3. There's no way you can become rich doing something that feels this good.
4. Big hearted women don't make good CEOs.
5. I'm an artist not an entrepreneur.
6. I don't have key messages because I'm too distracted.
7. I don't know anyone who is really wealthy so what chance do I have?
8. If it was going to happen for me, it would have happened by now.
9. If I become more successful, I'll end up with no friends.
10. I can't do all the things I want to do and have babies at the same time.
11. I will work incredibly hard and it won't work and I'll be full of regret.
12. I am destined for a life of loneliness.
13. I will have to work so hard I will have no life.
14. Why do you always want more, you should just be grateful.
15. It shouldn't be this hard, you shouldn't have to think about it that much.
16. This whole thing is selfish and ridiculous.
17. People will hate me.
18. I will not be able to be a kind and generous person.

19. I don't have the network.
20. This business idea has no legs.
21. Genuinely brilliant people are just known for being brilliant and do not need a brand.
22. Building a personal brand is over-engineered and dumb.
23. I'll never succeed because I'm not known for one thing.
24. I don't have a thing because I'm jumping about and not focused enough.
25. People will think I'm full of myself.
26. People will realise that I don't have depth in any one area.
27. People will make up stories about me behind my back.

When I read the list from 2018, I winced, not because I was embarrassed but because every line was wired with one underlying fear. If I go too far, too big, too loud, too UPFRONT, people will stop liking me.

And it hit me, this wasn't just my fear. It was a reflection of something much bigger. We've been taught that likeability is our lifeline. That being liked is how we stay safe, how we stay hired, how we stay included. For women, especially those who challenge norms, lead visibly or speak up, the risk of being disliked carries real consequences, personally and professionally.

Carol Gilligan's research shows us that girls start to lose their voice around adolescence not because they lack opinions, but because they learn it's safer to stay quiet.[1] Staying likeable becomes a survival strategy. Dr Thema Bryant and Dr Julie Hanks call this *Good Girl Conditioning*.[2] Be helpful, be humble, be nice and be small. Never too loud, too opinionated, too successful. Never too much.

Being disliked is not a personal failure. It's often a political inevitability. When you step into your power, speak your truth or dare to lead in ways that don't fit the mould, someone will flinch. Someone will frown. Someone will label you as too much. But that doesn't mean you did something wrong. It means you're disrupting something that needs disrupting.

That list of fears wasn't proof that I lacked confidence. It was proof that I was beginning to practise it, by naming the stories I'd been told and preparing myself to let them go. Especially the one that says 'You have to be liked to be successful'. But you don't. You have to be honest. You have to be brave. You have to be respected.

From childhood, girls are rewarded for being pleasant, agreeable, accommodating. We're praised for sharing, for smiling, for keeping the peace. Boys, on the other hand, are allowed, even encouraged, to challenge, interrupt, dominate.[3]

This conditioning shows up in performance reviews that call women abrasive while calling men assertive. It shows up when a woman in leadership is critiqued for her tone rather than her decisions. It shows up when women of colour, especially Black women, are labelled angry or intimidating for expressing valid emotions.

A study on performance reviews found 76% of women received negative personality feedback, phrases like '*she's too abrasive*', '*she's not a team player*' or '*she comes on too strong*'. For men? Only 2%. This is not a coincidence. This is systemic.

So when we worry about being liked, it's not vanity, it's survival. But survival mode is not where confidence thrives. Confidence needs space. It needs room to disagree. The most common question I get asked in the Bond is, '*How can I be confident without upsetting anyone?*' My answer is short: *You can't.*

Confidence will upset someone. Especially if you're a woman. Especially if you're challenging norms. Especially if your voice was never meant to be in the room. The question isn't '*How do I avoid upsetting people?*' The question is '*If I want to Be UPFRONT, who am I willing to upset?*'

Likeability is a moving target. You can contort yourself to an unrecognisable degree to meet it and still you will miss it. What one person loves, another will loathe. You can do everything 'right' and still be too much for someone. Because likeability is variable, it is a multiple of all the people who know you and it changes on their whim, it's impossible. So what if we stopped aiming for likeability, and aimed for honesty, confidence and kindness? What would your life be like if being liked was less important than being yourself?

Every woman I admire, those I've worked with and learned from, has been disliked for something. They've ruffled feathers, challenged norms, spoken truths others tiptoed around. There's irony in that. Being disliked is not the end of your story. Sometimes, it's the beginning of a better one.

When we decide to step up and lead, there's often this nagging fear of what will others think of me? This fear often stops us from speaking up, taking action or making bold decisions. When you're navigating something as challenging as running a business, especially as a woman, those fears can get even louder.

How do we remain confident without coming across as bossy or difficult? My answer is short: *You can't*. We've all been there, on the verge of doing something important, something that felt like it could change the trajectory of our lives. Whether it's starting a new business, advocating for salary transparency or calling out harmful behaviour, there's that hesitation, that fear of the labels we might earn. Bossy, aggressive, intimidating are combative words that carry a different weight for women than they do for men.

For me, it's always bossy, sometimes it's been aggressive. Throughout my career, I've worn that label, and as I've gotten older, it's become one I'm more sensitive to. I've been called intimidating, combative and, once, a flowery steamroller—a term I've come to realise, oddly, has a certain charm. But these labels, no matter how flattering or unflattering, can be hard to shake. We start to ask ourselves, is this how I want to be seen? Then we have to throw that question away, as far as we can, and ask a better question: Does it matter?

These labels hit hardest in my role as an entrepreneur. You are the face of your brand and every move you make is scrutinised. You can't please everyone. Sometimes, especially in business, that means you will inevitably be labelled as too much. You'll be seen as difficult, unpalatable or intolerable because you're pushing boundaries, questioning norms and being UPFRONT.

You can't avoid it. The labels will come, and if you're not careful they may stick. What you can control is how you react to them. Being seen as difficult doesn't mean you're failing. It means you're doing something right. It means you're challenging a system that needs disruption. And that's exactly what happens when you start a business, especially when you're a woman.

Owning a business as a woman comes with a unique set of old rules and nonsensical expectations, old rules that are rarely said aloud, but everyone knows them. I'm going to say them out loud to you now.

- Make some money, but not too much. God forbid you out-earn your partner.
- Be lovely to everyone. Always. Smile through the bullsh**.
- Have a sound opinion on every news headline, including foreign policy, climate change and celebrity scandals.
- Work hard, but not too much. If you neglect your family, you'll be labelled a terrible mother.
- Be a visionary, but make sure you're nice about it. We wouldn't want anyone to feel uncomfortable with your ambition.

- Be a leader, but never ever be bossy. Don't even think about being short with anyone.
- Make tough decisions, but be liked by everyone. God forbid you prioritise your business over people's feelings.
- Be an influencer, but don't overexpose yourself. Share your fashion, family, holidays and husband because your customers want to see it all. But remember, not too much. No one likes a show off.
- Achieve big success, but have no boundaries. Be available 24/7 because everyone deserves a piece of you.
- Be an expert in your domain, plus an expert in all domains of diversity, inclusion and capitalism. And you'll be asked to educate everyone, pro bono, of course.
- Build a high performing team and be everyone's friend, mother, mentor and psychologist at the same time. No pressure, just don't let anyone down.
- Never show off. Downplay your accomplishments because modesty is everything.
- Always look good, but not too sexy. If you're too sexy, no one will take you seriously.
- Never sell. Heaven forbid you try to make a profit.

Meanwhile, men in business face not one of these contradictions. They can command respect with authority and do whatever they want without fear of being labelled too much. They can make billions, flaunt their success and take all the credit without being called bossy.

It's not just women in business, women in public life are routinely disliked for simply doing their jobs well. Nicola Sturgeon, praised and punished in equal measure, was called divisive for standing firm in her convictions. Kamala Harris, as the first female vice president of the United States, has faced relentless scrutiny and double standards, her every move dissected through a lens men in her position have never faced. Anne Hathaway was hated for being too earnest. Gwyneth Paltrow for being too much. Kate Winslet for being too fat. What do all these women have in common? They kept going. They stayed rooted in their purpose. They didn't shape-shift to become more palatable. They proved that being disliked is not a detour from leadership, it's often a sign you're on the right path. They're also all very successful.

So what do you do? The first step in overcoming these challenges is recognising that the labels will come. And they'll come not because you're doing something wrong, but because you're doing something right. You're stepping up, taking risks and challenging norms, and judgement from others is part of the work. You can't change how others view you. You can't control their perception of your ambition, your vision or your leadership.

Accept that people will label you as difficult, aggressive or bossy. It's a painful, yet liberating, reality. It doesn't mean you're failing. It means you're challenging something bigger than yourself. The respect you'll earn for staying true to your values will far outweigh the approval you might have been seeking.

The second step is to gather support. Seek out mentors, create a network of women who are walking the same path, and learn from their experiences. Build a community around you that reinforces the message that you are not wrong for being UPFRONT. Your voice matters. Your ideas matter. Your work matters.

Finally, understanding privilege is crucial. Many women, especially white women, are closer to power than others. For women of colour, women from working-class backgrounds and women who don't fit traditional beauty or education norms, the consequences of being labelled difficult can be far harsher.

Staying true to your values and who you want to be will earn you respect over likeability and reward you in ways that are far more meaningful. So being UPFRONT and learning confidence, is not about being liked. It's about being brave enough to be disliked. The next time you feel the heat rise in your chest because someone doesn't like what you said, or how you said it, pause. Ask yourself: was I kind? Was I clear? Was I true to myself? If the answer is yes, then you made someone uncomfortable with your confidence. And that is not your burden to carry. Onwards.

UPFRONT Moment

I don't know what label you're carrying around. Maybe it's bossy, cold, demanding, too much, not enough. Maybe it's all of them. I just want you to know: I've carried them too. They were heavy until I learned how to put them down.

I hope this chapter stirred something in you, something fierce. Because I didn't write this book to make you feel better. I wrote it so you'll act. So you'll have something to grip when the world tells you your confidence is too loud or too quiet. So you'll remember, especially when it's hardest, that your voice belongs.

Here's what we're going to do. One last moment, together.

Write the label that's followed you the longest. Write it HUGE. Flip chart paper. Blackboard. Back of the gas bill. Write it big. In capital letters. Then cross it out. Physically. With a line through the middle.

And write this above

'I am not here to be liked. I am here to be UPFRONT'.

Then send me a picture. But seriously, this would actually make my day. In fact, why am I making light of this? I'm not joking. This matters more than almost anything I can think of. Send me a picture of your label. I'm building a gallery. I'm going to publish a book full of women from all over the world choosing UPFRONT over likeability. A book full of hands holding paper and rage and relief. A book full of women who decided to set down what never belonged to them in the first place. This is not an exercise, this is a confidence revolution!

Because the world will keep handing us these labels. Over and over. Until we say enough already. We are here to be UPFRONT and we are not going anywhere.

May our confidence upset them.

MAY OUR CONFIDENCE UPSET THEM.

Notes

1. Gilligan, C. (1982). *In a Different Voice: Psychological Theory and Women's Development*. Harvard University Press.
2. Hanks, J. de A. (n.d.). *Good girl conditioning discussions* (concept referenced in clinical commentary and practice). DrJulieHanks.com. https://www.drjuliehanks.com/.
3. Hentschel, T., Heilman, M.E., and Peus, C.V. (2019). The multiple dimensions of gender stereotypes: A current look at men's and women's characterisations and leader-ship evaluations. *Frontiers in Psychology* 10: 11. https://doi.org/10.3389/fpsyg.2019.00011.

Afterword

You've walked through every page, rule, story and truth this book holds. That alone is worth pausing for. Because finishing this book isn't a tickbox. It's a commitment to yourself, to your confidence and to being UPFRONT.

Back in the Introduction, I told you that learning confidence is an act of rebellion. Now you know why. Choosing confidence, practising it, protecting it and passing it on pushes against everything we were told to be: small, grateful, quiet, liked (but not too much). You've met the old rules of the status quo and set them alight.

You've unlearned the lies—that confidence is a fixed trait, that you were never the imposter, that you had to be fearless, humble, perfect or silent to belong. You've seen how patriarchy, scarcity and shame have shaped your story, and you've replaced them with new rules rooted in power, visibility and self-trust.

You've relearned the truth that confidence is a skill, a choice, a practice. That it grows in small moments and big leaps. That it grows louder in community. That it's visible, vulnerable, vocal and never selfish.

Now, you are UPFRONT.

Adjective
Honest, direct, and fearless in expression.

Noun
A member of a collective movement; a bond of women rewriting the rules.

Verb

To step forward before feeling ready; to build ladders for yourself and others.

Being UPFRONT doesn't mean doubt will disappear. It means you're learning how to dance with it. Fear may still sit beside you, but you'll choose action anyway. You'll honour your own voice and invite others to do the same.

Because confidence isn't just for you. It's for the women watching. The daughters and sons you're raising. The teams you're leading. The communities you're shaping. Every single time you take up space, you make it safer for someone else to do the same.

The stakes are high. We are living in a time when women's rights, safety and autonomy are not guaranteed. When policies are being written without our voices, and narratives about us are being crafted without our consent. We cannot, and will not, stand by.

The world is full of ordinary, extraordinary women sitting on ideas, art, opinions and solutions that could spark change. Stories that could flip scripts, rewrite rules and light the path forward. This isn't the end of your confidence story, it's the start of your practice. I can't wait to hear about your Woohoos, your skateboards and the bigger life you build. Remember: you're in a lifelong relationship with your confidence, and there is no right way to learn it, there is only trying.

The world needs you now more than ever. This book is a match. Your voice is the spark. Now, go burn the old rules down. I have endless confidence in you.

Be UPFRONT.

CONFIDENCE ISN'T JUST
FOR YOU. IT'S FOR THE
WOMEN WATCHING.
THE DAUGHTERS
AND SONS YOU'RE
RAISING. THE TEAMS
YOU'RE LEADING. THE
COMMUNITIES YOU'RE
SHAPING.

Where We Meet Next

This isn't the end. It's the beginning.

Confidence doesn't grow in isolation. It grows when we practise it together. That's why UPFRONT exists: to build a world where women's confidence is seen, celebrated and rewarded. A world where speaking up, showing up and taking up space is the norm, not the exception.

We call our spaces Bonds. Some are long, some are short. Some you pay for, some you don't. But they're all built on the same truth: confidence is built, not born. In every Bond, women unlearn the old rules, practise new ones and remind each other what's possible when we stop trying to do it alone.

We host Bonds for individuals and for organisations. Sometimes that means a group of women joining together online for six weeks. Sometimes it means whole teams or sectors; charities, local and central government, law, HR and more, committing to practise confidence together. Wherever a Bond happens, it creates ripple effects far beyond the individual.

Maybe your next step is a Bond. Maybe it's a conversation you've been avoiding. Maybe it's simply sharing this book with a friend. What matters most is that you keep going. If there's one thing I hope this book has shown you, it's that confidence is not something you complete.

It's something you practise in different ways, at different moments, across different seasons of your life. The stories in this book are a testament to the amazing things that happen when women practise confidence together. When you share what you're trying, what you're unlearning, and what you're noticing about yourself along the way.

If you'd like to stay connected to this work beyond the final page, in whatever way feels right to you, you're invited to become a Book Bonder.

Book Bonders are readers who want to keep exploring these ideas in the real world, at their own pace, and in their own way.

You can join by scanning the QR code below. There's no fixed path, no expectation, and nothing to "keep up with".

However you choose to go on practising confidence from here, I'm cheering for you wildly.

And if you're raising or caring for children, you might also love my children's book *Taylor Meets The Trick*. I created this book to help children, and the grown-ups around them, see through the unfair rules of patriarchy and start imagining a fairer world together.

Start here: the-trick.co

Here's the part worth remembering: confidence spreads through people. Ideas spread through people. If this book gave you something, pass it on. Because every spark of confidence you share builds the world we're all longing for.

Acknowledgements

I'm sitting down to write these acknowledgements on the day I welcomed 3,025 new women into the Bond. That sentence alone feels wild to write.

This book exists because I refused to wait for permission. Because I do things even when they feel scary. And while I wish I could say I was carried on a tide of support, it wasn't always like that. But there were people, the right ones, and they mattered deeply.

Thank you to every woman who shared a story, a quote or a spark of truth that made these pages real. You trusted me with your voice. I will never stop honouring that.

To every single person fighting for women: thank you. Around the world, our rights are being stripped away—our bodies, our voices, our freedoms. We're dismantling a system and it will take every single one of us.

To my team at UPFRONT, thank you. You make this work possible. I see you. I appreciate you.

To **Matt Desmier,** for saying yes when I asked if I could bring a sofa on stage with me at Silicon Beached. That moment was the start of an amazing adventure.

To **Kim Taylor,** thank you for everything.

To **Sarah Wright,** for seeing me and helping me fall in love with my Tall Poppyness.

To **Mr John Grant,** my art school teacher—your belief in me changed the course of my life.

To **Aunt Irene,** for always making me feel like a super star. I hope I'm as fabulous as you when I'm 88.

To every **Bonder,** past, present and future, you inspire me. Our collective power has no bounds.

To my **online community,** thank you for listening to me bang on about confidence for the last ten years. Every comment, like, share and message helps me stay brave.

To **Lorna,** thank you for making me write these 24 new rules down on a napkin in Sugo, for making me laugh until I cry, and for always asking me the right questions. I love you.

To **Mum and Dad,** thank you for your unconditional love and support. Imagine buying eight-year-old me a typewriter so she could retype *Fantastic Mr Fox* word for word. That says it all.

To **Christopher,** you are the most incredible believing mirror (and so tall! And handsome as hell!). I love you. Thanks for letting me take all the credit.

To **Atlas,** you are everything. Being your mamam is the joy of my life.

And to every woman who knows what it feels like to build something without the safety net, no flood of support, no soft landings, just a vision and a big, brave heart, this is yours as much as it's mine. Keep going.

Lastly, to the women who came before me. Lily and Margaret, my grans, I think you'd be proud. Even though we never spoke the same language of confidence, your lives made mine possible.

About the Author

Lauren Currie OBE is an entrepreneur, author and global voice on confidence as a tool for economic justice.

She is the founder of UPFRONT, a company redefining confidence as a core leadership competency, essential to culture change, equity and performance. UPFRONT's flagship programme, *The Bond*, has upskilled over 15,000 women across more than 50 countries and is trusted by organisations such as Nike, Spotify and the Ministry of Defence.

Lauren believes confidence is not a personality trait, it's a social and economic lever. She's spent the last decade building businesses, products and ideas that prove it. Lauren was awarded an OBE for services to design and diversity, and was named one of the UK's top businesswomen under 35. She spent seven years as chair of the UK's leading maternity discrimination charity, Pregnant Then Screwed.

Her children's book, *Taylor Meets The Trick*, is helping young people and grown-ups all over the world name the patriarchy for what it is and begin to unlearn it together.

She grew up in Kilmarnock in Scotland and now lives in Uppsala in Sweden with her family.

www.laurencurrie.co

Index